ADDITIONAL PRAISE I

"An alarming study of an economi    d
entirely avoidable."

                                                                    vs

Mitchell explains why: "If you remember the days of people working their way through college, doing shifts on the docks or driving a cab— or lived that yourself—you might be wondering why those days are long gone . . . government policies designed to help Americans compete in the global technological race, but also an unholy alliance of funding systems, lax regulation, and institutional competition that has bid up the price of a college education far beyond the rate of inflation and far beyond the ability of many people to pay."

—NPR

"Proves the old adage that the road to Hell is paved with good intentions."

—*Forbes*

"Vivid and compelling"

—*Chicago Tribune*

"The book is sure to garner attention, as well as make readers take a close look at the cost of higher education. Parents, students, and educators will find it enthralling and possibly be moved to push for industry reforms."

—*Booklist* (starred review)

"A deeply reported, jaw-dropping book. A must-read for every student, parent, and educator. Through engaging storytelling, this timely book helps us understand, in the same way as *The Big Short* did with housing, how we allowed a student-loan system started with good intentions during the Great Society to grow into an uncontrolled behemoth that has left tens of millions of Americans saddled with trillions in debt."

—Jeffrey Selingo, *New York Times* bestselling author of
Who Gets In and Why and *There Is Life After College*

"A masterfully written, surprising, and deeply reported book that is studded with breathtaking insights on every page. *The Debt Trap* is about more than student debt—it's the true story of how America's ladder of opportunity was turned into a debtor's prison. It's all here: well-intentioned government programs gone awry, corporate corruption, exploitation, and the unbreakable hope of American people working tirelessly for a better life. An indispensable book to understand one of the most urgent problems in our country today."

—Christopher Leonard,
New York Times bestselling author of *Kochland*

"A powerful investigation into one of the most important economic crises of our time. The storytelling is lively and emotive, which is crucial for understanding the human impact of towers of student debt on everyday Americans. The book should be read by politicians, parents, and students alike as a cautionary tale of how government policies can bring enormous gains while also wreaking havoc on lives."

—Bradley Hope, *New York Times* bestselling coauthor
of *The Billion Dollar Whale*

"Almost out of nowhere, student debt became a one trillion dollar problem—not just for the 43 million people who suffer under its weight but the entire society. In his rich and poignant book, Josh Mitchell traces this harrowing history, how policy makers' good intentions in Washington, DC, and corporate executives' greed and exploitation has led to stifled lives and snuffed out dreams of betterment."

—Jesse Eisinger,
author of *The Chickenshit Club*

The

DEBT
TRAP

How Student Loans Became
a National Catastrophe

Josh Mitchell

SIMON & SCHUSTER PAPERBACKS
New York   London   Toronto   Sydney   New Delhi

Simon & Schuster Paperbacks
An Imprint of Simon & Schuster, Inc.
1230 Avenue of the Americas
New York, NY 10020

Some names and identifying details have been changed.

Copyright © 2021 by Josh Mitchell

All rights reserved, including the right to reproduce this book or portions thereof in any form whatsoever. For information, address Simon & Schuster Subsidiary Rights Department, 1230 Avenue of the Americas, New York, NY 10020.

First Simon & Schuster trade paperback edition August 2022

SIMON & SCHUSTER and colophon are registered trademarks of Simon & Schuster, Inc.

For information about special discounts for bulk purchases, please contact Simon & Schuster Special Sales at 1-866-506-1949 or business@simonandschuster.com.

The Simon & Schuster Speakers Bureau can bring authors to your live event. For more information or to book an event, contact the Simon & Schuster Speakers Bureau at 1-866-248-3049 or visit our website at www.simonspeakers.com.

Interior design by Carly Loman

10 9 8 7 6 5 4 3 2 1

Library of Congress Cataloging-in-Publication Data has been applied for.

ISBN 978-1-5011-9944-8
ISBN 978-1-5011-9947-9 (pbk)
ISBN 978-1-5011-9950-9 (ebook)

*For my mom, who taught me how to laugh,
even when times were tough*

*Kathleen Diane Mitchell
1951–2017*

CONTENTS

The

DEBT
TRAP

Introduction

L isa's lawyer needed an answer.

The government isn't budging, her bankruptcy attorney said on the other end of the line. *How much more money should we offer?*

It was Monday, August 13, 2018. The midday sun beat down on Lisa as she stood in a plaza dotted with palm trees at the University of South Florida in Tampa, pacing in front of the doors to the student center, phone pressed to her ear, as she discussed her fate with the attorney, Bob Lohr.

She had just dropped off her 18-year-old daughter, Stephanie, for freshman orientation. The long drive down I-95 from their home in Chester, Pennsylvania, had been eerily quiet. Stephanie, normally bubbly, had jitters about starting college in a new city. Lisa didn't feel like talking, either. She was suffering another bout of agony over her own student debt. She had been paying off her federal student loans for 17 years, starting when Stephanie was an infant. Lisa still owed nearly $100,000. She worried she would go to her grave with it.

In a prior generation, a mother dropping off her daughter at college would be cause for celebration, the first step toward the

American Dream. In 2018, Lisa, a 54-year-old single mother of two, was two years into bankruptcy in a seemingly endless struggle with the U.S. government over the price of her education.

Before Lisa, no one in her family had gone to college. In the early 1990s, she was a secretary in her 20s when she decided to give college a shot. She enrolled at Fairleigh Dickinson University, a private college across the street from her work. As her studies progressed, she realized that her dream of becoming a psychologist required a graduate degree, thanks to state licensing rules. After she received her undergraduate diploma, she enrolled in a graduate program at nearby Widener University. As she piled new loans on top of old loans, the financial counselors at each school reassured her that student debt was "good debt," an investment in her future.

Exhibit 1 of her bankruptcy documents listed how much she had sent over the years to Sallie Mae and its spinoff, a company called Navient, to repay her student loans. Month after month, year after year, she mailed off those payments, each check for more than $700. After some 160 checks, she had paid $135,603.34. Most of it, $100,000, went toward interest, padding the profits of Sallie Mae. Her balance now sat at $96,820. At this pace she'd be well into retirement before it was paid in full.

Exhibit 2 was the document from Main Line Health laboratories, dated 08-31-2016. "LEFT BREAST," it said, followed by these words underlined in pen: "WELL-DIFFERENTIATED LOBU-LAR CARCINOMA."

Congress, hoping to claw back every penny it lent to students, had made it so hard for borrowers to discharge student loans in bankruptcy that Lisa's breast cancer wasn't a sufficient reason to escape her debt. That's what the lawyers representing the U.S. Department of Education told the judge.

How could this happen? she had asked herself over and over.

Her daughter Stephanie was about to get into student debt herself. Instead of the American tradition of parents passing wealth to their offspring, daughter was about to join mother in debt. Lisa cringed at the thought that Stephanie might be headed for the same fate: years of sleepless nights worrying about how she'd ever pay it all as her children slept in a bedroom nearby.

As she paced in front of the student center, Lohr told her the government wanted another 14 years of payments totaling $150,000. She reflected on the years of payments, the times when the student loan bill came before putting away savings for her children's college education, how it had prevented her from having a house with a yard. She thought about how she might not have much longer to live.

No, she told Lohr. She wouldn't do this anymore. *Give them my retirement money*, she said defiantly.

I don't think they're going to accept that, Lohr said.

I don't care, she replied. She was done living under the cloud of student debt.

She logged into her Vanguard account, snapped a screenshot of the balance—$12,086.43—and emailed it to him. It was all she had. And it was all the government was going to get out of her, she said.

How could this happen?

Millions of Americans have asked themselves Lisa's question. Today, 43 million people owe $1.6 trillion in student debt, an amount that has tripled since 2006. Americans owe more in student debt than they owe in credit card debt and car loans. Combined, student debt in the U.S. is the size of Canada's economy.

The program began with good intentions, as a way to pry open the gates to America's respected universities. By the late 20th century higher education had become intertwined with the American experience. It embodied the nation's promise of upward mobility: If you could get into college and worked hard enough while there, you were guaranteed a lifetime of success. For millions of Americans—poor and middle-class, fifth-generation and new immigrants alike—college was the first step on the ladder to prosperity in the world's biggest and most dynamic economy.

Elected leaders wanted to give every American the chance at that prosperity by removing the financial barrier to college and graduate school. They did so by providing loans, combining the American ideals of education, upward mobility, and individual responsibility. Americans would be guaranteed a shot at the American Dream—while paying their own way, without a handout.

Families put their faith in institutions—Congress, banks, universities—as they signed up for loans. They assumed those institutions had their best interests at heart. Students thought they were making an investment, and in fact they were told they had no choice. Radical shifts in the U.S. economy placed growing emphasis on the need for a degree to succeed. College wasn't a luxury but an economic imperative.

For too many, that investment has gone bust.

Far from making college more affordable, student debt enabled schools to raise tuition faster than family incomes, creating a higher-education industrial complex that has driven up the price of college and graduate school to unprecedented levels. Average tuition and room and board at four-year private colleges has risen nearly 800 percent since 1980, more than five times the rate of inflation. Today a four-year degree at a private college costs nearly $200,000 on average, before discounts. The same degree at a public college costs more than $100,000 on average. Scholarships and grants bring the price down for many students, but the average obscures massive problems.

A substantial and growing share of students pays far more than the average and gets into tens of thousands of dollars—and in some cases hundreds of thousands of dollars—in debt just for a shot at making it in today's economy. At the University of Alabama, a state flagship profiled in this book, most students come from out of state and pay $45,000 per year, or $180,000 over four. Even after grants and scholarships are factored in, many Alabama students and their parents take on tens of thousands of dollars in debt, and in some cases more than $100,000.

Then there's graduate school—including medical and law school—which accounts for nearly 40 percent of all student debt in the U.S. Taking on six figures of student debt for grad school has become routine. At the University of Southern California's dental school, tuition and room and board cost $152,000—*for the first year.*

Student debt is both a cause and consequence of those higher costs. The government gives families a blank check to allow students to attend the school of their choice, regardless of that school's price. Colleges have abused their tremendous pricing power. This is the never-ending chase of college pricing: The more colleges raise tuition, the more Americans borrow. The more Americans borrow, the more colleges raise tuition. More than two-thirds of undergraduates borrow, and those who do graduate owing an average of $29,000. Those with larger balances are among the fastest-growing groups, even accounting for inflation. A generation ago it was rare to owe $60,000 in student debt; now more than seven million Americans owe that much. A million borrowers owe more than $200,000. At least a hundred owe over $1 million.

Balances have grown faster than Americans' incomes. For many borrowers, the well-paying jobs promised by universities never materialized, leading to a wave of defaults on par with those of the 2000s housing crisis. Eight million borrowers are in default on a student loan as of this book's writing. That's not far from the number of people who lost their homes after the housing crash. In recent years, despite a strong pre-pandemic economy, 3,000 people a day defaulted on a student loan.

The program was supposed to reduce inequality, leveling the playing field for society's most disadvantaged. Instead it has increased inequality, harming many of the borrowers it was intended to help. Minority students struggle the most with student debt. Black households with student debt typically owe far more than households of any other race. Black borrowers are three times as likely as white students to default. Nearly 4 in 10 Black borrowers who started college in the early 2000s defaulted.

Student debt has shaped how Americans live, work, and form relationships, research shows. The homeownership rate among young Americans fell to the lowest level in decades just as America's student debt tab soared in the 2000s and 2010s. Student debt was one big reason why. Couples are delaying marriage because of their high student loan bills. They are holding off on starting businesses. They are delaying saving for retirement. They are choosing jobs solely for higher salaries, rather than jobs that best suit their talents and interests, so they can pay off their debt.

A college degree once led to higher wealth. Debt has eroded that advantage. Among Americans born in the 1980s—the millennial generation—college graduates are only modestly wealthier than those who never went to college. While they earn far more than nongraduates, they have failed to build the savings that prior generations of graduates did, in no small part because their debt has consumed so much of their earnings.

It's not just the young. Student debt has become multigenerational. Just over half of all borrowers are over 35; a fifth are over 50. Many older Americans are still paying their own debts; others borrowed to pay tuition for their offspring. The debt is depriving them of a financially secure retirement. Over the past decade, hundreds of thousands of senior citizens have had their Social Security checks reduced as the government collects on unpaid student debt. Many seniors have no other income. The reduced checks have left many living below the poverty level.

Meanwhile, the program has become a drain on the federal budget. When borrowers fail to repay, taxpayers cover the tab. The cost of covering defaults is absorbed in the budget. The losses are growing so large they are bound to drive up the federal deficit in coming years. Of the $1.6 trillion in student debt, borrowers are on track to pay back only two-thirds, leaving taxpayers on the hook for more than $500 billion. That's almost the amount of subprime mortgage debt that private lenders wrote off after the housing crash. It's seven times what the government spends on food stamps each year.

How could this happen? The Debt Trap attempts to answer Lisa's question. This book is the culmination of eight years of reporting, including hundreds of interviews with borrowers, college presidents, members of Congress, congressional aides, presidential advisers, lobbyists, and Wall Street investors. The reporting includes interviews with the first four CEOs of Sallie Mae, the company that, with a mandate from Congress, created the student loan industry.

Student debt was supposed to be an equal partnership among those parties and America's families. Banks and schools would lend, with a little help from the government; students would borrow, work hard in school, and pay back their loans with interest as they got the job of their dreams and lived happily ever after.

Elected leaders thought they were helping families by putting more money in their hands. The problem is Congress failed to provide guardrails to ensure borrowers weren't overcharged for their degrees. The program became a profit center for schools and the student loan industry, which put none of their own money at risk as they encouraged students to sign up for tens of thousands of dollars in debt.

Over the decades Congress passed a series of laws that created perverse incentives for lenders, schools, and borrowers alike. The student loan program is the quintessential form of crony capitalism. It privatized profits and socialized losses. In an echo of the housing bubble, all the risk fell to students and their families, who have been told repeatedly that college and grad school are safe and necessary investments. The narrative of higher education as a ticket to the American Dream fueled the exploitation of good intentions by bad actors.

The most important actor in the evolution of the student loan system was Sallie Mae, a quasi-public agency that Congress created in the 1970s to kick-start the student-loan industry. The company served as a money laundering operation—as its main congressional defender, the late Michigan congressman Bill Ford, once described it—and the money it laundered was taxpayers'. Sallie Mae, under an agreement with Congress, funneled untold billions of public dollars to schools and banks, and itself made enormous profits off the whole operation.

The actors who have benefited the most—banks, Sallie Mae, and universities—shaped that system, hiring armies of lobbyists to push for laws that improved their bottom lines while often leaving borrowers in the lurch. Universities employ more lobbyists than any other industry except pharmaceuticals and technology. They have fended off attempts at federal regulation that would have prevented many borrowers from getting into financial trouble.

College presidents have done quite well from the system. Eighty-one university leaders, including 17 at public colleges, earned more than $1 million in 2019. Wall Street, too, made a killing, earning tens of billions of dollars from the student loan program each year by investing in for-profit colleges that left students with low salaries and deep in debt.

Congress and multiple U.S. presidents encouraged borrowing

while ignoring red flags that the loans set up borrowers to fail. Congress used shoddy accounting to mask the consequences of the reckless lending, engaging in behavior that would be criminal in the private sector. All of the practices that the government accused private lenders of in the mortgage market—predatory lending, deceptive math, willful ignorance—occur routinely in student lending.

How could this happen? This book tells the story of how we got here, starting from day one of federal student lending in the late 1950s. It chronicles how the program evolved into a grand social experiment in the 1960s, how it unleashed an era of runaway tuition in the 1980s and '90s, how Sallie Mae became a Wall Street behemoth and the biggest student lender in the early 2000s, and how investors stoked the for-profit college crisis in the 2000s.

Many people—more than are included in this book—played a role in creating this mess. Most had good intentions, putting their faith in higher education and student loans as they sought to uplift families and the country. Many now say they got it wrong. The late economist Alice Rivlin, the first head of the Congressional Budget Office and first female White House budget director, provided the ideological framework for the student loan program. As part of the Lyndon Baines Johnson administration in the late 1960s, Rivlin oversaw a landmark report calling for a major expansion of student lending.

The idea was to help the poor and the middle class, through scholarships and student loans, move up in a rapidly maturing economy, and to reduce poverty and income gaps in American society.

I asked her in early 2019, two months before she died, how that system turned out.

She didn't hesitate: "We unleashed a monster."

ONE

The Visionary

(1957–1969)

After nightfall on October 4, 1957, Lyndon Johnson stood on a dusty country lane and stared up at the wide Texas sky. His wife, Lady Bird, stood beside him, craning her neck to look up at the stars strewn across the heavens. Guests who had dined with them at the ranch that night stood nearby, gazing skyward. No one spoke.

Everything around Johnson should have been familiar. Every night that he and Lady Bird had been home since Johnson's heart attack two years earlier, they had walked this road tracing the path of the Pedernales River, the lights of their ranch blazing behind them. All his life, the stars above his beloved Hill Country had aligned in his favor.

Not this night. For Lady Bird, what was usually a comforting stroll felt long and strained, the familiar stars above strangely alien. Earlier in the day, the Soviet Union had surreptitiously launched Sputnik, an aluminum sphere the size of a beach ball. By that evening, humanity's first artificial satellite was hundreds of miles above Earth, orbiting the planet every 98 minutes.

Johnson had been hosting dinner at his ranch near Austin when the news broke. As the Senate majority leader, he was the second most powerful man in Washington, after President Dwight D. Eisenhower. He was now confronting a humbling and terrifying reality: The Russians had a rocket powerful enough to send an object into space—and, in all likelihood, a nuclear bomb to the U.S.

Johnson was stunned. After the starlit walk, he went back to the ranch and picked up the phone, calling fellow senators and their aides. Sputnik marked a national emergency, he told them, and Congress needed to rise to the challenge. "I also remember the profound shock of realizing that it might be possible for another nation to achieve technological superiority over this great country of ours," Johnson later wrote.

He concluded that beating back the Soviets relied on higher education. This was a cold war, after all, not a conventional war. Winning would require brainpower—scientists and engineers—as much as military force.

The country, he concluded, needed more college graduates.

At the time of Johnson's walk under the stars, middle-class families were worried about the soaring cost of college. Universities were complaining they didn't have enough money. Employers were saying they couldn't find talented workers. And the nation as a whole was becoming anxious about the United States' standing in the world, stoked by rising tensions with the Russians.

That year, 1957, was a pivotal one. It was right around this time that the idea of a universal right to education started to take hold, and Americans began to think about college as the ticket to the American Dream. It was also at this time that the idea of securing access to higher education through debt—rather than scholarships—gained prominence.

Understanding how today's student loan system became so dysfunctional requires understanding how that system took root six decades ago. It requires understanding the rapid economic, political, and social shifts that occurred early in the 20th century that spurred the government to increase its role in higher education in the first place.

At the turn of the 20th century, most Americans worked with their hands: In 1900, about 4 in 10 workers toiled on farms, while nearly 1 in 3 worked in factories, mines, and construction sites. But the country was in the middle of a historic period of rapid technological change, the second Industrial Revolution. This period had started in the 1880s with the development of the modern electrical grid. Advances in machinery and production—including Henry Ford's creation of the assembly line—followed. Urbanization— the shift of employers and employment to big cities—was well underway. Technologies such as the radio and air travel changed how Americans lived and worked.

At the same time, there was a related shift in Americans' education. It's hard to fathom now, but at the start of the century the vast majority of Americans had never graduated high school, let alone college. In 1910, only about 14 percent of all Americans above age 25 had a high school diploma. But that was changing dramatically.

In the ensuing decades, no country invested in primary and secondary education like the United States did. Cities, towns, and counties built schools and trained teachers. States passed laws requiring attendance. High school graduation rates soared.

Most students never went to college. By the 1920s, fewer than a tenth of young adults matriculated. For many, the biggest barrier was money. While public primary and secondary schools received funding from state and local governments, most colleges charged tuition. Private colleges charged the equivalent of a quarter of the typical household's annual earnings. Public colleges charged as much as 8 percent. Families tended to be larger than today. If parents could afford to send one child to college, they often couldn't afford to send another.

In the 1920s, as the economy boomed, America entered an era of mass consumerism. Households started to borrow to pay for all types of goods and services—including college. "Everything from automobile tires to real estate can be bought on the deferred-payment plan," reads a 1929 pamphlet distributed by the U.S. Department of the Interior. "Higher education is no exception to the rule."

Philanthropists set up funds to lend to students. Schools such as Stanford and the University of Minnesota lent to their students. Banks lent to students who showed "honesty, character, industry and ability."

One of those early bank borrowers was a tall young man named Lyndon Baines Johnson. He'd been raised by tenant farmers in southwest Texas, in a house with no electricity or plumbing. In 1927, he waited anxiously in line to enroll at Southwest Texas State Teachers College, unsure how he would pay tuition. When the bill arrived weeks later, he panicked. "Unless I can arrange in the next 10 days for a loan, I am going to be compelled to leave school," he wrote a family friend. His local bank lent him $75, which he augmented by working as a campus janitor and as secretary to the college president.

Johnson was lucky. The student loan market was exclusive. Many banks refused to make loans, because unlike mortgages or auto loans, student loans had no tangible asset backing them, such as a house or a car. Those that did typically required students to put up "collateral"—stocks, bonds, or real estate—that the banks could sell if borrowers failed to repay. Students needed money to get money.

This was a societal problem, because as America's economy matured and technology was incorporated into the workplace, employers increasingly needed workers with new skills—but they couldn't find enough of them. In 1940, while half of all teenagers graduated high school, only 9 in 100 young adults enrolled in college. In 1944, everything changed.

Up to this point, the idea of education as the ticket to the American Dream didn't quite exist—at least not for a wide swath of the country. The United States had only a decade earlier emerged from a long period of turbulence and trauma—the stock market crash of 1929, followed by the Great Depression—in which unemployment skyrocketed above 20 percent. Higher education still mainly served upper-income and elite families.

As World War II neared an end, President Franklin D. Roosevelt faced pressure to provide aid for the 16 million veterans destined to return home. Administration officials wanted to prevent the kind of debacle that occurred during the Great Depression, when unemployed World War I veterans marched in Washington demanding federal bonuses they had been promised but hadn't received. Protesters clashed with police and army troops, resulting in bloody mayhem.

Roosevelt and Congress feared more social unrest and another depression if employers failed to hire World War II veterans fast enough. To buy time, Congress unanimously passed the Servicemen's Readjustment Act, more widely known as the G.I. Bill of Rights. Signed by Roosevelt in June 1944, the law provided each veteran with unemployment checks, loan guarantees to buy homes, and $500 a year for college tuition, plus a "subsistence" payment of $50 to $75 a month. For the first time, college across the U.S. was free to the masses.

The dream of moving up in society through education was now a very real ambition for millions of Americans who otherwise lacked the money to go to college. College enrollment exploded. By 1946, two million Americans were taking courses, half of them veterans. Colleges, unprepared for the crush, set up "trailer towns" to house and teach them.

The flood of $14.5 billion in federal aid for training and education had unintended consequences. Entrepreneurs eager to tap into the sudden federal largess opened thousands of for-profit trade schools. "Fly-by-night" schools charged exactly $500 a year to collect the maximum G.I. voucher from the Veterans Administration, which paid schools directly, a Congressional investigation found in 1952. They offered "courses in fields where little or no employment existed." Schools falsified data and attendance records and overcharged for books and supplies. "Hundreds of millions of dollars have been frittered away on worthless training," the report concluded.

The G.I. Bill had another flaw: Not every American benefited. Many Black veterans were blocked from using G.I. money because colleges, particularly in the South, refused to admit them. Among Black veterans who sought to go to college, only one in five were able to enroll by 1946. Few women qualified for the money. While many women served in the war, the military labeled their units civilian, making them ineligible for G.I. benefits.

Veterans who did use the aid tended to graduate and land well-paying jobs, earning far more than those who never used the benefits. The law kicked millions of veterans into the middle class.

In 1946, President Harry Truman appointed a panel to draft a long-term plan for paying for college. In a sign of colleges' influence in Washington, Truman turned to the universities' top lobbyist, George Zook, to head the panel. The so-called Zook Commission called education "a birthright" that was being undermined by tuition "so high as to eliminate almost completely the enrollment of students from low-income families." It urged the government to make the first two years of college free and to offer a limited number of scholarships for students in their final two years.

Congress rejected the plan. The nation's rivalry with the Soviet Union had provoked a sharp break from the New Deal era's big government and collectivism. Republicans had taken control of Congress in 1946 by campaigning to defend the free world against Communism. They tarred proposed federal aid for education as socialism.

Southern Democrats feared federal involvement in education would force schools to desegregate. Other lawmakers warned that a federal scholarship program would fund religious colleges and, in their view, breach the separation of church and state.

After the 1948 election, a newly elected Democrat from Alabama, Rep. Carl Elliott, approached Truman about the prospect of a new federal college scholarship program. Truman, a champion of the New Deal, personally favored scholarships. But the president flatly turned Elliott down, telling him, "There's probably never going to be any federal aid to education in this country, at least not in your lifetime."

Nine years later, the satellite that whizzed through the night sky swiftly improved Truman's dim prognosis for federal student aid. But it didn't immediately change the mind of the sitting president, Dwight D. Eisenhower. The same weekend that Lyndon Johnson and Lady Bird stared up at the Texas sky, Eisenhower and his wife, Mamie, settled in for a weekend at their bucolic vacation home in Gettysburg, Pennsylvania. President Eisenhower had been preoccupied with the Little Rock Nine episode in Arkansas, where the governor sought to block the enrollment of nine Black children in a white school. Eisenhower learned of Sputnik from his press secretary. He was not impressed. The next day, he went golfing. "The Russians have only put one small ball in the air," Eisenhower told reporters.

Newspapers ran front-page stories about Sputnik for weeks. Reports focused on the skills of America's scientists against their counterparts in Russia, which had been frantically training engineers to win the space race. Under the media pressure, Eisenhower met with renowned American scientists in the Oval Office eleven days after the satellite's launch. The scientists told the president that the Russians had nearly caught up to the U.S. in science. "They could pass us swiftly," Nobel Prize winner Isidor Rabi, a Columbia University physicist, told the president, "just as in a period of 20 to 30 years we caught up to Western Europe and left it far behind." Eisenhower committed to finding a way to inspire young Americans to study science in college.

Three weeks later, the Russians launched Sputnik 2, a bigger satellite that carried a stray mongrel named Laika into orbit. In December, the Eisenhower administration tried to launch its own satellite. The rocket rose four feet before falling back on the launchpad and exploding. News reports called the incident Flopnik.

Lyndon Johnson realized the two Sputnik launches made Eisenhower politically vulnerable ahead of the following year's midterm elections. Johnson, who chaired the Senate's Preparedness Investigating Subcommittee, held hearings on the "missile gap" between the U.S. and the Soviet Union. Scientists testified that the key to reclaiming the lead in the space race was boosting the nation's ranks of scientists. "We were finally coming to see that our defenses did extend even to the classroom," Johnson wrote.

With the leaders of both parties on board for some type of student aid program, the country faced a pivotal moment: Should college be free to students, through taxpayer-funded scholarships?

Or should households bear at least some of the cost, through student loans?

Other Western countries subsidized education with grants to institutions of higher learning. In Britain, for example, the state stepped up direct funding of universities after World War II to make college free to citizens, relieving the pressure on schools to raise money through tuition and fees.

In the U.S., where at least one state—California—had provided tuition-free public college since the late 19th century, prominent figures came out in favor of a system that shifted a greater share of the cost of higher education onto students. In a 1955 essay, the conservative economist Milton Friedman wrote that students should be treated like companies, with investors lending them money as a type of equity investment and the student repaying them with future earnings. Months before Sputnik, a higher education panel commissioned by Eisenhower recommended government-backed student loans. The panel's chairman, the investment banker Devereux Josephs, told *Fortune* magazine that loans would promote independence and responsibility among students.

The Eisenhower administration believed loans would burden students who went into low-paying fields. But it also didn't like the idea of a wide-scale scholarship program, which would undermine the president's limited-government philosophy. In January, Eisenhower proposed a mere 10,000 college scholarships a year over four years for students studying the sciences.

The man who would decide this debate was Carl Elliott, the Alabama Democrat who had unsuccessfully pressed Truman for a college scholarship program. Elliott headed the House Subcommittee on Special Education, which crafted higher education policy. The son of tenant farmers, he had worked as a houseboy and groundskeeper to pay for a degree at the University of Alabama. He ran for Congress in 1948 telling coal miners there was no reason their children shouldn't have the same opportunity to go to college as wealthy elites in the city.

Elliott had fought for years for a universal scholarship program, to no avail. He saw only one way to bring together liberals and conservatives: student loans. In the summer of 1957, he held hearings at which a University of Minnesota official testified that his school had extended loans to students for decades. Few borrowers defaulted. Elliott pointed out that college graduates on average earned $100,000 more over 30 years than nongrads—so a modest loan would be a high-reward investment. He proposed a massive new student loan program. In a deft political strategy, Democrats gave their bill the patriotic name the National Defense Education Act and attached a requirement that each borrower sign an oath of loyalty to the U.S. government, appeasing McCarthyites. Conservatives approved.

"The House denounced scholarships—'it was a waste of money and socialism and all of that,'" Stewart McClure, a Senate Democratic aide who worked on the bill, later recalled. "The minute the damn scholarship issue was done for, dead, the bill swooped through."

Lyndon Johnson focused on passing a law to create the National Aeronautics and Space Administration, which Eisenhower signed that summer. The next month, on September 2, 1958, Eisenhower, under intense political pressure, signed the National Defense Education Act, which created the National Defense Student Loan program.

Eleven months after Sputnik, the United States government entered the student loan business.

The new student loan program represented a seminal moment in the evolution of higher education. The federal government adopted a de facto policy: Students are obligated to pay a substantial share of the cost of their education, rather than having government cover it entirely.

The loan program funneled hundreds of millions of dollars to schools, which decided who received loans of up to $1,000 a year. In the first year, schools requested twice as much as the government had projected. Eisenhower officials suspected schools of inflating their needs but told Congress the law explicitly forbade the government from overseeing how the loan money was spent.

Because Congress approved a finite amount of money for the program, many students were rejected for loans. Less than a year after the new law was established, at least one prominent university advocate pushed to greatly expand the program. The Harvard economist Seymour Harris, who would later advise President John F. Kennedy, argued in the *New York Times* that a bigger program would allow colleges to extract more money from students, money that could be used to raise professors' salaries. Senator Lyndon Johnson, who had his eye on the White House, introduced a bill to create a new loan program to allow more middle-class students to borrow. The bill went nowhere, but Congress did approve more funding for the National Defense Student Loan program.

College enrollment climbed rapidly, in part because many students who otherwise wouldn't have been able to pay now got loans. As borrowing soared, few Washington policy makers considered whether students would be able to repay their debt. Increasing Americans' access to college was the primary focus.

After John Kennedy won the White House in 1960—with Johnson as his vice president—Kennedy worried about poor students getting into too much debt. He asked Congress to provide them scholarships, which they wouldn't have to repay. "Half of all American families earn less than $5,600 a year, and they simply cannot take on that kind of debt," he told reporters in early 1962.

After another surge in applications from schools, the loan program ran out of money in 1963. Colleges scaled back lending. A front-page story in the *New York Times* warned that hundreds of thousands of students would be rejected for loans. Kennedy, seeing that Congress had little appetite to set aside more money for scholarships, asked Congress for another increase in funding for the loan program.

By the end of November, Kennedy was dead, killed in Dallas by an assassin's bullet. The presidential mantle passed to the Texan who had once gazed up at the stars above his ranch and worried about what the future would hold.

On the evening of Saturday, November 23, 1963, Lyndon Johnson stared pensively out of a window in the Oval Office, a day after he had been hastily sworn in as president on Air Force One. Walter Heller, the White House's top economic adviser, waited by the president's desk.

As grieving staffers roamed the halls, Heller told the new president that Kennedy had been looking into ways to reduce poverty. *Do you want to make that a priority in your own administration?* Heller asked.

Johnson paused. One in five Americans lived in poverty. He thought about how 35 million poor citizens needed someone to represent their interests in Washington, he later wrote.

"Full tilt ahead," Johnson told Heller.

Johnson, a former schoolteacher, viewed education as the most effective tool to reduce poverty. He may have been the first president to say a college degree was essential. "Higher education is no longer a luxury but a necessity," Johnson told Congress in January 1965.

He linked education to the civil rights movement. In a famous speech at Howard University, a historically Black college in Washington, D.C., in 1965, Johnson said that after centuries of slavery and oppression, Black Americans were in a societal race they had begun far behind the starting line. "They lack training and skills," he said. A national investment in education would help close the gap.

Johnson's vision for college marked a crucial shift. Congress passed the first student loan program to win the Cold War. Johnson wanted to deploy colleges to solve a more complex problem: racial and income inequality.

Doing so would require a huge sum of money.

Congress was already under political pressure to help families pay for college. Congressional Republicans proposed tax breaks, which would reimburse families after they paid tuition. The Johnson administration viewed tax breaks as a costly handout to wealthy families, who were the ones most likely to have enough money to pay tuition out of pocket. Poor families needed assistance up front to cover tuition.

College groups warned of a separate problem: Tax credits would, perversely, encourage schools to raise tuition, to collect the extra money the government put in families' hands. "Many educators who advocate tax relief do so explicitly with the aim of raising tuition levels," Allan Cartter of the American Council on Education, the universities' main lobbying group, told Congress. "Thus, what the parent who bears the burden of college costs views as a partial 'cure' may turn out to be quite illusory."

Johnson developed a compromise: scholarships for the poor and loans for the middle class. He proposed a much bigger loan program than the National Defense Student Loan program, one that would essentially make student loans an entitlement, available to any middle-class family that needed them.

One obstacle stood in his way: the federal deficit.

*　*　*

Congress, at Johnson's urging, had passed a flurry of bills that were bound to drive up the deficit. It had just created Medicare and Medicaid and approved aid for elementary and secondary schools. Defense spending surged as the U.S. deepened its involvement in the Vietnam War. Overall federal spending topped $100 billion for the first time in 1965 and was set to rise further in coming years.

The Johnson administration worried the deficit would spook the investors who lent to the government by purchasing Treasury bonds. Interest rates on those bonds would rise, officials feared, increasing the government's borrowing costs and crowding out private funding, which threatened to slow the economy.

A large-scale student loan program would push the deficit higher because of arcane budget rules that made a loan program look expensive. Under those rules, any money flowing out of the U.S. Treasury—whether to pay for army tanks or to build highways—was considered spending. Any money flowing in—like when Americans paid their federal taxes—was income. If the government originated $1 billion in student loans, spending increased by $1 billion. This was a mirage, since the spike would be temporary; years later, students' monthly payments would reduce the resulting deficit. But what mattered at the time was the immediate budgetary hit. This is why Johnson didn't seek to simply expand the National Defense Student Loan program, which drew money from the Treasury.

Instead, Johnson turned to banks.

He had a model to follow. The government had long promoted homeownership by incentivizing banks to lend to families to buy houses. In the wake of the Great Depression, Congress created the Federal Housing Administration to insure, or guarantee, mortgages made by private lenders. If a borrower defaulted, the government reimbursed the bank for most of the loan. The federal insurance encouraged banks to lend to borrowers they would otherwise deem too risky. Because the loan money came from banks, not the Treasury Department, the federal budget was unscathed. The program was, in Washington-speak, "off the books."

Johnson had proposed a similar agency for student loans in his 1959 bill, which he now revived as president. The plan called for colleges to borrow from banks at a 4.5 percent interest rate and lend that money to students at a 5 percent rate. The school would pocket half the proceeds and put the other half into a pool that—combined with federal tax dollars—would cover losses if a student failed to repay.

All three institutions—banks, schools, the federal government—would have money at stake. The risk of losing money would discourage banks and schools from extending loan amounts that would be too high for students to repay.

Johnson urged Congress in 1965 to guarantee loans for college students. The new program would be "a more effective, fairer and far less costly way of providing assistance than the various tax credit devices which have been proposed," he said. Just about any American, excluding the wealthy, would qualify for the loans.

The administration assumed that everyone would come out of college with a degree, land a well-paying job, and repay the debt with ease. "The idea of a guarantee was that this wasn't going to cost us any money," Johnson's Treasury secretary, Joseph Barr, later said. "Everybody would pay it off."

Ever the avuncular arm-twister, Johnson invited bankers to the White House, hoping to convince them the new college loan program would be good for their business and good for the country. In the grandeur of the Oval Office, he described how a bank thirty years earlier had extended him a student loan, salvaging his college career. It was the best investment that bank ever made, he told them.

One of the fixtures in those back-slapping Oval Office meetings was Charls Walker, a friend of Johnson's and the head of the American Bankers Association, the industry's top lobbying group. (Walker's mother left the *e* off his name because she didn't like the name Charlie. He went by that anyway.) Walker loved cigars and bourbon. He also loved helping his industry make money, and he was skeptical of Johnson's enthusiasm for federal college loans. Walker had a natural disdain for the federal government, which he viewed as an obstacle to the ability of his 14,000 member banks to make profits.

By 1965, banks had gotten into student lending without federal assistance. A group of corporate CEOs had created a loan insurance fund similar to what Johnson proposed but using private donations from philanthropists, schools, and other sources. Banks lent to students. If the students defaulted, the fund reimbursed banks. By early 1965, the program, called United Student Aid Funds (USAF), had insured nearly $40 million in student loans— or about $335 million in today's dollars—and was growing quickly. Some states had also set up nonprofit insurance funds, known as guarantee agencies.

USAF's default rates were low, for one main reason: They didn't let just anyone have a loan. Banks reviewed each student's credit history for red flags, such as a bankruptcy. They refused to lend to freshmen, who were at the highest risk of dropping out and defaulting. They often turned down Black applicants and poor students. "Parent and student of above-average income are the only ones who are able to take advantage of it," Armour Blackburn, dean of students at Howard University, told a House committee in the spring of 1965.

For Johnson to meet his vision of universal access to higher education, he needed banks to make loans to anyone who needed one.

Walker lobbied Congress to defeat Johnson's version. "His intention was to create a Federal bureaucracy to run the program—and surely kill it with red tape and mismanagement," Walker wrote in notes for a book that he never finished. "Our group banded for lobbying and in the oval office [*sic*], told LBJ we strongly supported the concept but were unalterably opposed to federal ownership and operation."

In Congress, Charls Walker's proposal—to create a program using hundreds of millions of taxpayer dollars, with no federal oversight—became known as "the bankers' bill."

Senator Ralph Yarborough was skeptical. The Texas Democrat was a former state prosecutor who had sued oil companies to ensure public schools gained a share of the industry's profits. He was sitting next to then–vice president Johnson in the presidential motorcade in Dallas when Kennedy was assassinated.

At a Senate committee hearing in March 1965, Yarborough said bankers had told him how eager they were to get Walker's bill passed. Banks had already set up branches to process the loans. That rankled Yarborough, who warned that banks would find ways of "making a killing" off of college students. "I don't think we ought to hang three balls of the pawnshop over the college door and treat this like an automobile loan," Yarborough said. "There ought to be a scholarship program instead of mortgages on these students before they are 21 years of age. It's getting away from the American concept of this country and its families educating students."

Other members of Congress felt constrained by the federal budget. Johnson's proposal called for scholarships of up to $800 a year for poor students—not enough to cover a year of tuition and living costs at many schools. Poor students would have to borrow to make up the difference. "You are never going to be able to get enough money appropriated for the number of scholarships that qualified students need in order to go to college," Senator Wayne Morse, an Oregon Democrat, said at a hearing.

Policy makers found themselves in a bind that endures to this day, caught between the ambition to provide universal access to education and the need to pay for it. The U.S. already had more colleges per capita than many other countries. With more buildings and more college faculty, the system was becoming expensive.

Student loans became the answer. Senator Morse equated access to loans with access to college. Without loans, Morse said, "there are thousands and thousands of students to whom we are going to deny a college education to in the years ahead, thereby not only doing them a great damage but causing a great damage to the economy and security of this country."

Congress went with Walker's proposal. It passed the Higher Education Act, which included a scholarship program for the poor and the Guaranteed Student Loan program for the middle class. The latter provided tens of millions of dollars to the USAF and state nonprofit guarantee agencies to insure student loans. The program allowed a student to borrow up to $1,000 a year for college or $1,500 for graduate school. The guarantee agency co-signed the loan. If the student defaulted, the agency fully reimbursed the lender for the loan principal and accrued interest. Then, the federal government reimbursed the agency for 80 percent of the principal.

Congress set an interest rate of 6 percent on the loans. The government paid that rate to banks while students were in school and for a brief period after they graduated. Then, starting nine months after graduation, students paid the interest. This benefit was limited to students from households earning less than $15,000 a year.

On November 8, 1965, Johnson returned to his alma mater, Southwest Texas State Teachers College in San Marcos, Texas, to sign the Higher Education Act. Organizers set up a wooden desk outside a gymnasium called Old Main for the president to sign the bill. Johnson had swept the floors of the gymnasium as a janitor.

That morning, a heavy downpour forced the ceremony indoors. The rain couldn't dampen Johnson's spirits. The president's goal of universal access to higher education had been achieved. No longer would lack of money prevent Americans from getting into college and achieving the American Dream. "The path of knowledge is open to all who have the determination to walk it," Johnson told the packed auditorium.

While Johnson spoke loftily about helping Americans achieve their middle-class hopes, schools gained access to a huge source of money with few restrictions. "Recently the thick doors of the national Treasury have begun to swing open much wider," Keith Spalding, Franklin and Marshall College's president, said at an industry convention shortly after Johnson signed the bill. "We are quite suddenly confronted by a munificence on the part of the federal government for which we truly were not fully prepared."

Within months, Johnson's hopes for the program to become a middle-class entitlement ran into a wall: inflation. The cost of living started to rise sharply. Banks raised interest rates on other types of products—mortgages, car loans, commercial loans. Soon, the 6 percent interest rate on student loans was less than the banks' own borrowing costs, or what they could earn on other investments. Many refused to participate in the program.

It was the first sign that Congress's and Johnson's attempts to steer private markets had gone awry. Not long after he signed the Higher Education Act, Johnson hosted bankers in the Oval Office to celebrate the new law—and to bend banks to his will. He pulled Walker aside to a window overlooking the Rose Garden. "Charly, your goddamn banks are raising interest rates sky-high," Johnson said. "I want you to tell them to stop."

While the bankers mingled in the background, Walker explained that interest rates were rising in part because the president's own policies—the surge in spending from the Great Society programs—were stoking inflation. "Mr. President, this is not something the banks pulled out of the air," he said. "It's the market."

"To hell with that Charly," the president snapped. "Tell them to stop."

The banks didn't stop. They told Johnson if he wanted the student loan program to survive, they needed more money. In 1968, Congress raised the student loan interest rate to 7 percent. In 1969, it raised it to 10 percent.

Even then, many banks refused to lend to students. That created a big problem for policy makers, because college enrollment was exploding with the full onslaught of baby boomers. Eight million students, including one in three young adults, took college and graduate courses in 1969, more than twice the number of students in 1957. Many were only able to matriculate because of federal loans and grants. Many others complained that their banks wouldn't lend to them.

The seeds of another problem had been planted. Colleges were raising tuition faster than before. Economic theory predicted that would happen. The economist Milton Friedman once posited that inflation happens when too much money is chasing too few goods. The more dollars consumers have, businesses will raise prices to collect those dollars. The government had put dollars into families' hands through the defense loan program and the Guaranteed Student Loan program. The loan dollars increased the number of people willing and able to pay for college. Colleges responded to that increase in demand by raising prices. In the 1960s, colleges raised tuition 30 percent above inflation. The cure for high tuition was worsening the disease.

Colleges said they needed more money to meet their students' needs. In 1968, the Carnegie Foundation, the influential nonprofit that advocated for professors' pensions, released the first of several reports urging an expansion of student loans. The group warned of a looming "depression" for colleges as baby boomers aged into their 20s, shrinking the colleges' customer pool. More loans would enable the schools to raise tuition and ease colleges' financial plight.

Banks needed more money. Colleges needed more money. Students needed more money. The government's foray into student lending was already a mess, producing unintended consequences. Congress had passed the two loan programs hastily, with deference to banks and schools and little thought to the perverse incentives that might lead to even higher tuition and taxpayer costs. Johnson needed someone to craft a long-term plan to fix the mess.

Enter Alice Rivlin.

Rivlin was in her 30s and assistant secretary of the Department of Health, Education, and Welfare. Born in Indiana, she had graduated Bryn Mawr College with an economics degree and gone overseas to work on the Marshall Plan, the U.S. effort to help Europe's economy recover from World War II. When she applied to the graduate school of public administration at Harvard, the university rejected her as a dropout risk because she was of "marriageable age." (She eventually got into Harvard's graduate school for economics.)

Rivlin adhered to "new economics"—an idea in the '60s that economists, through excruciating analysis, could identify societal problems and design policies to fix them. Johnson handed Rivlin her biggest task yet: Draft a plan to finance higher education for future generations. Rivlin headed a panel consisting mostly of government officials to come up with the plan.

Rivlin's main focus was on how best to reduce poverty, the

most vexing problem of the era. She believed, as did Johnson, that college was part of the solution. College graduates earned far more than nongraduates. How better to reduce inequality than to help the poor earn degrees?

Rivlin saw two big problems in higher education. First: Youths who needed college the most were the least likely to enroll. Students from wealthy families were twice as likely to enroll in college as those from poor families. Whites were far more likely to enroll than Blacks.

Second: Upper-income students went to better-funded schools than lower-income students. The first group tended to go to big state flagships; the second group tended to go to community colleges.

The debate Rivlin had to decide was philosophical: Should the federal government give money directly to colleges, or to students?

College groups argued for direct aid to schools. If the government gave them money they wouldn't have to charge such high tuition to pay their bills, they said. Some educators acknowledged that student loans provided an incentive to raise tuition to collect more money than the schools needed. Loans would lead to an "escalation which would require ever-increasing student financial aid funds to enable students to meet the ever-increasing costs of going to college," Allen W. Ostar, head of the American Association of State Colleges and Universities, wrote at the time.

Rivlin's panel supported the position that the federal government should continue to give money to students, in the form of loans and grants.

Rivlin believed in harnessing the power of consumers, through their choices on what and where to buy, to force companies to innovate and become efficient. She believed higher education could benefit from such pressure. Giving money to students would empower students as consumers. By shopping around for different colleges and armed with a federally funded voucher—a scholarship, a loan, or a combination of the two—students would stir competition among colleges, which would be under pressure to hold their tuition in check. If a school charged too much, a student would go to a cheaper school. Also, the most prestigious schools would open their doors wider to the poor and minorities, the Rivlin panel argued.

Colleges "will presumably be more responsive to student needs (and thereby more effective) if they must compete for students who have the financial flexibility to choose among a greater number of institutions," it said.

To satisfy schools' needs for more money, Rivlin's panel envisioned them modestly raising tuition. Wealthy students would bear the brunt. The poor would have their tuition covered by grants.

The biggest group—the middle class—would take out loans if they needed to. The report characterized loans as an investment in students' future. Just as companies borrow money to upgrade their facilities with new machinery, young Americans should borrow to increase their "human capital"—the knowledge and skills that make them valuable to employers and lift their lifetime earnings. "It evolved into an almost fixation—among economists anyway—with the idea that higher education added to your future income and therefore loan finance was a sensible thing," Rivlin said in a 2019 interview. "You could pay it back out of your future income."

Who would lend to students? The Rivlin report proposed a nonprofit, federally controlled agency to originate loans, eliminating banks from the program.

Rivlin delivered the report in January 1969, two weeks before President Richard Nixon took office. The incoming administration—advised by Daniel Patrick Moynihan, the liberal antipoverty crusader who believed in giving money directly to the poor—adopted Rivlin's main recommendations for wide access to loans and grants.

The U.S., in just the span of a decade, had made a huge investment in higher education. The country's spending on higher education had risen from 1.4 percent of the economy at the start of the decade to 2.3 percent by the time Rivlin released her report. The 1960s became known as the "golden era" for the nation's universities, a time when the country invested heavily in them—both spiritually and with its citizens' pocketbooks.

The Rivlin and Carnegie reports reframed the national discussion about who should go to college, and about how society should pay for it. Each carried a strong message that higher education played the role of the Great Equalizer, leveling the playing field for the poor. Loans allowed borrowers to invest in themselves.

After Nixon's election in 1968, Johnson called outgoing Treasury secretary Joe Barr to ask if Nixon's economic team was any good. *Oh yes*, Barr said, and listed some of the incoming staff, which included Paul Volker, the future Federal Reserve chairman, as undersecretary for monetary affairs. Johnson approved, and then asked who would occupy the number two spot as Nixon's deputy Treasury secretary. *Charly Walker*, Barr said.

That's good, Johnson said. "Every administration needs a tough guy somewhere and that son-of-bitch Walker's got elbows," he said. Walker's sharp elbows would help usher in a new era in college lending, one that would depend upon a new private corporation. Its nickname sounded innocent enough—Sallie Mae. Yet it would become the backbone of Rivlin's monster.

TWO

When Ed Met Sallie

(1969–1990)

Samuel Welch clutched his pistol as he made his way to the ninth floor of an office building in the shadow of the U.S. Capitol.

At 63, Welch couldn't afford to retire after a long career managing banks. He had three children to put through college. It was 1969. After two decades of an economic boom, America's middle-class families had raised their ambitions. As employers increasingly required workers to have degrees, families viewed college as a ticket to prosperity. Parents like Welch wanted their children to live more prosperous lives than they did. In the late 1960s, that meant ensuring they went to college.

As a bank manager in Atlanta, Welch had reached his company's mandatory retirement age without enough saved to cover his children's tuition. Desperate, he took a job in Washington, D.C., at the Federal Home Loan Bank Board, an agency that helped Americans obtain mortgages.

Welch moved alone to D.C., temporarily leaving his wife and three kids behind in Atlanta while he began the new job and searched for a house for the family. That April, after the assassination of Martin Luther King Jr., protesters rioted in the streets of D.C. for four days. Businesses went up in flames, the stench of tear gas filled the air, and the National Guard patrolled the streets while the Southern transplant cowered inside his motel room.

Welch bought a pistol. He was a white conservative Southerner who would have been more at home in the 19th century than in the 20th. His experience in Washington left him shaken and bitter. Months later, on a Monday in early November 1969, Welch snapped.

That afternoon, he met with his boss Clarke Fauver, the home loan bank board's operations manager, on the ninth floor of the board's offices on First Street N.W. Welch and Fauver frequently clashed, the former viewing the latter as a condescending liberal. During the meeting, Fauver told him he was being demoted, reassigned to a basement office. To Welch, the bigger humiliation was that he would share the office with a Black employee. Welch stormed out of the meeting in a fury.

When Welch returned, he pulled his pistol out of his coat pocket and shot Fauver in the chest. An assistant tackled Welch and wrestled away the gun. Fauver died. After Welch was arrested, he strangled himself in his jail cell.

The murder proved to have an impossible-to-foresee consequence for the student loan industry, which evolved through a series of events—many planned, others random—over six decades. The assassination of John Kennedy brought to the Oval Office Lyndon Johnson, whose nostalgia for his own student loan led him to champion a new student loan program. The murder of Fauver brought to Washington a Wall Street investment manager who would create the first manifestation of Alice Rivlin's monster: an industry of lenders, investors, and loan-service companies all motivated to make money from America's college students. Higher education would become a hot commodity on Wall Street, enabling a new era of runaway tuition and debt, forever changing the nature of America's college system.

The first domino to fall was the murder. The second domino was a phone call. The bank board's chairman, Preston Martin, reached out to friends on Wall Street to see if they knew anyone who could succeed Fauver. *Yes*, one said. *His name is Ed Fox.*

For the student loan industry to become a monster, someone had to turn on the juice. The person who flipped the switch was Fox.

When Fauver was murdered, Edward Alan Fox managed global investments for Mobil Oil, the energy conglomerate. At 33 years old, he was tall and lean with bushy dark hair and a boyish face. He'd been raised in a middle-class family in Long Island and had gone to Choate Rosemary Hall, the prestigious boarding school. His father, a dentist, wanted him to follow in his footsteps. In 1954, Fox enrolled in Cornell's premed program, only to drop out six weeks later. He switched his major to American studies—it required the fewest credits—and graduated Cornell near the bottom of his class.

Opportunity found him. After a marketing stint at Procter & Gamble, he joined Mobil Oil as a financial analyst. The company's profits were exploding thanks to the economic boom of the 1950s and '60s, which drove up demand for electricity and gasoline. Fox helped decide where to invest the company's money. "Out of nowhere the treasurer pulled me in one day and said he was going to send me off to advanced management training," a six-week program at Princeton, Fox says. "When I came back they told me I was now in charge of the domestic portfolio."

Fox stood out for being a risk-taker, choosing investments that others shied away from. "I fell in love with it," he says.

In 1969, Fox got a call about the Federal Home Loan Bank Board vacancy that resulted from Fauver's murder. The board was part of the intricate financing network Congress stitched together during the Great Depression to kick-start the housing market. The board oversaw a system of regional banks that provided cash to mortgage lenders.

Fox knew little about the housing market and less about Washington politics, and the job would pay less than he earned on Wall Street. But he loved a challenge and the idea of being in a position of authority. To reach a similar leadership role at Mobil would have taken years, if not decades, of climbing the corporate ladder. He took the job.

His first task was reviving the mortgage industry, which in the late 1960s had run into trouble. America's growing middle class and the aging of baby boomers into adulthood pushed up demand for housing—so much so that lenders were running out of money to make mortgages. The system needed investors to put up more money to keep the financial gears churning.

Months into his new job, Fox helped do that. He oversaw the creation of the first asset-backed security, an investment vehicle that would forever change Wall Street and eventually play a role in the 2008 financial crisis. Fox's employees, along with Ginnie Mae—another federal housing agency—bundled a bunch of home loans into one package, against which it borrowed money frominvestors. Years later, banks would take this process a step further, by dicing up such loan packages and selling the pieces to investors. Selling the pieces made more money than selling the package as a whole. This process, called securitization on Wall Street, removed the loans from lenders' books, freeing up cash to make new mortgages. In creating securities, the government deepened its ties with the financial system in the name of helping American households achieve wealth.

Word got around D.C. that Fox was good at what he did. Within months he was summoned to a second job on the side as an aide to Charls Walker, the former banking lobbyist who was now deputy secretary of the Treasury Department. Walker eventually turned to Fox to save the floundering Guaranteed Student Loan program. The banks needed more money for student loans. Fox had to find that money.

At the time, the U.S. had just come out of an economic boom that was due in part to a surge in college graduates, whose skills helped the American economy become more innovative and efficient. Living standards had risen quickly—and none reaped the economic benefits more than college graduates, who earned a decent premium over nongraduates.

President Nixon, like Lyndon Johnson, believed wholeheartedly in the ability of education to improve peoples' lives. Like Johnson, Nixon wanted to make college largely free for the poor by providing cash grants, while having the middle class pay at least a portion of their costs through loans.

But student lending had come to a halt, despite the federal guarantee program. Some banks had made a lot of student loans but had run out of money to make more. Normally, to raise cash, banks would sell to investors the student loans that they had made. Then the investors would collect and keep any payments that the borrower paid; the bank would use the cash from the sale to make new student loans.

But investors believed student loans weren't worth buying. The biggest uncertainty was the interest rate. Congress had agreed to pay up to 10 percent interest on each student loan (students would pay 7 percent and the government would pay the rest). Investors had little confidence that 10 percent would make them money. Inflation and interest rates on other financial products were rising. Investors feared a situation in which they would earn 10 percent on student loans while having to pay 12 percent to borrow. They'd lose money.

President Nixon's advisers proposed creating a new nonprofit entity to lend to students, cutting out the banks. That would have saved the government tens of millions of dollars a year—the interest it paid banks—which could have gone to students in the form of scholarships, easing their reliance on loans.

Banks had a powerful ally in Charls Walker at Treasury. Walker wrote a scathing memo criticizing the proposal and insisted that banks stay in the program. "Some members of the working group suspected Treasury of greater concern for the interests of bankers than those of college students," Nixon aide Chester Finn Jr. later wrote.

Walker proposed that Congress create a corporation, infused with taxpayer cash, to provide money to banks. The agency would be modeled after Fannie Mae, which Congress created after the Great Depression to buy mortgages from banks.

Few of Nixon's other advisers objected to Walker's arguments, Finn wrote, and the administration went with Walker's idea. In Congress, lawmakers were skeptical. Some balked at the idea of bolstering banks with taxpayer money, particularly when it came to funding education.

Bank lobbyists argued that young Americans would be shut out of universities without Walker's proposed agency. Congress hastily crafted a bill that enacted Walker's vision. "They copied some paragraphs out of Fannie Mae's legislation," Fox says.

In 1972, Congress created the Student Loan Marketing Association, with a mandate to inject money into banks. A congressional aide gave it a nickname that made the company sound like a doting aunt serving up a slice of hot apple pie: Sallie Mae.

Sallie Mae's creation rested on the hope that a corporation could balance two separate goals. The first goal was the social mandate of opening up America's universities to the poor and middle class. The second was making money.

Partnerships between private enterprise and the government weren't new. In the 1940s, the government gave money to colleges and universities—many of them private—for research and development to create rocket technology. The government had intervened in housing, through agencies like the Federal Housing Administration and Fannie Mae. It subsidized the farming industry.

This mix of social good and private profit was reflected in Sallie Mae's ownership structure. Sallie Mae was privately owned—only universities and lenders could hold shares—and controlled by a 21-member board, a third appointed by the U.S. president, a third by schools, a third by banks.

At the beginning, Sallie Mae did not have the authority to lend to students. Its purpose was to inject money into the private lending market so college students could borrow. The company did that in two ways. Both involved providing money to banks. Sallie Mae's first method was to buy loans that banks had already made to students, taking those loans off the banks' books. The banks could use the proceeds to make new loans to students.

Sallie Mae's second method was to extend commercial loans to banks, which would put up student loans as "collateral." These commercial loans were called "warehouse advances," and the title wasn't a euphemism. Sallie Mae would store the student loans—actual pieces of paper—in a warehouse, and keep them if the bank defaulted.

Both functions expanded the amount of loans banks made. But Sallie Mae had a third, ancillary function that was vitally important to Congress, which was to essentially outsource the accounting for student lending. By making Sallie Mae responsible for maintaining the complex bookkeeping around federal loans, Congress created an illusion that the federal government wasn't spending money on student lending. It was a smoke screen, an opaque Wizard of Oz curtain around machinations so complicated that few members of Congress—let alone the general public—understood.

To build this novel lending structure from the ground up, Sallie Mae needed cash, and congressional largess only went so far. Initially, Congress gave the company the option to use $5 million in taxpayer money to get started; the rest was supposed to come from shareholders. Sallie Mae was required to raise money from banks and schools, which would thus have "skin in the game," earning profits if students repaid and losing money if they didn't.

When Fox heard of the venture, he loved the idea of starting a company in a new industry that he knew nothing about. "I love challenges," he says. He told Charls Walker he wanted to be its CEO. Walker recommended him to Sallie Mae's board, which selected him over 75 other candidates, at a salary of $70,000 a year—more than $400,000 today.

The board met for the first time in February 1973 in a restaurant at the Shoreham Hotel in northwest Washington. During a break, Fox went to the restroom, where he overheard two board members—Joseph Barr, Lyndon Johnson's former Treasury secretary, and Bill Spencer, the head of Citibank—bantering at the urinal.

"Do you think this will ever work?" Spencer asked, unaware Fox was in a stall nearby.

"Not a chance," Barr replied.

Fox spent the next month flying from city to city meeting with potential investors, hoping to raise $100 million. His pitch: They'd earn profits while contributing to a social cause. Only one investor chipped in during that tour—a mere $100,000—as a form of charity. Investors were skeptical the government could manage such a large program and pay them on time at a profitable rate.

A year later, Congress passed a law allowing Sallie Mae to borrow almost as cheaply as the federal government itself. Congress created the Federal Financing Bank, an arm of the Treasury Department, to lend taxpayer dollars to Sallie Mae, Fannie Mae, and the other so-called government-sponsored enterprises. Sallie Mae could now borrow up to $5 billion at an interest rate just a shave above the government's own borrowing costs.

The advantage this gave Sallie Mae was tremendous. No other institution—public or private—can borrow as cheaply as the U.S. government, whose own debt is considered among the safest assets in the world. Investors that lend to the government—by purchasing Treasury bonds—accept low interest rates in exchange for knowing there's almost no chance the government will fail to repay. Sallie Mae—a for-profit entity serving the interests of banks—now had the same advantage. This kept Sallie Mae's costs extremely low.

Sallie Mae was part of a circuitous route between lender and borrower. To recap: The Treasury Department gave money to the Federal Financing Bank, which lent to Sallie Mae, which provided cash—through warehouse advances and student loan purchases—to banks, which lent to students, who paid schools.

If the student defaulted, the guarantee agency reimbursed the bank all of the loan principal plus all accrued interest, no questions asked. The federal government then reimbursed the guarantee agency 80 percent of the loan principal but no interest—until 1976, that is. That year, with some states refusing to set up guarantee agencies, Congress sweetened the deal by agreeing to cover 100 percent of financial losses. Congress also allowed states to sell tax-exempt bonds to finance student lending, giving them another source of ultra-cheap cash.

This absurdly convoluted system was in place solely to keep the student loan program off the federal budget. The cruel irony: To give the mirage of spending restraint, Congress had increased taxpayer costs. It had to pay lenders tens of millions of dollars in interest each year simply for the lenders to front the money to the student.

"Almost from the beginning the quilt to cover the Treasury had to be patched," John F. Morse, the former head lobbyist for the American Council on Education, wrote in 1975. "Nobody planned it that way; there were just too many seamstresses called in to work on it. We could scarcely, over the years, have devised a more confusing, more expensive, or less efficient program than the one we now have."

The federal government had severed the financial link between borrower and lender. The only money at risk was federal tax dollars. The government had created what economists call a "moral hazard." Studies show that the more an activity is insured, the more people take risks. A bicyclist with a helmet will actually ride more recklessly than a bicyclist without one. A homeowner with flood insurance will buy a home closer to the ocean. And lenders with a 100 percent federal guarantee will extend loans to borrowers who are unable to repay their debt, knowing the lenders won't suffer any losses either way.

The first sign of the coming train wreck came a few days after Sallie Mae opened on K Street, not far from the White House. The company operated out of the third floor of an office building with—appropriately—furniture borrowed from the Treasury. Fox was still getting settled into his new office when a group of people in suits walked into the lobby. They represented a Delaware-registered corporation named Advance Schools Inc.

Fox had never heard of the school. But it was huge. It taught 80,000 students—more than most traditional universities—even though it didn't have a campus per se. It was a "correspondence school," one of a new breed of colleges that taught students by mailing materials to their homes. It was online learning before the internet.

Hundreds of corporate-owned correspondence schools like Advance Schools had cropped up around the U.S. since the establishment of the 1965 law that created the student loan program. They targeted older workers and military veterans, offering the opportunity to learn a trade without having to leave their homes or jobs. Veterans were particularly appealing because they had both student loans and G.I. Bill vouchers to pay the schools' tuition.

Advance taught students how to repair cars, air-conditioning units, refrigerators, and televisions. It offered certificates in those fields, not degrees. Advance found a way to make a lot of money off of taxpayers. It would lend to a student under the federal loan program. Then it would sell that student loan to a bank and use the proceeds to pay employees and make loans to other students. Once the original student graduated, Advance would buy back the loan from the bank and collect payments from the student. If the student defaulted, the government would reimburse Advance for the loan. Advance earned $200 million in 1974, most of it from the federal student loan program.

The men in Fox's office told him the school needed a $10 million loan from Sallie Mae, ostensibly so it could make more loans. They weren't asking; they were demanding.

Fox was suspicious of the huge sum. He told the group he needed to send an auditor to Chicago to inspect the company's books, mainly to see how successfully students repaid their loans. The auditor randomly called borrowers, and couldn't reach a third of them.

Sallie Mae's mandate was to provide money to institutions to educate American citizens. Fox agreed to the loan but required that the school put up as collateral student loans held by borrowers that the auditor was able to reach. By 1975, the school's borrowers were defaulting in droves and the company went bankrupt. More than $100 million in student loans—held by 45 banks, along with Sallie Mae—were outstanding.

Advance was part of a broader trend. Congress had allowed students to spend their loan dollars at for-profit schools in accordance with the 1965 Higher Education Act. By the mid-1970s, businesses like Advance Schools had opened up 7,000 to 8,000 schools, training truck drivers, auto mechanics, computer programmers, and secretaries. They catered to new types of students: those from poor households, those who had struggled in high school, veterans.

But these new schools charged higher tuition than their public school counterparts, in part because they had to. They didn't receive direct money from states or have public endowments. Tuition was their main source of money. The federal loan program provided 90 percent of the funding for many for-profit schools.

In the early 1970s, newspapers around the country ran front-page investigations on how for-profit schools abused the program, failing to provide an adequate education and deceiving students into believing they would land high-paying jobs.

"I could go down in the ghetto and stand on the corner and enroll all kinds of people if it is free," one salesman told the *Chronicle of Higher Education*. "He doesn't care if the course is airlines, insurance adjusting, hotel-motel management, or what, if it is free, going to be paid for by the government and you can get him a job.

He would have to be crazy not to do this. This is a salesman's dream."

Student loan defaults soared. Taxpayer losses on defaulted loans doubled each year in the early 1970s. By 1974 they totaled more than $230 million. Thousands of borrowers declared bankruptcy each year.

Congress held hearings on the scandals. It was the first red flag that the government's loose lending encouraged risky behavior. Toxic debt piled up on Sallie Mae's books, just a couple years after it had been created.

Lawmakers, particularly Democrats representing manufacturing communities, shrugged off the concerns. Trade schools taught blue-collar workers who couldn't get into four-year schools. Factory workers, they argued, deserved student loan access just as much as the children of well-off families in the Northeast sending their kids to Ivy League schools. *These schools are providing opportunities*, they said.

The for-profit schools' biggest supporter in Congress was Bill Ford. The Michigan Democrat was the gatekeeper of higher education policy as head of the House Subcommittee on Postsecondary Education in the late 1970s through the '80s. If anyone was responsible for the laws that erected Sallie Mae and the student loan industry, it was him.

William D. Ford was raised near Detroit, the son of Scottish working-class immigrants. Neither of his parents graduated high school. His mother was a florist, his dad a security guard. "They understood the value of education and told me it was the only way I could keep from replicating their hard struggle," Ford once recalled. After serving in the navy in World War II, he enrolled in an apprenticeship program at Ford Motor—no relation—and went to college on the G.I. Bill.

When Ford was a young adult, his father narrowly escaped a fire at the factory he worked at but died of a related illness. His mother, faced with a mortgage on their new house, had a nervous breakdown. The factory's union successfully fought for her to get compensation for her husband's death. After that, Ford staunchly defended unions. In Congress, he forbade aides from parking a car on Capitol Hill that wasn't made by one of Detroit's big three auto companies.

He was a complicated man. On one hand he was a populist, with a natural distrust of banks and their unrelenting push for profits. On the other hand, he supported profit-seeking trade schools.

Ford didn't understand how Sallie Mae worked—few in Congress did. But Sallie Mae kept money flowing so students could attend college or trade school. That was enough to make Ford an ally of the company.

Ford's support of for-profit schools was in part due to seismic shifts in the U.S. economy. America's manufacturing industry peaked in the late 1970s and then began a decades-long decline as automation replaced workers and companies bought parts made overseas. The displaced workers needed retraining, and Ford felt for-profit trade schools were their only avenue for that. "He would just explain, he just couldn't sell the notion of student loans in his blue-collar district in Michigan if the blue-collar kids didn't get those loans," Fox says.

Ford once said at a hearing that he knew many borrowers were defaulting. The students most likely to default had grown up poor. They lacked the advantages of wealthier students—access to good high schools, stable families, family connections—and many dropped out of college. These students were, from the perspective of many traditional colleges, a bad risk. Those schools rejected such students to avoid lowering their graduation rates or having to spend on resources, such as additional instruction, to improve the students' chances.

Ford felt those students deserved a shot at college. Loans allowed them to go to schools that had no admissions standards, such as for-profit trade schools.

"We knew that trouble was developing, we know why, and it has more to do with the type of person that is being served by those loans than it has to do with anything else," Ford once said at a hearing. "You are faced with a choice: We either quit protecting and affording education to low-income people because they are bad risks, or we continue."

Fox developed a close relationship with Ford. He had to, given Sallie Mae's role as a so-called quasi-public agency. Sallie Mae was privately owned but was propped up entirely by the federal government. It had two layers of insurance provided by Congress. It borrowed from the Treasury at exceptionally low rates—no questions asked. And it earned a hefty, taxpayer-funded profit on each student loan it purchased with that money—no questions asked.

At Mobil Oil, Fox had to guess which investments would make money. There was always the risk that the investments he chose would go bust, losing the company millions. At Sallie Mae, there was no guesswork. The investments were chosen for him, the profits guaranteed. Instead, Fox had to manage two other risks. The first was operational. He had to ensure that the student loan market operated efficiently—that Sallie Mae's money found its way to banks, and then to students, as quickly as possible. The more students borrowed, the more money Sallie Mae made.

The second risk—the bigger one—was political. Fox had to make sure the people who signed the company's checks—members of Congress—were happy. They could kill Sallie Mae's unheard-of deal.

Bill Ford, the man in charge of higher education policy in Congress, effectively signed Sallie Mae's checks. For a while Ford and Fox got along. Ford wanted to help Americans pay for college in the quickest, most efficient way possible. Fox wanted to make money.

So they found ways to do both, and it usually involved expanding loan programs. In 1976, Senator Edward Kennedy (D., Mass.), Ford's counterpart in the Senate, wanted to end a federal scholarship program for medical students, which the liberal senator considered a handout for soon-to-be-wealthy doctors. Medical schools objected, contending they'd lose money and the quality of their programs would suffer. Ford fretted about what to do.

One night over drinks with Ford, Fox proposed a compromise: a new loan program for medical students. The schools would continue to get money, the students would pay their own way—and Sallie Mae would profit by having a new type of loan it could buy from banks. Ford backed the idea, championing a law that allowed medical students to borrow tens of thousands of dollars more than other types of students.

Other measures that Ford championed and Congress passed expanded who could borrow. Congress opened up the program to part-time students, for example, and to students who never graduated high school. It increased loan limits, allowing each student to borrow more.

The biggest measure came in 1978. Congress faced pressure from middle- and upper-income constituents to provide more help paying college tuition. These people's incomes prevented them from enjoying the full benefits of the Guaranteed Student Loan program, which covered some of the interest on loans only for students from families earning less than $25,000 a year. Lawmakers proposed tax breaks for upper-income families to help with tuition.

President Jimmy Carter opposed the plan, saying it would be a handout to wealthy households, who were likely to spend the most on tuition since they sent their kids to prestigious private schools.

As a compromise, Ford proposed the Middle Income Student Assistance Act, which removed the loan program's income threshold, entitling anyone—no matter how wealthy—to interest-free loans while in school and then to pay 7 percent interest once out of school.

These moves deepened the government's involvement in the complex world of finance. To open up higher education to all Americans—while hiding the costs of such an endeavor—Congress had created layers of for-profit scaffolding. The biggest layer was Sallie Mae, which served as a funnel between the Treasury Department and banks. Banks sent that money to students, who sent it to schools.

Sallie Mae's profits rose, and Ed Fox was being paid handsomely for it. Defaults, too, rose, driving up taxpayer costs. The equal partnership Lyndon Johnson envisioned among lenders, schools, and students was actually highly unequal. The banking industry profited, as did schools; students and taxpayers incurred all the costs.

The Carter administration realized the system was inefficient and costly. It proposed revamping the system to remove private investors from the student loan program, folding Sallie Mae into a government agency or killing the company.

Bill Ford also turned against Sallie Mae, which he compared to a money-laundering operation using taxpayer money. "In the process everybody who touches it makes something off of it and the student is left with a loan to pay back," he said during a hearing. "The system is so complicated that everybody forgets that we started these programs for the purpose of buying education."

Sallie Mae's future was in jeopardy.

To navigate the political thicket on Capitol Hill, Fox needed a lobbyist. He turned to Williams & Jensen, a dominant lobbying firm, which assigned a woman named Mary Whalen to the Sallie Mae account. She had been an aide at the Library of Congress and then the Senate Committee on Veterans' Affairs before joining Williams & Jensen in 1976 as a law clerk. She was in her mid-20s, energetic, and had the drive and smarts to match Ed Fox and Bill Ford. The firm promoted her to lobbyist.

Her presentations and writing were meticulous. "She was incredibly, incredibly, incredibly, insanely focused on details," a former colleague recalls.

The key to influencing lawmakers was to establish a rapport with them. Mary Whalen did that, immediately becoming close with Bill Ford. According to an internal company document recounting Sallie Mae's history, Whalen and other Sallie Mae executives met with Ford shortly after Whalen was hired. The Sallie Mae contingent spent hours arguing that the company would be more efficient than the government at managing the student loan market, with some necessary tweaks to the law. The meeting proved pivotal: Ford dropped his opposition to Sallie Mae and became its chief congressional ally. He began incorporating the company's interests into the higher education legislation drafted by his committee. Whalen helped write that legislation, according to Fox, and lobbied other members of Congress to get behind it.

Fox and Whalen convinced Ford to champion two measures that solidified the roles of Sallie Mae and the banking industry in the federal student loan program. In 1979, Congress promised to pay Sallie Mae an interest rate of 3.5 percent, on top of the company's own borrowing costs, on each student loan it purchased. With this move, Sallie Mae was guaranteed a big profit margin regardless of how high inflation rose. Guaranteed profits. Absolutely no risk of losses.

A year later, Ford pushed through a law that solidified Sallie Mae's autonomy. The law allowed Sallie Mae to raise money by selling shares of the company to the public.

Congress had just opened up higher education to Wall Street.

A decade earlier, Wall Street had shunned the student loan market. That was about to change. The program was about to make all sorts of people money.

The 1978 law that opened up the student loan program to wealthy families provided an opportunity for households to make money. Student loans were interest-free while borrowers were in school and for nine months after graduation. Wealthy families who had enough savings to pay tuition on their own could now take out a $2,500 student loan each year—interest-free—and stuff it in a savings account, which at the time could earn upward of 14 percent interest. Following graduation, families could pay back the loans, after they had earned hundreds of dollars in interest.

Financial advisers urged families to take advantage. A popular personal-finance magazine ran a story apprising students of the scheme. Indiana's higher education commissioner told parents to take out student loans to make a profit.

"You were a fool if you didn't take money out and put it in a money-market fund when you were in college," says Terry Hartle, a former adviser to Senator Edward Kennedy. "We would have been better off dropping the money out of a plane over Cincinnati."

Student lending exploded. Millions of new borrowers applied for loans—because they genuinely needed them or they wanted to make money through arbitrage. Banks happily lent them money now that they could earn a guaranteed profit—or sell the student loan to Sallie Mae for a chunk of change.

This was big business for Sallie Mae. In 1980 it had $3 billion in assets—student loans it had purchased or commercial loans it had extended to lenders—which was a 75 percent increase from a year earlier.

The surge in loan money pushed up demand for college. Schools responded the way any other business would if customers suddenly banged on their door armed with money. They raised prices—by a lot. Universities had put out reports and written newspaper op-eds warning they needed to raise tuition to expand campuses and pay professors more. Now they had the means to do so, with all the new money flowing through the system and the higher loan limits Congress had approved. In the 1970s, tuition on average had risen at the same rate as inflation. In the 1980s, tuition started rising at double and triple the rate of inflation.

Students complained about the tuition increases, but in the end, they paid. "Sure, there's a lot of negative reaction, but people are going to pay," Charles Dervarics, a George Washington University student, told the *Washington Post* after the school raised tuition 17 percent, to $4,211, in the early 1980s. "They'll scrounge up the money somehow. They'll take out more loans."

Schools benefited directly from Sallie Mae. Some of the company's biggest shareholders were colleges that charged the most—Ivy League schools like Brown and Harvard. The more business Sallie Mae got, the more their shares went up. "Harvard made a fortune in the stock," Fox says.

The key to Sallie Mae's profits was that students borrowed. The more students owed, the more money Sallie Mae made. In the 1982 school year, a record 3.6 million students borrowed $7.8 billion. That comes out to about $2,200 per student—or nearly $6,200 today. Sallie Mae bought up a big chunk of those loans. If a student borrowed $2,200 from a bank, Sallie Mae bought that loan and collected interest—a rate of 3.5 percent above Sallie Mae's own borrowing costs. Congress paid banks that interest while students were in school. After graduation, students paid Sallie Mae a rate of 7 percent, and the government paid whatever else was needed to ensure that Sallie Mae achieved the 3.5 percent spread.

In the 1981 school year, the government spent $3 billion in interest payments on student loans—six times the figure that it spent in 1978, before Congress opened the program to families at all income levels. Much of the cash generated by those interest payments went to Sallie Mae. Sallie Mae's after-tax earnings rose to $9 million in 1980 and would double every year after, to $18 million in 1981, $38 million in 1982, $67 million 1983. In 1984, its profits hit nearly $99 million.

Lawmakers scrutinized Sallie Mae, but many didn't know how it worked. "If most members of Congress were asked what they thought of Sallie Mae, they would respond with a question, 'Who is she?'" Senator Jennings Randolph (D., W.Va.) said during a 1981 hearing.

Fox argued to the committee that Sallie Mae operated as Congress had intended. Because of the company's support to banks, roughly 2.5 million students had received loans in its first nine years of existence, he said.

In 1981, Fox told a magazine that by 1990, the company would have $20 billion in assets on its books. "With a legislative change that made it easier to get student loans, rapidly increasing educational costs and rising interest rates all coming together, I just sensed a surge," he later said. Sallie Mae's critics thought such growth impossible.

To grow, it needed more money. Fox turned to a 35-year-old accounting executive named Al Lord. A tireless worker, he was abrasive and opinionated. Lord felt he knew finance better than just about anyone. He obsessed about making lending more efficient, and about making money. He joined Sallie Mae in 1981 as its comptroller, or top accountant. Within a year he would become its chief financial officer. Within two decades he'd take Sallie Mae to heights no one ever imagined.

Lord had initially told Sallie Mae he'd join the company on one condition: that it commit to becoming a private entity and sever its ties to the government. He wanted to sell stock to the public, a move that Fox had already been plotting. Even though Congress had passed legislation in 1980 that permitted Sallie Mae to sell stock to the public, the company hadn't taken that step. Sallie's shares were owned exclusively by universities and banks. Going public would allow Sallie Mae to raise cash from investors around the world and boost its profits without meddling from bureaucrats or congressmen. When Sallie Mae mailed him a job offer letter with such a promise, Lord said yes.

His first week at work, Lord took the company's financial statements to his house in Pennsylvania. That evening, as he looked them over, his heart raced. This place is a gold mine, Lord said to himself.

The company's return of 3.5 percent on student loans was unheard of. Since the mid-1980s, the average return that banks got on all types of assets has not exceeded 1.6 percent. The federal government guaranteed Sallie Mae a return at least twice what other banks could get on the average investment. (Fox says that the company's expenses–including taxes, the interest it paid on its own debt, and the cost of keeping the lights on–ate up most of the money that it

Fox and Lord realized this good deal wouldn't last. Sallie Mae was coming under fire from members of Congress for its growing profits. They feared Congress, under political pressure, would kill the arrangement. Fox and Lord concluded the company needed to stop relying on the government for its money and find other sources. It needed to go public.

"With just plain people in a sizeable number now holding our shares—in addition to the banks and schools—we're much more the private company and less vulnerable than before—less vulnerable to government tinkering," Sallie Mae's chairman, Edward McCabe, once said.

They believed Sallie Mae didn't need government financing anymore. Even without low-interest loans from the Federal Financing Bank, Sallie Mae would still have access to cheap credit. The company had what's known as an "implicit guarantee"—a broad assumption among investors on Wall Street that, as a government-sponsored enterprise, Sallie Mae was in no danger of defaulting on its debt or going bankrupt. Congress would step in before that happened. It was considered an ultra-safe asset.

In the summer of 1983, Sallie Mae's board approved a plan to sell shares of nonvoting common stock to the public. In September it made an initial public offering, selling 10 million shares at $20 apiece. The stock was hotter than expected. Within a week, all shares had sold. Seven months later, in April 1984, Sallie Mae joined the New York Stock Exchange. The company earned a triple-A rating from Standard and Poor's—the equivalent of a perfect credit score. Investors bid up the stock price. "Stock Analysts Take a Shine to Sallie," the *Washington Post* declared in a headline in November 1984. Wall Street analysts put Sallie Mae's stock on a "priority selection" list, advising investors to buy it above other products. The stock had risen to $33 a share, jumping 65 percent from its initial price.

Overseas investors bought shares, making money off of America's burgeoning student debt pile. "We were shocked to find out who owned our stuff," Fox once told an interviewer. One year, he was touring Asia when a government official from Singapore said, "We own some of your stock."

This was all enabled by a grand illusion that everyone should go to college, and that student debt was a surefire investment. All involved told themselves they were making money while achieving a social mandate, which was giving Americans access to college. Investors and banks told themselves they were helping Americans invest in their future.

That changed by 1985. Sallie Mae had infused banks with nearly $23 billion. It owned nearly a third of federally guaranteed loans. Fox stated unabashedly at the time that his primary duty was to serve the interests of investors, not the interests of students. "Since day one we have run this corporation as a business," Fox told the *Washington Post*. "We're not educators and we don't pretend to be. We know there are people out there primarily interested in education who have no notion what the banking business is. Somebody once suggested at a hearing that people would be willing to put money into Sallie Mae stocks and bonds at a lower return to themselves . . . even if we were losing money, because they would know in their gut we were doing something good. That is the most naive, simplistic pap I've heard in my life."

If he was confident, he had reason to be. Mary Whalen had become the top lobbyist on education in Washington. Ford and Fox would discuss big ideas over drinks, and Whalen would help craft the legislation—she knew the law better than the congressional aides on Capitol Hill.

The relation between Whalen and Ford grew to become more than professional. After Ford's wife left him, he became involved romantically with Whalen. Ford's chief of staff at the time, Dave Geiss, sensed there was a relationship. He says members of Congress knew about it, too. Terry Hartle, Senator Kennedy's aide, says Congress deferred to her on legislation involving Sallie Mae because of her relationship with Ford. "Everybody dealt with her with kid gloves because she was so close to Bill Ford," Hartle says. "It was a different time in Washington."

Fox says few people were as important to Sallie Mae's history. "So my lobbyist was sharing a pillow . . . ," he says, without completing the sentence. Pressed further, he reverses course and says he wasn't aware of an improper relationship.

Lord says the relationship was well known and that Fox had become obsessed with the effectiveness of Whalen's lobbying, to ensure Congress supported the company. "You see these shows on TV, like that show *House of Cards*?" Lord says. "That's what it was."

Sallie Mae didn't only break ground in finance; the company invested in new technology, including an electronic platform in the 1980s that made taking out a loan as easy as pressing a computer key. "They were so far ahead of everybody," says Thomas Stanton, a former Congressional Budget Office researcher who studied Sallie Mae. "They were ahead in technology. It was really an Amazon model before Amazon was invented. You created this platform and suddenly have a lower cost structure than anybody else and you could go to town."

Banks realized they could make a killing off of financing college tuition. One lender offered Sony Walkmans, records, and alarm clocks to students who took out a loan. Chase Manhattan Bank installed computer terminals at high schools to allow students to apply for student loans for college.

Banks sent flyers to parents, along with their credit card bills, advertising student loans. Banks held seminars on the virtues of borrowing for college. "You really sell the parent, not the student," one executive at Chase Manhattan told the *Wall Street Journal*. Some banks paid financial aid offices—the departments at universities that help students apply for student loans—"$5 to $10 a head to influence students to take out loans with them," the *Journal* reported. "It's ridiculous," Polly Gault, staff director of the Senate Education, Arts and Humanities Subcommittee, told the paper. "It was not the intent of the program to have big banks warp the local financial markets by going in and competing with the local banks."

States also profited from student loans. By 1986 most states had set up nonprofit agencies to lend to students or to buy student loans from banks, performing the same task as Sallie Mae. The agencies raised money by selling tax-exempt bonds—the buyer of which was often Sallie Mae—which allowed them to borrow at interest rates below 7 percent, exceptionally low at the time. They would then collect interest rates of 9 to 14 percent on every student loan on their books—rates that had been set by Congress and that students paid on their loans. Such a spread was unheard of among private companies.

"You've got a spread you could drive a truck through," Fox told IRS researchers in 2006. "The states love it. All sorts of politicians go to work for those state agencies. They make profits that go into other parts of the state coffers. It's a transfer mechanism that benefits the states at the expense of the federal government."

The agencies reaped millions in profits, a Congressional Budget Office report showed, and paid handsome salaries to their executives. The state profits had an important, unintended side effect: They eased pressure on states to directly finance public colleges through annual budget appropriations. Instead, states allowed a greater share of college costs to shift to students, through the loan program.

By 1986, 50 state and local government agencies across 39 states performed these tasks. They collectively held 12 percent of the $39 billion in total outstanding student debt across the U.S. that year.

David Bayer, the former chief of the Education Department's student loan branch, told an interviewer that the state incentives were like "a small key to Fort Knox." "Used to be when you attended meetings of these state guarantee agencies everybody brought his own can of beer," Bayer said. "Now they have elaborate receptions and everybody seems to be doing quite well."

As tuition soared, Congress increased loan limits. Sallie Mae helped shape laws regarding them. One of Fox's biggest priorities was a new program called "loan consolidation." This allowed a borrower who owed multiple loans to combine them into one new loan. If the new loan exceeded a certain amount, the payments would be spread over 30 years, instead of the standard 10 years. The program enabled Sallie Mae to expand its reach in the student loan market and American households' finances. Under the new consolidation program, Sallie Mae shifted loans from banks' books to its own. The new loans stayed on Sallie Mae's books for decades, allowing the agency to collect thousands more dollars in interest charges from each borrower.

Student loans began to resemble mortgages. The U.S. pioneered the 30-year mortgage as a standard home loan. Extending payments over 30 years, instead of 10 or 20, allows the borrower to buy a bigger, more expensive house, since the payments are spread over a long period. But the 30-year loan pushes up home prices and the borrower pays more in the long run. Student loan consolidation had the same effect. Students able to spread payments over 30 years instead of 10 can pay more in tuition while keeping their monthly payments low. The school then can charge more.

By 1990, Sallie Mae had outstripped Fox's earlier estimates that it would be worth $20 billion in assets. It had almost $40 billion in assets, including half of all student debt that Americans owed. Its top executives earned $1 million annually. Sallie Mae ranked 39th on *Fortune* magazine's list of largest U.S. corporations.

"Its luxurious Georgetown offices have the power-quiet of a major law firm; corridors are decorated with immense modern paintings and sculptures bearing names like *The Drama of Space* and *The White Peacock*," *Time* journalist Steven Waldman wrote. "The glass doors never seem to have fingerprints."

That year marked a decade and a half of explosive growth that few predicted. For decades, banks had refused to lend to college students; now banks profited handsomely from student loans. Schools had become addicted to the program. A growing share of students had to borrow as colleges raised tuition. Tuition rose at twice the rate of inflation, increasing faster than even health care costs. Student loan defaults soared. Yet, counterintuitively, the financial industry earned huge profits from this toxic debt.

In one major way, Sallie Mae helped achieve a public good. College enrollment and graduation rates soared in the 1980s and '90s. By 1991, the United States had the world's most educated workforce. Its economy was the world's strongest, in large part because of its commitment to education, including college.

The loose lending was in the name of helping the poor, the middle class, and the country as a whole. Student loans provided access to higher ed and a path to the American Dream. It also made many people wealthy, including Ed Fox.

In the summer of 1990, Fox shocked Sallie Mae's board by announcing he was resigning to become dean of Dartmouth University's business school. Fox says he had accomplished what he set out to do—turn Sallie Mae into a profitable company—and had always wanted to be a business school dean. He says he left with $7 million in Sallie Mae stock.

Congressman Ford, during a House committee hearing several years later, spoke with regret about the industry that he had helped build, piece by piece, through a series of laws over two decades. "We protected them," he said of Sallie Mae. "We spent a whole decade piling on bribe after bribe after bribe.

"We didn't start out here to create a banking system," he added. "We started out to find a way to help people go to college."

In 1990, the same year that Fox left Sallie Mae, Ford got married. The wedding was in early August on a cliff overlooking the Pacific Ocean in southern California. The bride at his side was Mary Whalen.

Mary Whalen declined to be interviewed. In an email, she disputed the idea that her personal relationship with Bill Ford was improper.

It would be a mistake to say Ford protected Sallie Mae solely because of his relationship with Whalen. Sallie Mae received support from bipartisan majorities in Congress and became the backbone of a system that granted access to millions of Americans who hoped to move up in society. In 1991, he explained why he defended Sallie Mae.

"We don't care what they do as long as they are there when we need them to make sure that our train runs on time," Ford said at a hearing. "In the case of this committee, the trains that we want to run on time are the Guaranteed Student Loan program."

For Ed Fox, the reason the industry exploded in scope and profit was simple. "The money was there," he said. "It was available. Schools took it."

THREE

Our Greedy Colleges

(1974–1990)

Students crowded the hallway of the Florida State University law school as Eleanor Hill shouldered her way toward her next class. She had studied on the sun-drenched campus for six years, as an undergraduate and then as a law student. She was a few weeks from receiving her J.D. She had no idea what to do after commencement.

As she jostled through the noisy throng, a hand grabbed her arm. It was one of her professors, pulling her aside to offer career advice. *Become a federal prosecutor*, he said. She agreed to meet later in the day to talk.

It was fall of 1974, and Hill was in her early 20s. Slim, with dark, shoulder-length hair, Hill had grown up in Miami, where her father, an air force veteran, worked as a meteorologist and her mother as a teacher. As a child, she spent her days involved in piano lessons, debate club, and the school newspaper. She read voraciously, spending hours in her home library consuming historical biographies. In college, she was a fiery idealist, a liberal child of the '60s who debated her conservative parents about the merits of big government and helping the poor.

Her idealism waned in the 1970s. The economy was sputtering

after an oil shock, President Nixon had resigned amid the Watergate affair, and crime—the drug trade, robberies, white-collar corruption—was on the rise. Her law professor knew she had no career plans, and when they met again later that autumn day, they talked about whether Hill might be cut out for work with the Department of Justice.

After graduation she joined the U.S. Attorney's Office in Tampa. Nineteen-seventies Florida was a good place to be a young lawyer fighting fraud. Hill helped prosecute one of the biggest corruption cases of its kind at the time, an insurance fraud ring of 23 people with ties to La Cosa Nostra. The Mafia was no match for Hill. Three members of the arson ring pleaded guilty, and the jury convicted 16 of the remaining 20.

By 1980, Hill wanted a bigger challenge. A friend told her of one. A Democratic senator from Georgia, Sam Nunn, was looking for young, aggressive prosecutors to staff a congressional committee embarking on a bunch of investigations to root out fraud and abuse. Was she interested? the friend asked.

Hill said, *Yes, I'll do it*. At 28 years old, she moved to D.C. on Labor Day of 1980.

Hill learned in Tampa that to find corruption, follow the money. By the early 1980s, a lot of money was flowing into federally backed student loans. Sallie Mae had flooded the college market with billions of dollars in cheap cash—laying tinder on the forest floor of American higher education. All that was needed was a match to light the system on fire.

When Hill began her new job, colleges had begun aggressively competing for students and their loan dollars. In that sense, putting vouchers into students' hands had stirred competition, as Alice Rivlin's report had predicted. But colleges—particularly private middle- and upper-tier schools that went after students with the strongest grades and test scores—didn't compete on price. Instead, they competed on prestige, which had the opposite effect on tuition, causing prices to skyrocket.

In 1983, a new factor pumped steroids into this collegiate race to rake in loan money. *U.S. News & World Report* published its first annual issue of college rankings, declaring the 25 best colleges in the U.S. To develop the rankings, the magazine surveyed college presidents, asking which schools they believed to be the nation's best. Presidents often listed schools that were "selective," or those that admitted only a fraction of the applicants who applied each year. The lower the school's acceptance rate, the higher it rose in the rankings. That translated into more money: Families paid more for degrees from reputable schools.

Colleges became savvy in how they set their tuition. They started acting like airlines setting fares, charging different prices to different students for the same service. Presidents from LBJ to Ronald Reagan had effectively urged variable pricing based on students' financial needs, with the poorest getting the biggest discounts. In the 1980s race for prestige, colleges often did the reverse—giving the biggest discounts to academic stars, who tended to be from upper-income families. These discounts became known as "merit aid," and this form of price discrimination boosted the colleges' bottom lines.

David Breneman hated the ruthless nature of the system but learned to use it to his school's advantage. A University of Colorado graduate with an economics Ph.D. from Berkeley, Breneman became president of Kalamazoo College, a private liberal arts school in Michigan, in 1983. It was a tough time for colleges across the country. Slowing birth rates had led to a decline in the number of Americans graduating high school, universities' main customer pool. When Breneman took over, Kalamazoo College's enrollment had in just a few years fallen by a quarter, to 1,100.

The school employed 250 people. Breneman faced an ugly choice: lay off employees to cut costs, or raise tuition to increase revenue. He raised tuition. Breneman felt justified—this was the era of individual responsibility, one ushered in by President Reagan. "When Ronald Reagan came in you had this sea change in attitude toward higher education," Breneman says. "It started being looked upon by policy makers as, this is a private good rather than a public good."

If Breneman worried that higher tuition would dampen enrollment, he learned to his surprise that the opposite was true. Breneman discovered that students were perfectly willing to pay more. Higher tuition made a school more attractive to families, not less. Breneman later applied a popular economic phrase to describe this phenomenon in higher ed—the Chivas Regal effect, named after a high-end Scotch whisky. The theory goes that if consumers know little about the quality of a product—whether it be mattresses, whisky, or colleges—they will often go with the more expensive brand, on the assumption that higher price means higher quality.

Kalamazoo's annual sticker price crossed $10,000 for the first time under Breneman. The school then strategically offered discounts to boost its reputation as a selective school. If the school sensed that a sought-after student—one with good grades and high SAT scores—would balk at the high sticker price and go to a competitor, it offered a scholarship, effectively a discount. For less desirable students, it charged full price. The biggest discounts went to high achievers, who would raise the school's average SAT scores and GPAs and thus its chances of rising in the rankings.

The amount students paid rose faster than average family incomes in the '80s. Students and their parents had to turn to loans. "The students were being told that this was a great investment and it was worth borrowing for," Breneman says. "The Feds made it pretty easy to get enough money to cover the gap that you had between parents' assets and money the students had."

Breneman's strategy was a bellwether for higher education across the country. Nationwide, colleges adopted the same approach: Set the sticker price high, then offer varying discounts. So began the era of runaway tuition. College tuition had been flat in the 1970s, after accounting for inflation. In the 1980s, tuition at both public and private colleges rose at double and triple the rate of inflation each year.

The higher prices affected different students in different ways. Kalamazoo turned away the poorest students who needed the biggest discounts. Better to give several high-achieving students from wealthy families a partial scholarship, say, than one-high achieving student from a poor family a full scholarship. The former would lead to higher revenue overall. The latter would be a cost.

For Breneman, the pressure to raise revenue overrode the pressure to serve the neediest students. "I would have loved for a lot of reasons to bring in more African American students," Breneman says. "But I knew every African American student I admitted was going to take a full ride. For the same amount of money I would pick up three other students who would pay all the way. You were forced into those horrible trade-offs."

He adds, "Nobody was pure in this business."

By the 1980s, colleges like Kalamazoo saw the federal student loan program as their lifeblood. Higher education lobbyists fought any cuts in students' ability to borrow. George H. W. Bush once recalled a college president visiting his office when he was vice president. "Oh, don't tighten up student loans," the official told him. "It's going to kill us."

President Reagan wanted someone to stand up to the trade-group lobbyists. He had been a critic of elite colleges since his days as California governor, when he went after violent protesters at the University of California, Berkeley. He needed an attack dog who could convince the public, and their congressional representatives, that colleges weren't do-gooders, but profit-seeking entities that needed oversight. Reagan found that attack dog in a former college offensive tackle who had a personality to match his 6-foot-2, 220-pound stature.

Bill Bennett had gained the nickname "the Ram" as a student at Williams College after using his head to break down the door of his dorm suite when his roommate locked him out. ("He was in there with his girlfriend and he didn't want to let his two room-mates in to sleep in their own beds," Bennett says.) He earned a Ph.D. in political philosophy at the University of Texas at Austin and a law degree from Harvard, financed with student loans.

In early 1985, Reagan appointed him secretary of education. Five days later, Bennett publicly accused colleges of "ripping off" their students by raising tuition and saddling them with debt. He accused students of spending their student loan money frivolously. Cutting student aid would be "divestiture of some sorts—stereo divestiture, automobile divestiture, three-weeks-at-the-beach divestiture," Bennett told reporters.

His timing, politically, was impeccable. Spring break mania had peaked. The images of bikini-clad beachgoers and pumped-up fraternity brothers on a bacchanalia of debauchery spilled into popular culture with movies like *Spring Break* and a remake of *Where the Boys Are*. In 1985, 350,000 collegians swarmed Fort Lauderdale for the annual rite. Three young people died, police arrested thousands, and vice stings documented gross-out contests and semi-public sexual acts in clubs.

Meanwhile, defaults on student loans were soaring. Politicians from both parties blamed students for not honoring their obligations. The Reagan administration aggressively pursued borrowers who failed to repay, garnishing their wages and tax refunds.

Bennett felt that both sides—students and schools—were to blame. Many schools were providing a bad education, he argued, leaving students with few skills to land a job. But Bennett found himself hamstrung. While the government could go after deadbeat students, it had few tools to go after schools. Congress had long resisted regulating colleges, fearing that if schools worried about appeasing bureaucrats, they might make decisions—such as what subjects to teach—that would undermine the quality of their academic offerings.

Bennett turned to the op-ed pages. In February 1987, the *New York Times* published a column by Bennett titled "Our Greedy Colleges." Universities and colleges had been raising their tuition by 6 percent to 8 percent each year. Congress enabled them, he argued. "Higher education is not underfunded," he wrote. "It is under-accountable and under-productive."

Bennett laid out an argument that came to be known as the Bennett Hypothesis. By increasing financial aid to students, Congress had created a vicious cycle of tuition inflation, he said. Congress then provided students money to pay tuition, through higher loan limits. Colleges raised tuition to collect that extra money. Congress provided more money to cover the higher tuition. Schools raised tuition. Congress was feeding a beast with an insatiable appetite.

Colleges pushed back against Bennett's theory. They argued they had to raise prices because their own costs were rising beyond their control. They suffered from what economists call "cost disease"—the theory that industries that can't counteract rising costs through greater efficiencies must raise their prices. While factories cut costs through automation, for example, colleges delivered education the same way they'd done for centuries, with a professor lecturing at the head of a class.

This was a self-serving argument, of course. It ignored the fact that college costs rose in part because institutions went on a hiring and construction spree. University employment grew 43 percent between 1976 and 1989, far faster than the 25 percent rise in students. Colleges added "more palatable food in the cafeterias, fitness centers for those who want to work out in style, more amenities in residence halls, better campus security, counseling programs, health services, job placement programs," the *Denver Post* reported in 1989.

It was a vicious cycle: Colleges charged more, students in turn borrowed more and expected more, and colleges spent more. "The students who are unpacking their Ralph Lauren polo shirts and personal computers in the residence halls of college campuses across America this month have a different set of expectations than their predecessors," the *Post* wrote. "If they are going to invest an estimated $8,000 to $23,000 a year in higher education, these kids and their parents expect to see a little more for their money."

Few colleges represented this era of runaway tuition more than George Washington University. Under its president, Stephen Joel Trachtenberg, the middle-tier school in Washington, D.C., drastically raised tuition in the late 1980s, and spent the proceeds upgrading libraries, dorms, and other campus facilities, and on higher pay for professors. Trachtenberg's experience shows that the ready availability of student loans shielded colleges from making changes that a normal business would make to become more efficient, such as working more days per year. Thursday night was party night on many campuses because so few students took classes on Fridays. Trachtenberg says he wanted to move to a six-day-a-week, 11-month academic calendar, which would, in theory, have allowed students to graduate sooner—perhaps in three years instead of four—saving them thousands of dollars in tuition. "I would have taken what is essentially a structure that was crafted in the Middle Ages and brought it into the twentieth century," he says.

When Trachtenberg proposed expanding the academic year, professors revolted. The faculty senate didn't even bring his plan up for a vote.

Two years after Bennett wrote his op-ed, his disdain for the pricing behavior of elite universities was vindicated. In 1989, the *Wall Street Journal* reported that 23 elite schools, including all eight Ivy League colleges, had convened to compare notes on students who had applied to their schools. The schools had colluded to decide how to discount prices for different students. It was an alleged act of price fixing, apparently designed to take away negotiating leverage from students and maximize the amount of money schools earned from tuition. Wrote *Journal* reporter Gary Putka: "The Ivy schools are part of a price-fixing system that OPEC might envy."

Eleanor Hill started to see the same systemic problems as Bennett. Hill had risen to become chief legal counsel of the Senate's Permanent Subcommittee on Investigations, a panel with a tarnished history. It became famous after the anti-Communism hearings in the 1950s when its chairman, Senator Joseph McCarthy (R., Wisc.), smeared the reputations of those summoned to testify. Now Hill's boss, Senator Sam Nunn, wanted to overhaul the committee's image and turn it toward rooting out corruption and fraud.

Hill was his protégé. He told her investigations had to be done right or not at all. "If you do an investigation, it has to be done professionally, it has to be accurate, and it has to be fair," Hill says, describing her old boss's philosophy. "We don't want to do it by grandstanding or cheap shots."

Her team investigated fraud, abuse, and bad governance—issues that affected everyday Americans. Senator Nunn had long had his sights on the student loan program, and particularly the for-profit schools that were profiting handsomely from it. Other Democrats, including Bill Ford and Ted Kennedy, defended the schools as providing opportunity for blue-collar families. But Nunn, a so-called conservative "Blue Dog" Democrat who believed in limited government spending, was skeptical of the schools. He'd served on the same committee in 1975 that investigated the for-profit college scandals of that decade. In 1989, with student loan defaults soaring again, Senator Nunn directed Hill to oversee another sweeping investigation of the industry.

Hundreds of schools had opened in the 1980s—culinary schools, barber schools, brick-and-tile-laying schools—charging thousands in tuition, to teach skills in jobs that would pay little. A company owned by two brothers in Pompano Beach, Florida, trained secretaries and travel agents. It had just 23 teachers—and 109 sales representatives. The brothers paid the sales reps, which included the company's secretaries, bonuses related to the number of students they enrolled. They enticed students with cash, color televisions, and other rewards. Students applied for student loans, which went to the school for tuition, reimbursing the school the up-front costs and then some. Over four years, the school earned $150 million from federal student loans. The two brothers each earned $1 million annually.

"There is no way to escape being a slave to the quarterly report," the president of another school said, according to Hill's investigation. "Quality education and higher earnings are two masters. You can't serve both."

Another school owner said, "I'm a businessman out to make a profit."

"The floodgates opened and a lot of people got into the business that really didn't belong there," Hill says.

As Hill interviewed school owners, the structure of the system came into focus. She was stunned. The Education Department, the steward of a massive taxpayer-funded program, had no travel funds and only three staffers to oversee hundreds of for-profit schools and student lenders throughout the country.

"They just were not checking" for fraud, Hill says. Entrepreneurs "would buy a school that was accredited in one place and then 600 miles away they'd open a branch of the same school that did something totally different."

The accrediting agencies—a collection of private, regional bodies across the U.S. that the Education Department relied on to police the quality of schools—were staffed part-time by employees of universities, who rarely, if ever, disciplined schools. "They didn't have the resources to check these schools. The accrediting agencies were used to accrediting universities. They weren't used to going out in the field really being tough on the oversight to make sure that what they were teaching was legitimate, that students were learning things, that people were graduating," Hill says.

Hill identified an inherent conflict of interest. The biggest beneficiaries of the system—schools—were regulating it. Schools of dubious quality aggressively recruited naive students. Banks lent to those students and sold the loans for a quick profit, usually to Sallie Mae. Finally, Sallie Mae got paid by the U.S. government—regardless of whether the students repaid.

Hill's findings were crucial to understanding how the student loan industry operated, and where the money was going. She had begun her prosecutorial career pulling back the curtain of secrecy that protected the Mob. Now, she was lifting an almost impenetrable veil over student lending and for-profit colleges, and what she found underneath—while entirely legal—was a morass of profiteering, dubious educational institutions, and unchecked greed that was almost completely lacking oversight.

After two years of investigation and a series of hearings, Hill compiled her findings into a report that Senator Nunn released in

1991. Schools have been "exploiting both the ready availability of billions of dollars of guaranteed student loans and the weak and inattentive system responsible for them, leaving hundreds of thousands of students with little or no training, no jobs, and significant debts that they cannot repay," the report concluded. "While those responsible have reaped huge profits, the American taxpayer has been left to pick up the tab for the billions of dollars in attendant losses."

Senator Nunn said at a hearing: "We have yet to hear of even a single part of the student loan program that is working efficiently and effectively. The testimony has been so discouraging that one has to wonder if even immediate and concentrated reforms can, at this late date, salvage these programs."

By the early 1990s, the consequences of the dysfunctional student loan program—high default rates and skyrocketing tuition—had been laid bare. Between 1980 and 1990, all consumer prices rose 62 percent. The annual earnings of the typical family rose 68 percent. Tuition? The price of one year at a private school soared an average of 145 percent. At a public college, it went up 113 percent.

For a period, Washington heeded the calls of Eleanor Hill and Bill Bennett to reform the student loan program. In 1991, the Justice Department sued the eight Ivy League schools and the Massachusetts Institute of Technology, accusing them of "illegally conspiring to constrain price competition." While those schools denied price-fixing, all of them except MIT signed a consent decree agreeing to end the practice of sharing students' information in determining their tuition.

Congress passed laws to crack down on the worst for-profit colleges. The rules blocked schools from making money from the student loan program if too high a percentage of their students defaulted on their loans within two years of entering the workforce.

Congress revamped its accounting. After the S&L crisis—the collapse of savings and loan institutions in the late 1980s—Congress realized it needed a more responsible accounting method so it knew how much bad debt was on its books. It passed the 1990 Federal Credit Reform Act, which required the federal budget to project how much money the student loan program would make—or lose—over the long term.

This law ended one set of perverse incentives but created another. The program now, on paper, could save the government money and potentially turn a profit. Each annual budget would estimate, up front, all the payments that students would make in future years. And because Congress had whittled away students' bankruptcy rights, making it hard to escape their debts, the government assumed it would recoup nearly all loans and interest charges.

Student loans could now, in theory, make the government money. Congress, rather than banks or Sallie Mae, could collect all the interest charges on student loans and use that money as it saw fit.

That is, if Congress found the will to cut Sallie Mae and the banks out of the program.

FOUR

American Dreamer

(1991–1995)

L isa stood in the shower in her cramped New Jersey apartment after a long day of mind-numbing work. A question flashed through her tired mind: *What if I don't die young?*

It was the summer of 1991. Lisa, 27 and single, had spent years toiling as a secretary for a law firm in Florham Park, New Jersey, a suburb west of New York City.

Born in 1964 to parents of Irish descent, she had grown up in the nearby town of Madison, where shopkeepers worked in brick storefronts and a giant Christmas tree towered over the town square every December. Her mother stayed home to care for Lisa and her three siblings. Her father sold cars. Neither had gone to college.

When Lisa was four, her father died of cancer. She remembers sitting under the kitchen table, confused, as her despondent mother, having just returned from the hospital, told Lisa's grandmother, "It's over."

Everyone in the family went through a crisis after that. Lisa often woke up in the middle of the night to her older sister screaming, traumatized by their father's death. Her brother ran away from home. One day, she and her brother found their mother on the floor, suffering a nervous breakdown. Her mother recovered at an inpatient program while Lisa's aunt took care of the kids.

Others close to her died: a grandfather, an uncle, her boyfriend's brother. "I was always at funerals," Lisa recalls. Her mother would say the family was cursed, like the Kennedys.

Throughout childhood Lisa suffered from attention deficit disorder and struggled in school. A guidance counselor advised she learn a trade rather than go to college. Her mother, for her part, gave her two pieces of advice: Learn to type, and marry a man with a good job.

After high school, Lisa had wanderlust. "We were from a family with people dying young," she says. "Live for today" was how she approached life. She moved from city to city doing whatever work she could find. She worked as a bartender in Fort Lauderdale, a clerk in London, a secretary in Washington, D.C.

By her mid-20s, she missed home. Lisa moved back to New Jersey to be closer to her mother and siblings. She earned a modest salary as a secretary and saw no path toward a promotion. Her lawyer colleagues earned six figures. She could hear young associates on the phone telling their fathers what color BMW they planned to buy. At a coworker's wedding, Lisa walked into the reception with two lawyers. As the trio headed toward a table with only two vacant seats, one of the lawyers pointed Lisa to an empty table nearby.

She felt a divide—and it came down to education. People who had framed degrees on their walls earned a lot of money and respect. Those with bare walls didn't. "You could just feel it socially—us and them," she says. "I thought, intellectually, if it wasn't for the lack of education, they were my peer group."

Under the comforting jet of hot water, she thought about making a change. *What if you don't die young? Is this how you want to live the rest of your life?*

She had an epiphany. She had to go to college.

* * *

That divide that Lisa observed wasn't a figment of her imagination. Across America, millions of workers in the early 1990s were getting left behind in a rapidly evolving economy that favored college graduates over nongrads. That shift pushed many Americans into college—and into debt.

The U.S. had entered the digital age. Computers and automation eliminated millions of blue-collar jobs. The collapse of the Soviet Union and a shift toward capitalism by countries like China and South Korea heralded an era of global commerce. Companies outsourced jobs overseas. Employers needed skilled workers, and bid up their wages to hire them. College graduates, about a fifth of the adult population at the time, were in high demand and benefited from rising pay and living standards. From 1980 to 1990, their average hourly wages rose 6 percent, after inflation. For nongraduates, the exact opposite happened: Real wages fell 5 percent.

Going to college paid off for the average graduate, and the need for a degree became a mantra among economists and societal leaders. "Higher education, which used to be a privilege, is now a necessity," Albert Merck, vice chairman of New Jersey's Board of Higher Education, told a local newspaper in 1990.

College became a rite of American young adulthood—the ambition of not just the elites and the middle class but also the poor. More than 90 percent of high school seniors in the 1990s planned to go to college, up from 55 percent in the 1950s, a landmark study showed. (Not all of those students followed through on those ambitions. About 60 percent of high school seniors in the early 1990s enrolled in college, up from 50 percent a decade earlier.) American teenagers and their parents pored over the *U.S. News & World Report* rankings, took SAT prep courses, and agonized over personal essays, all in the hopes of impressing college admissions committees.

Lisa, a child of the '80s, was trying to catch up. When she decided to go to college, she set out to become a psychologist, so she could make a living helping people cope with tragedy. When she looked across the street from her law firm, she saw one of two campuses of Fairleigh Dickinson University. The private, nonprofit school opened during World War II and served 3,700 students at its Florham Park campus. It had a reputable psychology program, and the location couldn't have been more convenient. Lisa would be able to keep her job and take classes on the side.

The day after her epiphany in the shower, she crossed the street on her lunch break and took in the bucolic grounds and grand buildings, with their massive pillars of marble and stone. "I want to go to college here," Lisa told the woman in the admissions office.

Unbeknownst to Lisa, FDU was struggling. The Florham Park campus's enrollment had dropped by more than half in the early 1980s—hit hard by the demographic slowdown that reduced the number of Americans graduating high school. While college enrollment across the U.S. recovered in the late 1980s, FDU's remained depleted.

To find new students, the school, along with other colleges nationally, started recruiting "adult learners," people like Lisa who had spent time in the workforce and wanted to improve their skills to adjust to the new economy. FDU also raised its tuition to make more off of each student who did enroll.

Lisa, unfamiliar with the federal student loan program, told the woman at the admissions office she had no savings. The woman said not to worry. "Apply for aid," the counselor said, referring to federal student loans. Lisa visited the school's financial aid office, where a woman handed her a form to apply for federal student aid.

Lisa was surprised by the ease of the process. Earlier that year, she had applied for a loan at her bank to buy a stereo. It took weeks to get approved. Here, the school didn't even check her credit. And it didn't tell her how much her education would total by the time she graduated. Only later would Lisa learn that opening a private psychology practice in New Jersey required a doctorate. She'd have to attend grad school and pay a whole lot more than she had first envisioned.

She needed to borrow incrementally, taking out loans to cover each semester. This form of incremental payment worked to the advantage of schools like FDU. Once students enrolled, schools could easily raise tuition in successive years, since students seldom went through the hassle and cost of transferring. Students were essentially captive to price increases.

Lisa says she told the financial aid officer she was concerned about going into debt, but that the officer assured her that she had nothing to worry about. *You'll be able to pay it off with the money you earn once you graduate*, she told Lisa.

Weeks later, she received her first loan from the Guaranteed Student Loan program. The money went straight to the school. The $1,497 loan, like most federal loans at the time, was "subsidized," meaning the federal government would cover the interest until she graduated.

Lisa was beginning her journey into student debt as Congress launched a pivotal debate about whether Americans were getting into too much debt for college, or not enough. By this point far more people relied on student loans than Congress had envisioned in the 1960s and '70s. Tuition had risen faster than family incomes, forcing more and more students to turn to debt.

One year at a private four-year college—including tuition and room and board—cost $14,258 on average in fall 1991, having shot up more than 150 percent since 1980. One year at a public four-year college cost an average of $5,693, up more than 120 percent over the same period.

Congress had only modestly increased its main student aid program for the poor, called Pell Grants, which didn't need to be repaid. Pell Grants went to poor families to defray tuition and ease their reliance on debt. In 1991 the maximum Pell Grant of $2,300 covered only about half the average annual cost of public college, and less than one-fifth the annual cost of private college. More and more poor students were forced to take on debt. Roughly half of all students who graduated college in the early 1990s borrowed.

The amounts they borrowed rose, too. In 1991, Americans with student debt owed an average of $16,417, double the average of what borrowers had owed just six years earlier. The average monthly payment on student loans more than tripled over that period to $987.

With tuition and debt rising faster than anyone had envisioned, Congress reached a crossroads. One avenue would allow students to borrow more, accelerating the nation's slide toward education debt. Another would approve more government grants so that taxpayers at large shouldered more of the burden, rather than individuals like Lisa.

The debate began in the summer of 1991, just before Lisa's first semester.

By this point, the political tide had begun to shift against Sallie Mae. Not long after Senator Nunn released his landmark report on abuses in federal student aid, Senator Edward Kennedy released another report, showing that the government was funneling more than $2 billion in profits each year to Sallie Mae and the banks. Sallie's top two executives each earned $2 million annually. At a time when constituents were growing anxious about the cost of college, that money—in the form of bigger Pell Grants, perhaps—could have helped students instead of investors.

As Congress soured on Sallie Mae, the company had also lost some of its most effective champions. Bill Ford's wife, Mary Whalen, relinquished her post as Sallie Mae's chief lobbyist. His longtime friend Ed Fox was out as Sallie Mae's CEO and now at Dartmouth. At the same time, a change in federal law suddenly brought Sallie Mae's costs into sharp focus. Congress had for decades paid banks to make loans in order to keep the program out of the federal budget, preventing a run-up in the national deficit—at least on paper. But a crucial change to the law in 1990 removed the accounting smoke screen around student lending. The change required the federal budget to reflect the program's long-run costs and profits. Sallie Mae's taxpayer-funded bonanza suddenly appeared in the annual budget.

Ford was in an awkward position. He had long protected Sallie Mae, but increasingly, leaders of his Democratic Party were livid at the high taxpayer costs of reimbursing the company and banks for extending and holding student loans. He wanted someone to appear tough on the company, as long as it wasn't him. Sitting behind his desk on Capitol Hill, Ford called into his office a freshman Democratic congressman from New Jersey named Rob Andrews. The irascible chairman of the House Committee on Education and Labor told Andrews he needed a favor.

"Tiger," Ford addressed Andrews affectionately, "I'm going to make your career here or ruin it."

As chairman, Ford had power over the junior congressman. Ford told Andrews to introduce legislation that would replace the Guaranteed Student Loan program with a new Direct Loan program, under which the Treasury Department, not banks, would lend to students. The government would save billions of dollars in bank fees that it could use to cut interest rates for students or increase grants. In turn, it would no longer need Sallie Mae to purchase student loans from banks. Ford, to avoid blowback from Sallie Mae and banks, asked the young congressman to introduce it for him.

Andrews introduced the bill in August 1991. "All hell breaks loose," Andrews says. Investors panicked, seeing their profits in jeopardy. Sallie Mae's stock fell 14 percent in the ensuing weeks. Banks, guarantee agencies, and Sallie Mae—the institutions that made loads of money off the federal program—revolted, lobbying Congress to beat back the proposal. Whenever Andrews gave a speech to constituents on the virtues of the proposed Direct Loan program, Sallie Mae planted representatives in the audience to ask hostile questions, he recalls.

President George H. W. Bush, a Republican friendly to the banking industry, threatened to veto the bill. Congressional Democrats buckled and scaled back the plan. When Ford introduced an updated Higher Education Act that fall, it only included a pilot program for direct loans, keeping intact the Guaranteed Student Loan program as the main form of student aid. Sallie Mae, for now, had won.

However, Ford's bill settled another debate—whether to expand loan eligibility and borrowing limits or to boost grants. Andrews was one of several Democrats who decided the outcome, which would accelerate the country's slide toward student debt.

Andrews, both of whose parents dropped out of high school, had used federal loans to go to Cornell Law. When he got to Congress in 1990, he realized that the original vision of the student loan program had been lost. The Rivlin Report of 1969 had advocated for people from modest or poor backgrounds like Lisa to have most of their tuition covered by grants. In the late 1970s, the maximum Pell Grant a student could get—$1,600 per year—covered 80 percent of the cost of attending the typical public four-year college. But over the years, while Congress occasionally increased the maximum Pell Grant, tuition had risen more quickly. By 1991, the maximum award of $2,300 had fallen to roughly 50 percent of the average four-year public-college tuition.

Loans increasingly went to poor families, not just the middle class. By the 1990s, Black students, who tended to be poorer than the typical student, were the most likely of any race to borrow. Andrews wanted to reverse this shift to loans by boosting Pell Grants.

A big obstacle stood in the way: the federal deficit. It had exploded under Reagan and Bush. Economists believed that unless Congress reduced the deficit, interest rates on government debt would rise, driving up the government's costs and harming economic growth.

Andrews and other Democrats came up with a solution. Cut funding for Pell Grants while expanding eligibility for them—in essence, helping more people, but giving less help to each individual. Then, give all families access to federal loans—regardless of their income—and increase the amounts they could borrow. The Democrats' bill increased undergraduate loan limits and allowed parents to borrow unlimited amounts to make up for any tuition their children couldn't cover.

Finally, the bill did something that lawmakers and economic advisers had previously warned would be catastrophic. For a significant portion of new student loans, the government would no longer cover the interest while students were in school. The interest would accrue on these loans—Congress called them "unsubsidized loans"—over those years and would then be tacked onto borrowers' total balance once they graduated.

The effect of this plan would be to shift aid from the poor to the middle class—and to greatly expand the nation's reliance on student loans overall.

Andrews, years later, gives two rationales for shifting Americans' reliance toward loans—one philosophical, one technical.

The philosophical one: "The government has to have a smaller deficit, which means we have to stop giving people things, and make people earn them."

The technical one: Under the new accounting rules, expanding student loans would make the government money, under the assumption Congress would recoup the loan dollars plus interest charges, some of which could be used to reduce the deficit.

That is, if Congress could defeat Sallie Mae.

"I refuse to be part of a generation of Americans that celebrates the death of communism abroad with the loss of the American Dream here at home," Bill Clinton said on a brisk morning on the steps of the Old State House in Little Rock, Arkansas, when he announced his run for president, in 1991.

He was running as a "New Democrat," representing a moderate wing of the party that took liberal stances on social issues like affirmative action and abortion and conservative stances on economic issues like free trade, regulation, and deficit reduction. Clinton was a deficit hawk. But he also centered his campaign around finding ways to help families cope with the rising cost of college, an anxiety he knew personally.

When he enrolled at Georgetown University, his undergraduate dream school, he was rattled by the high tuition. "It was so expensive," he wrote in his memoirs. "Although we were a comfortable middle-class family by Arkansas standards, I was worried that my folks couldn't afford it."

He worked part-time to pay for it and went on to Yale Law

School, where he borrowed from the National Defense Student Loan program as well as from a separate program administered by Yale. The Yale program didn't give students a specific dollar amount in loans; instead it required students to pay back a percentage of their salary for a number of years after they left.

Clinton credited the Yale repayment plan for allowing him to take a modest-paying job as an assistant professor at the University of Arkansas, since it kept his monthly payments manageable.

While running for president, Clinton called for everyone, regardless of income, to have access to federal student loans, and to have the option to pay back a share of their income, as under the Yale plan. He proposed an even more generous debt-forgiveness plan for young Americans who went into AmeriCorps, a new public-service program.

Clinton had identified a key flaw in student lending. There was uncertainty as to how much college students would earn after graduation. Yes, on average going to college boosted a person's income, but by a variable amount. Many graduates wouldn't earn a lot—at least not early in their careers. Clinton wanted to ensure that people like Lisa could go to the college of their choice without debt ruining their lives afterward. A program that allowed monthly payments to float with a borrower's income was a form of insurance. Such a program would protect a borrower in a time of crisis, such as a spell of unemployment, during which her payments would be suspended. Just as Congress insured banks, Clinton wanted to insure students.

"If you're asking what was on our minds, it was one very simple thing—getting loans to students at lower interest rates which would lower their monthly payments," says Bill Galston, who advised Clinton during his 1992 campaign and in the White House.

To save the government money, Clinton campaigned on ending the Guaranteed Student Loan program in favor of a Direct Loan program. In November 1992, Clinton won the presidential election in a landslide, beating the incumbent, Bush, as well as Ross Perot, a Texas businessman who had run as an independent on a platform of deficit reduction. More than 60 percent of the popular vote was cast in favor of candidates who saw the deficit as an urgent problem.

In his first weeks in office, Clinton pushed for a broad deficit-reduction package that included changes to the student loan program. In February 1993, the month after his inauguration, he abandoned his plan to forgive debt for those who entered AmeriCorps, but he successfully pushed Congress to create a permanent version of the Direct Loan program to compete against—and, Clinton hoped, ultimately replace—the Guaranteed Student Loan program. As part of a bill passed by Congress months after he took office, the Direct Loan program would steadily grow, and within four years originate up to 60 percent of all federal student loans. The bill created an income-based repayment option similar to the one at Yale—but only for borrowers with direct loans.

Sallie Mae's stock price tumbled again. "The student loan business is changed forever," Sallie Mae CFO Al Lord told *Barron's* magazine in June 1993. "Bill Clinton has won."

Most of the interest that Congress collected from students would help fund other programs, like Pell Grants. But some would go toward reducing the deficit. The government was cutting its own debt in part by enabling people like Lisa to get more into debt.

Lisa had enrolled at FDU as a part-time student. After getting all A's in her first three classes, she told her boss she was going to enroll full-time while continuing to work at the firm. He reprimanded her. "You're going to mess everything up," he said, urging her to stay a part-time student. "You'll stress out and fail."

Undeterred, she enrolled full-time anyway. She worked at the law firm from 8:30 to 5, then crossed the street to take classes from 5:30 to 11. She did that four days a week for three and a half years, including summers. At the end of one semester, she slapped a transcript on her boss's desk. All A's. He had been wrong. School was hard, but she was excelling.

In 1991, Lisa's first year, the school raised tuition nearly 9 percent. Her sophomore year, it raised tuition another 6.5 percent, to nearly $10,000. She took out multiple loans each year under the Guaranteed Student Loan program to cover the charges. For most of those loans, interest accrued while she was in school, thanks to the 1993 law that steered a portion of borrowers' payments toward reducing the federal deficit.

Lisa saw the loans as an investment. She proudly borrowed, believing the debt would lead to a better future. She didn't want a handout.

Colleges essentially acted as customer service agents of the federal loan programs, guiding students through the application process. School offiicals had few restrictions in awarding loans for students. Unlike with federally backed mortgages, Congress didn't require them to review a student's ability to repay loans. Congress didn't collect data on what students earned after graduation.

While the congressional architects of the student loan program praised debt as building character and promoting individual responsibility, that responsibility fell disproportionately on students and not enough on schools. Colleges suffered no consequences if the loan amounts were too high for borrowers to repay. Meanwhile, students such as Lisa often had few, if any, alternatives to debt for paying tuition, and limited repayment options to keep payments manageable.

It didn't matter to schools—or banks, or Sallie Mae, or even the government—that Lisa was on the path to owing six figures in student debt, far more than what she would earn in a single year as a psychologist. Those institutions had eliminated their risk. The government insured banks against losses, but it provided no such insurance for students. Larry Hough, who succeeded Ed Fox as Sallie Mae CEO, says schools have a conflict of interest. They sell a product while also acting as an agent for the lender financing that product—the government. Hough compares colleges to car dealerships, where the person selling the car sits next to the person financing it. The consumer lacks leverage to negotiate. "You figure out what new car you wanted to buy, you walk 100 feet, and you arrange the financing," he says.

At colleges, the loan application process took minutes. The school packaged loans with federal tax dollars. When schools like FDU told Lisa she was making a good investment, they had a vested interest in believing it. Their economic livelihoods depended on her taking out debt.

Al Lord, Sallie Mae's longtime CFO who would become its CEO, knew this as well. In retrospect, he says schools raised prices simply because they could. "All those funds which take twenty, thirty years to pay off, are current revenues to the university," Lord says, adding that once the students sign the documents, "the university has no obligations."

Lisa received her undergraduate degree in psychology from FDU in 1995 with a near-perfect 3.97 GPA. She had borrowed $21,000, and interest was accruing. The undergrad degree wasn't enough. New Jersey law required psychologists to have a Ph.D. to open a practice. This requirement was part of a broader trend called credential inflation. As college graduates flooded the labor market, employers and licensing bodies raised the bar, requiring more workers to have advanced degrees.

Lisa, determined to start a practice, set her sights on the required Ph.D. "I was so motivated," she says. "I knew everything hinged on getting strong enough grades to get into grad school. I knew this was going to be a long haul."

She enrolled at Widener University, another private school near her home in New Jersey, requiring tens of thousands of dollars in additional student debt.

Lisa was part of a cultural shift. Credit—long a part of American culture, dating back to the financing of cars for working-class families in the 1920s—was being even more broadly adopted by middle-class families toward the end of the 20th century. Americans started borrowing more overall in the 1990s—for education, cars, shopping, and homes. Elected leaders, while warning of the dangers of federal deficits, encouraged consumers to take on more debt. Bill Galston, Clinton's policy adviser, says the administration viewed federal debt as a drag on the economy but student debt as an "investment."

In June 1995, Clinton announced the National Homeownership Strategy, with the goal of substantially increasing the number of Americans who owned their homes. Homeownership had long been a pillar of American prosperity and, like education, was viewed as a class equalizer, a way for historically disadvantaged communities to gain a middle-class footing. The plan resembled the government's financing of higher education. In each case, government-sponsored enterprises—Sallie Mae in student loans, Fannie Mae and Freddie Mac in the mortgage market—infused banks with cheap money in the name of helping poor and middle-class Americans build wealth. The twin pillars of the American Dream—homeownership and college—were inextricably linked to debt. People like Lisa were told they had to borrow to make it happen. And they did.

In total, Lisa took out 16 different loans for her education, each with a 5 percent origination fee, totaling $95,000 in principal. By the time she entered the workforce, interest charges had pushed up her balance by $25,604, or 27 percent. Her total debt: $120,604.

Lisa achieved her goal of getting a college education. Clinton achieved his goal of eliminating the deficit. But Lisa was sunk deeper into debt than she could possibly repay. By the time she left grad school, her debt was the size of a mortgage.

Sallie Mae stood to make tens of thousands of dollars in interest off of her. But that business was in danger of going away. The new Direct Loan program was gaining market share and cutting into Sallie Mae's profits. Sallie Mae appeared to be headed toward defeat. That is, until one day, Al Lord received a call.

FIVE

The Lord of Wall Street

(1994–2008)

When Al Lord reached for his ringing phone in late 1994, he had been out of his job at Sallie Mae for more than a year. Fired as the company's chief financial officer, he was unemployed for the first time in his life. His involuntary exit had left him embittered, and plotting how to get back into the game he knew best: making money.

Andrew Barth, an executive at the investment company Capital Group, was on the other end of the line when Lord picked up. Barth was calling with a friendly invitation to connect in Pasadena, California, during the Rose Bowl in January. *Meet for breakfast over the weekend?* Barth asked.

Absolutely, Lord said. Not only was Capital Group Sallie Mae's top shareholder, Lord already had plans to attend the game to watch his beloved Penn State Nittany Lions play the Oregon Ducks on January 2, 1995.

When Barth called, Sallie Mae was in free fall, its stock plummeting and an adversarial president, Bill Clinton, in the White House. The Democratic-controlled Congress had created a new Direct Loan program—expanding Bill Ford's earlier pilot program. The new lending regime called for shifting most—and eventually all—of the student loan market to the public sector, with the Treasury Department, instead of banks, extending loans to students. If the government no longer needed banks to make loans, Sallie Mae would have no federal loans to buy. Sallie Mae had made billions of dollars in interest and fees off of such loans in the past decade and a half. The company's main line of business was about to evaporate.

Capital Group and Sallie Mae's other top shareholders—behemoths such as Fidelity and Lincoln Capital—were panicking. The companies managed Americans' 401(k) accounts and pensions, and their portfolios included millions of shares of extremely profitable Sallie Mae stock. As Sallie's stock plummeted, the funds were hemorrhaging money.

Barth's invitation wasn't just a social call to the former chief financial officer; he wanted to resuscitate the student loan giant and reverse its stock decline. When the two men met in Pasadena, Lord told Barth that the problem was Clinton's program. The Direct Loan program couldn't replace the Guaranteed Student Loan program overnight, and in the meantime the two competing programs created a bizarre situation. The federal government now had two student loan programs, each backed by taxpayers, vying for the same market. The result was an internecine battle over the financing of America's college and graduate students. Clinton wanted to use the interest that students paid on their loans to reduce the federal deficit and fund other government initiatives. Wall Street wanted to enrich investors. Clinton was winning.

Increasingly, schools steered their students to direct loans, under public pressure from President Clinton and First Lady Hillary Clinton. Sallie Mae was rapidly losing market share as more schools steered students to the Direct Loan program.

All of this had happened without Lord, who seethed as the company declined. Barth wanted more from Lord than just his advice.

Just before the check came at breakfast, Barth caught Lord off guard, asking, *Would you consider joining the board of Sallie Mae?*

Barth wanted Lord on the board to convince the other members to put in place his vision to turn the company around. Barth's employer had enough shares to install two board members, thanks to a 1992 law that gave private investors who owned Sallie Mae shares the right to vote on board membership. Wall Street now had new leverage over the financial backbone of America's universities, and Barth wanted to use it.

Barth's proposal took Lord aback. His unceremonious firing had been widely noted, and his disdain for the man who fired him, CEO Larry Hough, was well known. Joining the board would effectively make him Hough's new boss. Most people would have turned down the opportunity for the sheer awkwardness.

Lord wasn't like most people. He lived for confrontation. "Sure, I'll do it," Lord said.

Albert Leo Lord Jr. grew up a fighter, an eager pugilist who carried his combativeness from his working-class upbringing into Sallie Mae's boardroom, where he pushed for rapid growth and reaped millions in profits for himself and billions for the company.

Lord was the oldest of three boys in a blue-collar Philadelphia family. His mother, who wanted to go to college but couldn't afford to, worked as a secretary. His father, who dropped out of high school, worked as a linotype operator for the *Philadelphia Inquirer*. Both were labor Democrats. They divorced when he was young. His mother raised Lord and his brothers in a two-bedroom apartment.

Lord attended a Catholic elementary school and served as an altar boy. He and his friends got into street fights with public school kids. He was a dreadful student by his own admission, but knew he needed an education beyond high school. "My mom and my dad told me, 'You are going to college,'" Lord once told a newspaper.

He went to Penn State, covering the $175-per-semester tuition by bagging groceries and working at a construction site. Sixty years later, he remembers the drudgery of pushing grocery carts up a parking lot on a steep hill.

He earned poor grades at Penn State but graduated in 1967. He landed a job at a big accounting firm now known as KPMG. By age 32, he was treasurer of one of its biggest divisions. "This is as solid proof as you should ever need that you really don't need great grades to do well in business," he says.

In 1981, Sallie Mae's CFO called to ask if he'd be interested in becoming the company's comptroller, overseeing its accounting and payroll departments. Lord had only vaguely heard of the company and thought it would be silly to work for an employer with such a name, particularly one with ties to the federal government. No company could make big profits by being controlled by a bureaucracy, he felt.

He accepted the offer after the CFO promised that the company would eventually sever its ties to the government, and rely solely on investors for cash without meddling from bureaucrats or congressmen. A year later, after the CFO left, Lord succeeded him, overseeing the company's finances in the number three position. He was exceedingly ambitious. With his piercing blue eyes and silver hair combed gently to the side, he could be charming, nostalgic, or defensive, depending on the issue before him. Though he wore expensive suits for the boardroom, he preferred Miller Lite to $15 cocktails after hours. He wasn't shy about sharing his opinions, of which he had many. One of his most passionate beliefs was that college should not be free. His belief that students should pay their own way stemmed from his upbringing.

The man just above him on Sallie Mae's organizational chart was cut from altogether different cloth. Larry Hough had been one of Sallie Mae's first hires, and had risen to become chief operating officer, second in command only to Fox. Though close in age, Hough and Lord were a study in contrasts. While Lord scrapped his way through public high school, Hough graduated from Phillips Exeter, one of the nation's elite boarding schools. Lord had eked his way through Penn State, while Hough had sailed through Stanford. Lord went straight into the workforce after college; Hough enlisted in the navy and rowed at the 1968 Olympics, earning a silver medal, and competed again in 1972.

After Fox departed for Dartmouth in 1990, Lord and Hough were finalists to succeed him as CEO. The board went with Hough, the candidate with the prestigious pedigree, over the scrappy brawler from Philadelphia. "I was devastated when I lost," Lord says. "I think that's just competitiveness. But the fact that they took Larry was the most devastating part."

Fox had left Sallie Mae at an inflection point. The moment Clinton came to Washington in the winter of 1993, the company stock tumbled, starting a multiyear slide. The new president made clear he wanted banks and Sallie Mae cut off from the loan program. The head of Clinton's National Economic Council, former Goldman Sachs executive Robert Rubin, was a friend of Lord's. (Rubin later served as Clinton's Treasury secretary.) Months into Clinton's first term, Lord dropped by Rubin's office in the White House for what he expected to be a friendly chat. He also hoped to glean information about the status of Sallie Mae in the new administration. Rubin had a blunt message for Lord. There would be no relationship. The new administration wasn't playing nice. It planned to take over student lending, and in the process decimate Sallie Mae's profits.

Lord was so stunned by the chilly meeting that he walked the two miles to Sallie Mae's offices in Georgetown to clear his head.

The administration's posture raised an existential question for Sallie Mae: Should it stay the course as a part of the student lending industry, or shift into a new line of business when Clinton's lending plan began eating into company profits?

"Our shareholders wanted to know, 'What are you going to do?'" Hough says. "I would not address that." Hough privately planned to expand Sallie Mae into other types of consumer lending products for families, such as college-savings plans. But he worried that if he announced those plans, the banking industry's top lobbying groups—the Consumer Bankers Association and the American Bankers Association—would mobilize and lobby for legislation to prevent Sallie Mae from moving into their territory.

Taking the opposite position of Hough, Lord wanted Sallie Mae to stay in the business of student lending. That's where the real money was. With colleges raising tuition rapidly, he saw an opening. The government limited how much students could borrow per year. He wanted them to be able to borrow more—through Sallie Mae. If Sallie Mae could convince Congress to allow it to do so, Lord wanted the company to lend directly to students, becoming the biggest lender under the guaranteed program while also offering students private, nonfederal loans to augment their federal loans.

Lord sneered at what he viewed as Hough's lack of grit in taking on Clinton and Congress. "Sallie Mae's whole corporate culture, its whole public demeanor, was one of victim," Lord says. "Larry was complaining about what had gotten done to them. You can't fix it by complaining about it, particularly with the government, because that just motivates them to get you again."

Lord and Hough clashed over their respective visions. Despite Lord's stubbornness, Hough prevailed and ousted his competitor in 1994. Lord spent a year in limbo. During that time, as Sallie Mae's stock fell, he received calls from investors, including hedge fund managers, wanting to know how to revive the company.

Weeks after Andy Barth asked him to join Sallie Mae's board, Lord rode an Amtrak train to Philadelphia to meet with an old colleague he hadn't seen in years. Tim Fitzpatrick headed a consumer lending company that he and his partners had just sold, making Fitzpatrick richer than he'd ever imagined. He was thinking of retiring in the Caribbean.

Lord told Fitzpatrick about the mess at Sallie Mae, and how he wanted to wrest control of the company from Hough by taking over the board. He wanted Fitzpatrick to help him do it.

No one had ever done anything like this before, Fitzpatrick thought. There had been plenty of hostile corporate takeovers by rogue shareholders in the 1980s and 1990s. But Lord's plan involved no financial transaction, just a few outsiders forcing their way onto the board of a huge company with a philosophical argument, not money. The idea sounded crazy—and exhilarating.

Lord told Fitzpatrick he had a name for his fledgling group of mercenaries: "The Committee to Restore Value to Sallie Mae."

Fitzpatrick saw the possibility of a corporate coup as a daring endeavor for his career bucket list. "I was more intrigued by the rebellious process," Fitzpatrick says. "I had this ghost in me saying if there was anything that got me excited, it would be to defy the corporate veil of 'same old, same old.' This was historic, a Harvard Business School case." He agreed to join Lord's takeover team.

As a government-sponsored enterprise, Sallie Mae had a hybrid structure—part public, part private—that made a takeover gambit unlike a typical corporate raid on a private company. Sallie Mae's shares, since 1984, were traded on the New York Stock Exchange: Anyone could own its stock. Its main business was buying student loans from lenders and "servicing" those loans: staying in touch with borrowers, fielding their questions, collecting their monthly payments, tracking them down if they fell behind on payments.

However, Sallie Mae differed from other companies because its board of directors was controlled by both private investors and the federal government. The president of the United States appointed a third of Sallie Mae's board; financial institutions another third; schools, the final third. On top of that, Sallie Mae's governing documents—a charter created by Congress—restricted the company from engaging in the most profitable task in the student loan market: lending directly to college and graduate students.

Lord, above all else, wanted Sallie Mae to lend to students, taking over the role of banks. He needed the investor-appointed board members to overcome the government-appointed board members' allegiance to Hough and Clinton. While Lord could get on the board through Barth, he needed allies once there.

Lord met with potential investors at the offices of the Manhattan securities firm Furman Selz. Lord wanted to convince them to buy enough of Sallie Mae's stock to gain the rights to vote on who served on its board—so they could install his allies. Such a meeting typically included 75 interested investors. Hundreds showed up to hear what Lord had to say. Lord delivered a 10-page presentation titled "The Art of the Possible." He talked about cutting costs, selling loans as "securities" to investors to raise money, buying shares, and, most important, shedding the company's status as a government-sponsored enterprise. The last step would reduce congressional oversight of the company and remove the White House–appointed members from its board. It would also allow Sallie Mae to lend to students, going head-to-head against Clinton's Direct Loan program. Sallie could then play all three roles: lend to students, buy loans from banks, and service loans. (Even the Direct Loan program relied on private firms to service loans.)

The reception for Lord's approach was so enthusiastic that when some of the group gathered afterward at a bar, he became emboldened and aimed to get a slate of eight supporters on the board, instead of the four he had originally intended. That still wasn't enough to gain a majority, but it would expand his influence from the seven-vote bankers' bloc. In mid-1995, Lord got on the board, as did his allies, including Ed Fox as chairman. Then came the campaign to oust Hough.

Lord's opening came in 1996, when Congress—now controlled by business-friendly Republicans—and the Clinton administration agreed on a law to rid Sallie Mae of its GSE status, killing its charter and making the company private. Such a move would eventually remove the government-appointed members of its board and allow it to act like any other private company. That now included the option of lending to students. Hough had assured the Clinton administration and Congress that once Sallie Mae lost its GSE status, it didn't plan to lend to students, leaving that market to the Direct Loan program. Al Lord had other plans.

In 1996, Sallie's board held a series of votes to determine whether to fire Hough. Initially, Lord failed to garner enough board support, but more votes followed. With each round of voting, Lord incrementally gained support. It became clear that Hough was losing allies, and he left on his own. The board appointed Lord as CEO in 1997. Lord hired Fitzpatrick as chief operating officer, making him the second most powerful executive in the company.

Lord viewed his takeover of Sallie Mae as a triumph of Wall Street—interested solely in increasing a company's share price—over the government. Sallie Mae's investor-appointed board members prevailed over government-aligned allies.

"If you're a public shareholder in Sallie Mae and you buy stock at fifty bucks and it's at forty, you have a say at running the business," Lord says. "I proved that. That's how I became CEO of the company against the incumbent, telling the world that I could do better. And they decided—not the government, not a bunch of banks, not a bunch of colleges—but people that held specific return objectives in mind. It's pretty much as simple as that."

What was Lord's motive in taking over Sallie Mae? Lord says he was so angry at what he viewed as the prior board's indifference to Sallie's stock plunge that "I could not see straight. Their arrogance and contempt for the shareholders fueled my drive, not money," he says.

Asked what motivated Lord, Fitzpatrick says he believes it was the prospect of making money. Wolf Schoellkopf, a close friend of Lord's who joined the new board, answers the same question with a laugh, as if the answer is obvious to anyone who knew Al Lord: "He wanted to get rich."

By the late 1990s, higher education and housing were on parallel tracks. By the time Lord took over Sallie Mae, Wall Street investors were pouring more money into the federal government's deepening commitment to helping Americans buy homes and pay for college.

Wall Street invested through a money-raising and risk-reducing tool called securitization. Companies bundled consumer loans, sliced the bundle into pieces, known as "securities," and sold them to investors. Just like buying a tube of toothpaste is more expensive at the grocery store than buying in bulk at Costco, securities cost investors more on a per-unit basis than an entire bundle of loans would. This also reduced the risk of a company like Sallie Mae losing money, since the loans would be held by multiple institutions instead of being concentrated on the company's books.

Education and housing shared a second characteristic. At the heart of each industry was a highly sought-after asset whose price was rising. Homes and higher education each had acquired a mythical status as symbols of the American Dream. Prices rose as a result. Presidents Clinton and George W. Bush aggressively pushed homeownership, urging Americans to purchase homes through cheap credit and government subsidies. That increased demand for housing, lifting home prices. A similar phenomenon happened with college. Since Lyndon Johnson's administration, policy makers and economists declared a college degree essential. By the early 2000s, those calls had grown louder. The decline in factory employment that began in the 1980s accelerated in the late 1990s and early 2000s. Wages for college graduates had risen further in the 1990s while wages of nongraduates stagnated, pushing up demand for bachelor's degrees. Colleges continued to raise prices.

Still, there was untapped demand. In 2000, 6 in 10 recent high-school graduates went on to college. Colleges could still go after the 4 in 10 who didn't—as well as the tens of millions of potential "adult learners" like Lisa.

Lord saw the conditions for rapid growth. His goal: Dominate the market for lending to college and graduate students.

In December 1997, months after he became CEO, Lord gave the keynote speech to hundreds of bank executives at a conference hosted by the Consumer Bankers Association. The event in northern Virginia was one of the industry's biggest annual gatherings, and the organization had expected a friendly speech. Instead, Lord delivered a public scolding and issued a challenge.

"Nobody is putting any significant money into this business to improve delivery and technology," Lord told the audience. "You've got to get your tails out from between your legs and stop apologizing for making a profit.

"I'm certainly not embarrassed to make a profit," he added.

The bankers sat in stunned disbelief. One Sallie Mae official present at the speech described Lord's withering message as a challenge: *You're lazy, and we're going to take your market share. You used to be our clients. We're competing against you now. This is war.*

Lord's first step as CEO was to give everyone in the company— from the front-desk receptionist to sales reps to the chairman of the board—stock options. He wanted them all to have a stake in Sallie Mae's future, so that their principal focus would be growth and profits. The higher the company's stock price, the richer the employees would become.

Next, he needed to incentivize schools to ditch Clinton's Direct Loan program and return to the industry's Guaranteed Student Loan program. He wanted to crush the competition in two ways: By supplanting banks to become the dominant lender to students under the Guaranteed Student Loan program, and by making private loans that weren't guaranteed by the government. To achieve the first goal, Sallie Mae offered discounts on fees and interest rates if students used the Guaranteed Student Loan program. Sallie Mae made so much money from the program that it could afford the discounts. It was a small price to pay to reap the wider benefits of beating back the Direct Loan program. Lord wanted the whole market.

To sweeten the deal, Sallie Mae offered to upgrade schools' computer systems to quicken the financial aid approval process if they steered students toward the Guaranteed Student Loan program. Lord had a caustic pitch to schools. "He basically said, 'Look, the government fucks up everything,'" Fitzpatrick, his deputy, says. "It's only a matter of time before these schools see how inept the government is [in] transacting money to thousands of students on a daily, monthly basis and the nightmare they'd eventually create.

"We started one by one taking schools back from the Direct Loan program," Fitzpatrick says. By 1998, Sallie Mae had regained market share. Its stock was rising again. Lord and Fitzpatrick turned their focus to the next element of their growth plan: Get more American students to borrow—and to borrow bigger amounts.

In 1999, Fitzpatrick read the financial documents for a company called the University of Phoenix, a national chain of for-profit colleges. He couldn't believe the numbers. The company, which had gone public five years earlier, had nearly 70,000 students across the U.S. enrolled in dozens of programs. That made it one of the biggest educators in the United States, outweighing most state flagship universities. The company focused on a largely untapped market: adult learners. People in their late 20s, 30s, 40s, even 50s who had never gone to college, who had dropped out, or college grads who wanted additional degrees. It was using a tool that public colleges hadn't used yet: the internet.

University of Phoenix had figured out that online courses were highly profitable. They were cheap to run since they didn't require physical campuses. And they had unlimited reach: A fresh high school graduate living in Selma, Alabama, could take the same course as a 50-year-old secretary living in Sacramento. Its tuition in 2000 was $5,728, significantly lower than private nonprofit schools' average tuition of $22,300, but higher than the $3,800 that public schools cost that year.

Fitzpatrick flew to Phoenix to meet with the CEO of the University of Phoenix's corporate parent, Apollo Group, a man named John Sperling who went on safaris and hunted big-game trophy animals. The office was large and opulent, and when Fitzpatrick walked in, his eyes landed on a lion head mounted on the wall.

Fitzpatrick told Sperling the two companies could help each other. For-profit colleges like the University of Phoenix faced stricter federal regulations than nonprofit and public schools. A law passed by Congress in the early 1990s, known as "90-10," forbade for-profit schools from receiving more than 90 percent of their revenue from federal student loans and Pell Grants. The law reflected the belief that if a school relied entirely on the student loan program for revenue, it would enroll as many students as possible without regard to their ability to repay. Forcing schools to rely on at least one other source of cash would reduce their students' reliance on debt, while forcing the schools' owners to put some of their own money at risk to cover costs.

The law had an unintended side effect. Schools met the 90-10 rule with a trick: they raised tuition just enough to force students to hit the ceiling on their federal loans and then take out private loans to cover the balance. The private loans counted toward the 10 percent of revenue outside of the federal loan program.

The fates of Sallie Mae and the for-profit college industry converged. Sallie Mae told schools that if they used the Guaranteed Student Loan program, Sallie Mae would provide a pool of money—which it aptly called "opportunity pools"—from which their students could borrow, on top of their federal loans. The schools would make higher profits from tuition increases; Sallie Mae would profit both from the Guaranteed Student Loan program and the private loans. Sallie Mae could charge higher interest rates on private loans than the rates Congress set for federal loans.

Sallie Mae started offering this option to nonprofit and public schools as well. The private loans were riskier for Sallie Mae. If borrowers defaulted, the company and its investors, rather than taxpayers, would eat the losses. But the profits it made off of the Guaranteed Student Loan program were high enough to justify the risk. If it could convince a school to switch to the guaranteed program, the money Sallie Mae made from that program would offset any losses Sallie Mae suffered in the private program.

The only thing holding the for-profit college sector back was government regulation. Congress, after Senator Nunn's report, had passed a slew of rules in the early 1990s to crack down on for-profit schools. As a result of the rules, hundreds of for-profit schools lost their eligibility to receive students' loan dollars, sanctions that amounted to a financial death knell for the companies. Many went bankrupt. The colleges needed a powerful ally to roll back regulations.

Al Lord sat in the front row awaiting his guest's arrival, surrounded by bankers in Sallie Mae's new, gleaming headquarters in Reston, Virginia. It was Tuesday, March 28, 2000, a few weeks after Super Tuesday during the primaries of an election year.

Outside, a motorcade carrying George W. Bush approached. Inside Bush's vehicle, the Texas governor had just hung up the phone after a call with Arizona senator John McCain, who had ended his White House bid two weeks earlier. The cordial, if awkward, call marked the first time the men had spoken since McCain had dropped out of the bitter primary battle. Bush now stood as the undisputed front-runner for the Republican nomination for president.

The car came to a stop outside Sallie Mae's headquarters, a giant rectangular building overlooking a man-made pond and a stand of trees. Wearing a dark gray suit and a red tie with white polka dots, Bush walked into the building, where hundreds of company employees and business leaders awaited him in a packed room. Bush stepped to the lectern, and the crowd stood and cheered. "I appreciate so very much, Al, your hospitality," Bush said to Lord as people took their seats.

Bush was solidifying support to be the GOP nominee to oppose Clinton's vice president, Al Gore, in the November general election. Representative Tom Davis, a Virginia Republican and Sallie Mae ally, had arranged Bush's visit. Bush barely addressed higher education that day. But his appearance was a monumental victory for Lord, who had learned just how crucial the occupant of the White House was to Sallie Mae's bottom line. Bush was a free-market conservative who believed in the private sector's ability to drive reform in education.

Eight months later, after a Florida ballot recount and Supreme Court ruling sent Bush to the White House, his administration stocked the Education Department with for-profit industry officials and their allies.

Among them was Jeff Andrade. A big, gruff son of a Massachusetts factory worker, Andrade had served in the 1990s as a senior aide to one of Sallie Mae's top House allies, Rep. Buck McKeon (R., Calif.). Andrade, a deputy assistant education secretary, thought public and nonprofit colleges were hypocrites. They talked about providing opportunity to the poor but they weren't exactly swinging their doors open for them. They were too obsessed with rankings and enriching themselves as they charged students through the nose.

Andrade, who'd been raised by a single mother and took out student loans to attend American University, thought for-profit colleges played an important role. They pioneered online teaching, while nonprofit schools refused to innovate. "It was a tool for providing an opportunity for people who were basically shut out of the system because of their life circumstances," Andrade says. "They couldn't afford to leave their jobs and go away."

Early on, Andrade made a decision that would help drive a for-profit industry boom and unintentionally lead hundreds of thousands, if not millions, of Americans to take on student debt.

A week after Bush took office, a national chain of for-profit schools called Computer Learning Centers went bankrupt. The Clinton administration had accused the company of illegally paying recruiters based on how many students they enrolled, engaging in a practice known as "incentive compensation" that Congress banned in 1992.

Congress sought to prevent incentives for schools to aggressively enroll students unprepared for college, as those students would likely drop out and default on their loans. The Clinton administration ordered the company to repay $187 million in federal student loans and grants.

With a couple million dollars in reserves, the company went bankrupt. More than 1,800 Computer Learning Centers employees lost their jobs and thousands of students, nearly all of them in debt, were without a school.

The federal action and the company's collapse were a five-alarm fire for colleges. In the first days of the Bush administration, frantic colleges flooded Andrade's office with concerns they'd be found guilty of the same practices as Computer Learning Centers, even though they never intended to break the law. The line between acceptable recruiting and predatory recruiting was blurry, they said.

Andrade agreed. He led an effort to create a dozen exceptions, dubbed "safe harbors," to allow colleges to pay recruiters based on enrollment numbers. Andrade wanted to codify exceptions that the Education Department had been granting ad hoc. "I would rather work out the compliance issue with an ongoing entity than with a bankrupt zombie corporation," he says.

Not everyone in the Education Department agreed with Andrade.

David Bergeron, a midlevel staffer who had worked in the agency for years, stormed into Andrade's office. He warned that the exceptions would encourage schools to court naive students while offering education on the cheap. Schools would focus on making money rather than on students' well-being, and would throw open the doors to unprepared students, knowing they were likely to never graduate, increasing the risk they'd default on loans.

The argument grew heated. Andrade won. The administration adopted his proposal.

At that time, a new breed of for-profit college was emerging: corporate-owned conglomerates that offered associate's and bachelor's degree programs, competing for students who traditionally attended community colleges or four-year public schools.

For-profit colleges gained the interest of investors. With corporate profits rising, investors were flush with cash. After the collapse of the tech bubble and the September 11 terrorist attacks, the Federal Reserve pushed down interest rates by dramatically increasing the money supply. The goal: Make it easier and cheaper for companies and households to borrow so they could spend, lifting the economy out of recession. That gave investors cash to plow into new types of investments that offered big returns. Higher ed was a natural target.

For-profit schools took advantage of underinvestment in public colleges. State flagship universities had tightened their admissions as they sought to lower their acceptance rates and move up in national rankings. Meanwhile, public and nonprofit schools were slow to embrace the internet. In California, 90,000 students would be denied access to community college in the 2004 school year, which the CEO of the for-profit ITT Technical Institute blamed on the state's fiscal crisis.

"We have been approached by at least one Californian university who had capped its enrollment to invite our student recruiters to their campus to recruit some of their overflow students," ITT's CEO, Rene Champagne, said during an earnings call in October 2003. Sallie Mae was a big reason behind the schools' rise. Sallie Mae's "opportunity pools" allowed students to borrow on top of federal student loans. For-profit schools charged higher tuition than their public and nonprofit counterparts, and Sallie Mae abetted them.

* * *

By 2003, Sallie Mae had convinced dozens of schools to switch to the Guaranteed Student Loan program.

Sallie Mae and other banks lavished "free meals and drinks, golf outings, and sailboat cruises" on college officials, *U.S. News & World Report* said in a 2003 cover story. Sallie Mae's "opportunity pools" had enticed schools to switch to the guaranteed loan program, the magazine said. Between 2000 and 2003, more than 60 colleges and universities had switched to the program, generating $1 billion in loan business for Sallie Mae, the magazine reported.

That business translated into a windfall for Sallie Mae's executives. Lord made $33.6 million in salary, bonuses, and stock options in 2002.

The report caused a scandal. The public woke up to the fact that student lending—ostensibly for the public good—wasn't a philanthropic endeavor.

New York attorney general Andrew Cuomo launched an investigation of Sallie Mae and other lenders. Sallie Mae would later settle with his office, agreeing to pay $2 million into a fund to help educate borrowers about student loans. It stopped paying for trips for college financial aid officials.

But the company said it had done nothing wrong. A Sallie Mae spokesman told *U.S. News* that the guaranteed loan program injected competition in the student loan market that expanded students' choices. "Competition works," a company spokesman told the magazine.

Lord says the company's sales reps had indeed been buying meals for university officials as a form of "customer service." Asked about cruises, he says: "If one salesman or some salesmen did something they shouldn't have done, I suppose that's always possible. We would have conferences, right? So they [college officials] would come. And you bring in guest speakers, and introduce new products. So yeah, there probably were hotels taken care of, and dinners and so on and so forth."

While Sallie Mae spoke of the virtues of competition, one of the company's main strategies was to buy up competitors and consolidate its market share. Lord directed purchases that included those of USA Group, the nation's largest student loan guarantee agency, and Nellie Mae, a New England–based student lender. He then laid off employees of the former company, in a persistent effort to cut costs and boost Sallie Mae's profitability.

Sallie Mae spent millions on lobbying and campaign contributions, mostly to Republican lawmakers. The lobbying paid off: Key allies in Congress touted the Guaranteed Student Loan program and Sallie Mae, arguing that they injected healthy competition into the student loan marketplace. Bolstering the credo that private markets created efficiencies and encouraged innovation, they pointed to Sallie Mae's move to equip schools with computers and software to speed the application process for students getting loans.

"Know that I have all of you in my two trusted hands," Rep. John Boehner (R., Ohio), the House Committee on Education and Labor chairman and future House speaker, told executives of Sallie Mae and other student loan companies in late 2005.

As Sallie Mae made riskier loans, it lobbied for a law to make it harder for borrowers to escape those debts. Congress had already chipped away at borrowers' ability to discharge their federal loans. In 1976, Congress made it difficult for college borrowers to get out of their debts through bankruptcy. Legislation in 1998 set a nearly impossible standard for bankrupt borrowers to escape their federal student loans. That law forced borrowers to prove an "undue hardship"—no matter how long they had been making payments—to shed the loans. Judges applied the vague standard strictly, preventing most from getting out of debt. In 2005, Sallie

Mae backed a bill that similarly blocked student borrowers from declaring bankruptcy, but for private student loans. The 2005 law treated private student loans the same as federal loans, applying the undue hardship standard.

Removing bankruptcy protection for borrowers helped Sallie Mae's bottom line. The company would be able to pursue borrowers even when their debts were impossibly high, rather than eating the losses in bankruptcy court.

"They could appeal to the conservatives who thought that this was the private sector—that they were adding some value," says Jason Delisle, a former aide to Rep. Tom Petri (R., Wisc.). "And the Republicans and conservatives just gave them the benefit of the doubt. They were just, 'Oh, they're banks. The private sector works better.'"

In 2005, one Republican on the Senate education committee met with staffers who were going to tell him about the differences between the two federal programs, Delisle recalls. The senator stood up before they could finish. "That's enough for me," the senator said. "I know which one I'm for. I'm for the bank program."

Student debt took off. In 2000, Americans owed about $230 billion in federal student debt. By 2005, that figure had nearly doubled, to roughly $415 billion.

The percentage of that debt that went to for-profit schools rose sharply. In the late 1990s, just over a tenth of all new student debt went to students at for-profit schools; by 2005, that share had nearly doubled to a fifth of all student debt. For-profit colleges recruited customers shunned by many middle- and upper-tier colleges: poor people, homeless people, single mothers, grandparents.

One former Sallie Mae executive recalls touring one of the company's customer service call centers with Tim Fitzpatrick, then COO, around 2005. Fitzpatrick spent much of his time standing over customer service agents as they fielded calls from prospective borrowers, the executive says. Fitzpatrick reprimanded multiple agents for turning down applicants for having bad credit. "We should make that loan!" the executive recalls Fitzpatrick telling the reps. "We've got to be more aggressive on this stuff."

Fitzpatrick says he recalls the scene. He says the company was under pressure by the federal government and colleges that predominantly served minority students to approve loans for borrowers with subprime credit so that their children had a way to pay for the college of their choice.

It became a mantra within Sallie Mae, on Wall Street, and within the halls of Congress that higher education and student loans were a good investment. "The philosophy of policy makers and Sallie Mae was, 'Education is good,'" says another former Sallie Mae executive. "Go to college—it's good. Financing—borrowing money is good. And any questioning of that was anathema."

Al Lord believed for-profit colleges added value to higher education. He felt that because they were owned by investors, they had a incentive to innovate, to reach new types of students and deliver education in more dynamic ways. He agreed with people like Jeff Andrade that public schools had become elitist and lazy.

Sallie Mae controlled the student loan market like few companies dominated any industry. In 2006, Sallie Mae was the biggest lender in the federal guaranteed program, originating 27 percent of federally guaranteed loans. Its closest competitor, Citibank, originated 6 percent. Including private and federal loans, Sallie Mae owned $142 billion in student debt—roughly a third of all student debt in the United States.

Meanwhile, a decade after Senator Nunn's report exposed widespread abuses by for-profit colleges, the industry exploded. In 1999, the University of Phoenix's 70,000 students had made Tim Fitzpatrick's jaw drop. In 2003, the University of Phoenix had more than 225,000 students, nearly half of them online. Its corporate parent, Apollo Group, earned $1.34 billion that year, most of it from federal student aid.

David Hawkins of the National Association for College Admission Counseling described an "almost unbearable" pressure on for-profit schools to boost enrollment, a pressure that created incentives to misbehave. "We're seeing plenty of evidence that the 'recruit at any cost' mentality is becoming more the rule than the exception," he told the *Chronicle of Higher Education* in 2006.

That year, Sallie Mae's political fortunes shifted. One congressional aide says that among some Democrats, Al Lord had become "public enemy number one." Activist groups representing graduate students fumed at the high interest rates Sallie Mae charged for private loans while profiting from the federal program. Borrowers complained the company didn't explain their repayment options, or that interest would accrue if they suspended monthly payments.

Meanwhile, Congress felt renewed pressure to reduce federal spending, which had soared in the early 2000s due to the Iraq and Afghanistan wars and Bush-led tax cuts. With the midterm election looming, GOP lawmakers wanted to show constituents they still cared about the deficit, and crafted a broad budget bill that in part relied on undercutting Sallie Mae so that the government could make more money from graduate students.

Enrollment in grad school was rising rapidly at the time as the growing number of workers with bachelor's degrees sought a further leg up in the labor market by going for master's, law, or medical degrees. Graduate-school tuition was typically far more expensive than college tuition. The government capped how much students could borrow each year, and many graduate-degree seekers turned to Sallie Mae for private loans once they hit the ceiling on their federal loans.

The new budget bill, the 2005 Deficit Reduction Act, removed the dollar limit on how much graduate students could borrow by creating a new program called Grad Plus. This gave graduate students the ability to borrow solely from the federal program instead of having to borrow private loans from Sallie Mae. That also meant profits would shift from Sallie Mae's books to the federal budget.

Because graduate students historically repaid loans at exceptionally high rates—many are lawyers, doctors, and MBAs—the government could count on earning at least several cents on every dollar it lent to them. For good measure, Congress charged a higher interest rate for graduate loans than it charged for undergraduate loans. Congress could then use the proceeds for other initiatives, such as covering any losses incurred when undergraduates defaulted or, in the case of the 2005 law, reducing the federal deficit. The more graduate students borrowed, the more the government earned.

The new program was also a huge gift to universities. Grad Plus amounted to a blank check. Universities, law schools, and medical schools could now charge even higher tuition without restraint. Students would be able borrow any amount needed—with a minimal credit check—to cover the higher prices.

Sallie Mae's share price hit the stratosphere, quadrupling between 2000 and 2006. "Since 1995 its stock has returned over 1,900 percent, trouncing the S&P 500's 288 percent gain," *Fortune* magazine reported in December 2005. "Today Sallie Mae's stock sold for 22 times its earnings and almost ten times its book value, 'an almost unheard-of valuation for a financial institution,'" a Criterion Research report noted.

One analyst called Sallie Mae "high-growth, profitable, recession-proof, and almost 100 percent federally guaranteed."

Congress had set the interest rate on federal loans at 8.25 percent. Sallie Mae charged rates as high as 28 percent for its private loans. Nearly 90 percent of Sallie Mae's portfolio was federal student loans. The private student loan market was growing. Other banks had also started offering student loans, such as JPMorgan Chase and Wells Fargo. But few had gotten richer from the student loan market than Lord.

Lord earned over $225 million between 1999 and 2004. Tim Fitzpatrick earned $145 million.

Lord rode around in a personal bus emblazoned with the colors of his alma mater, Penn State, and chauffeured by a hired driver. By 2005, he had earned enough money to lead an unsuccessful bid with a group of investors to buy the Washington Nationals baseball team. He bought land in Maryland to build a 7,100-acre private golf course he called Anne Arundell Manor. He moved Sallie Mae's headquarters into a new glass building in northern Virginia. He retired as CEO in 2005 and became the company's chairman, an enormously rich man with most of his wealth tied up in Sallie Mae stock. He wanted to cash out.

In 2007, as chairman, Lord engineered a deal to sell the company to a consortium of investors and remove it from the New York Stock Exchange. Its shares would no longer be publicly traded—and Lord's shares would be converted into cash. In April, the consortium agreed to buy Sallie Mae for $25 billion, far above its stock value. The group included Wall Street behemoths JPMorgan Chase, Bank of America, investment fund Friedman Fleischer & Lowe, and private equity firm J. C. Flowers & Co. The value of Lord's stock would triple.

When Senator Edward Kennedy, chairman of the Senate Committee on Health, Education, Labor, and Pensions, heard about the sale, he was livid. If Sallie Mae became privately held, it would no longer be subject to the financial disclosure requirements—such as routinely publishing its earnings—that publicly traded companies face. Thus, Congress would have even less oversight of the company, the nation's biggest student lender. The Massachusetts

Democrat told Fitzpatrick to meet him in his Capitol Hill office. The senator ranted from behind his desk, issuing a chilling threat as he stabbed his finger toward Fitzpatrick's chest.

"If you dare try to take Sallie Mae private, I'm going to take your subsidies away," Kennedy roared. He was referring to the money that the government had long paid Sallie Mae and other banks to extend and service federally guaranteed loans. As chairman of the committee that oversaw higher education, Kennedy had the power to scuttle Lord and Fitzpatrick's plan. He wasn't bluffing.

Undaunted, Lord and Fitzpatrick forged ahead with the deal. Kennedy was true to his word. In September, months after the Sallie Mae sale, Kennedy pushed legislation through Congress that cut the amount of money the government paid banks to originate loans. President Bush signed the bill. In just a few years, Sallie Mae had become the biggest lender. Suddenly, with the cut in subsidies, Sallie Mae was far less valuable. A huge source of future profits— the interest it earned from the government on each student loan it originated—had been dramatically curtailed with the stroke of a pen.

When Chris Flowers, the CEO of J. C. Flowers & Co.—the company representing the group that bought Sallie Mae—saw the news, he panicked. The contract had a clause that allowed the buyer to pay a $900 million breakup fee and back out. Flowers retreated from the deal without paying the $900 million fee, arguing that Kennedy's new law had changed the material conditions of the sale. Sallie Mae sued to prevent the buyers from reneging. Flowers's investment team argued in court that the new legislation made the original deal null. The judge agreed. The sale was scrapped, and Sallie Mae had a royal mess on its hands.

Sallie Mae invited Lord back to rectify the situation. He took the CEO title for a second time in December 2007. Facing the decimation of the company and personal economic ruin, Lord was determined to salvage the deal with Flowers, believing he could negotiate the sale at a lower price. In early December, Lord and his wife traveled to New York City to attend the ceremony at the Waldorf Astoria Hotel in which Penn State coach Joe Paterno was inducted into the College Football Hall of Fame. Afterward, Lord met Flowers in a hotel room.

"So what's your number?" Lord asked, agitated, referring to Sallie Mae's dollar price per share. "When are we doing this deal? This is ridiculous. I'm willing to take fifty-six."

"Fifty," Flowers responded.

"Good," Lord responded, a hint of desperation in his voice. "The number is obvious, then. Fifty-three. Let's sign it and get going."

"I'm about to head out on a trip overseas," Flowers said. "Let's do it when we get back." Flowers left the room.

"He's not doing this deal," Lord told his wife, Suzanne.

A week later, Lord flew back to New York to meet with Flowers a second time at the Waldorf Astoria, hoping to secure the deal. While Lord waited in a hotel room, two associates met in another room with Flowers to see what price he was willing to settle for. When they returned, they had bad news for Lord. The deal was off.

Lord stood quietly for a moment, looking out the window at the sweeping view of Manhattan below him. Much of his wealth—valued at over $220 million months earlier—had just evaporated. "I never bought anything ever other than Sallie Mae, 'cause I was a fool," he says. "I preached it. And lived it. And I thought, 'What could be a safer asset than the one I'm managing?'"

He walked to the hotel-room fridge, grabbed a couple of mini liquor bottles, and poured a stiff cocktail.

Al Lord's world was unraveling. Days after he resumed his CEO duties, he got so testy with anxious investors during an earnings call that his profane comments made headlines in the press. "Let's go," he said toward the end of the call. "Let's get the fuck out of here." The next day's *New York Post* gleefully recounted what it called a "nasty conference call" with the headline, "Lord in Vain as Sallie Is Slammed." "Oh, Lord: Sallie Mae's Conference Call," headed one *New York Times* article, which described the call as "disastrous."

A few days after the call, Jack Remondi was working late in his office in Boston when the phone rang. Remondi was a 45-year-old hedge fund manager who had served as a deputy to Lord in the early 2000s. When he picked up the phone, Lord was on the other end. The familiar voice speaking in his ear sounded far different from that of the confident, hard-charging chief Remondi knew.

"I could really use your help," Lord said. He asked Remondi to fly down to Sallie Mae's headquarters in Virginia.

"Why don't I come down and see you in January?" Remondi said.

"No, I need to see you now," Lord insisted, and suggested that he fly down several days later, on Wednesday.

Incredulous, Remondi asked: "You mean Christmas Eve?" That was exactly what Lord meant. Remondi got a ticket and was on a plane on December 24.

After Remondi arrived at Sallie Mae's headquarters in Reston, Virginia, Lord revealed a disturbing trend. Hundreds of thousands of borrowers who'd taken out student loans from Sallie Mae weren't making payments. A huge chunk of Sallie Mae's portfolio—$5 billion to $8 billion—was toxic debt. These weren't government-guaranteed loans. These were strictly private. Sallie Mae's shareholders would eat the losses. Lord was confronting the reality that Sallie Mae had gone too far, too fast, in heaping debt on students who might not repay. This was part of a broader phenomenon. Most of Sallie Mae's bad loans had gone to students at for-profit colleges—companies like the University of Phoenix, the Art

Institutes, and ITT Tech. Those students defaulted at far higher rates than their counterparts at public and nonprofit schools.

Sallie Mae's fate mirrored that of the broader financial sector, which had crashed earlier that year amid a crisis in the housing market. Subprime mortgages repackaged into securities proved worthless. The subprime mortgage crisis, the result of lax regulation and years of ever more risky lending, sent the economy in a tailspin. Wall Street firms were on the brink of bankruptcy. The banking system was melting down. The eerie similarities between the housing market, undermined by credit default swaps and other novel investment strategies, and the risky student lending practices were sounding alarms among Sallie Mae's investors.

Lord needed Remondi to clean up the mess at Sallie Mae. Remondi accepted Lord's offer to become CFO. His first task: Ask Congress for a bailout. The company was running out of money, and financial markets were frozen. Sallie Mae needed its own secondary market. Its own Sallie Mae. Since the 1970s, the swaggering company had cowed Congress into filling its every need, but this would be its biggest ask yet.

"Action is needed now to prevent a crisis," Remondi told a Senate panel in April 2008. "We do not have weeks or months to decide the best course of action."

Nearly 18 million students were enrolled in college and graduate school in 2008, and most relied on federal student loans. If that system crashed, those students would be forced to drop out, and colleges would lose one of their biggest sources of money. Many would shutter. Sallie Mae was too big to fail. While it had shed its status as a government-sponsored enterprise in 2004, it was the biggest lender in the Guaranteed Student Loan program, which, under Lord's leadership, had reclaimed most of the market. Without Sallie Mae, the student loan market would collapse.

The Education Department considered turning to the Direct

Loan program to make loans. But there was a concern that schools would be unable to switch programs quickly enough.

President Bush, against his free-market principles, urged Congress to bail out Sallie Mae. In spring 2008 it did, passing the Ensuring Continued Access to Student Loans Act, which authorized the Treasury Department to buy Sallie Mae's debt. The company could then use the cash to originate new federal loans for the next fall's batch of college and graduate students.

With that, Sallie Mae became the first bailout of the 2008 financial crisis.

Facing financial ruin, the company made an abrupt decision. It would stop extending private loans to students to attend schools of dubious quality, particularly for-profit colleges. This move wasn't out of virtue, but self-interest. Loans to vulnerable students had lost Sallie Mae money.

Sallie Mae's move was part of a broader reckoning on Wall Street. Mortgage lenders, their balance sheets devastated because of the housing crash, cleaned up their lending practices. They imposed new underwriting standards to ensure borrowers didn't take on debt they wouldn't be able to repay.

But while risky lending ended in housing, it persisted in higher education. While Sallie Mae receded from the private student loan market, the federal government expanded student lending, increasing the amounts that students could borrow at a time when enrollment in colleges and universities was soaring.

The housing bubble had just burst. But the bubble in student lending was just getting started.

SIX

Hope and Hubris

(2006–2016)

On a sunny Friday afternoon in August 2006, Brandon stared in awe at the brick gateposts of Howard University, a historically Black university in Washington, D.C. Since he was a boy, he'd seen this place as a distant sanctum he would never reach. Now he was about to step onto the campus as a student.

Brandon had come to Howard that day to pay a bill before starting his freshman year. As he stood relishing the moment before he passed through the gates, self-doubt shivered through him. *Do I really belong here?* he thought. He was standing on the same ground that Thurgood Marshall, Zora Neale Hurston, Toni Morrison, and Sean "Diddy" Combs once walked. And then he shook off the shadow.

I'm here, he told himself. *I did it.*

Brandon came from a modest background. He and his three siblings were raised in Petersburg, Virginia, and Augusta, Georgia, by a single mother in the army and their great-grandmother. His elders taught him the importance of God, family, and education. He grew up poor, but at the time he didn't know it.

Socially awkward and with a speech impediment, he grew up to be polite and humble, seemingly without an ego. His great-grandmother taught him to appreciate what he had and to strive for stability in life. He went to church three days a week and got A's and B's in high school. When he graduated, he craved structure, so he joined the navy. He was stationed in Oklahoma City and specialized in communications, working 12-hour shifts behind two combination-locked doors in a windowless control room.

His time in the navy exacerbated his anxiety and feelings of isolation. Brandon suffered panic attacks over his worry that his speech difficulties would prevent him from speaking through a microphone in an emergency. After two years, he left with an honorable discharge and decided to try college. His great-grandmother, a retired hospital housekeeper who had dropped out of high school and later got her GED, had urged him throughout his childhood to go to college. "She was one of those people who thought if you went to college, then the doors were opened for you," Brandon says.

For many Black families across the U.S., no school held as mystical a status as Howard. Founded by missionaries in 1867, the school was one of hundreds that opened across the U.S. after the Civil War to educate Black Americans, many of whom were denied entry to other colleges because of the color of their skin. In its first five years, Howard taught tens of thousands of freed slaves. By 2006, Howard was the most prestigious of the nation's 100 or so historically Black colleges still in existence.

Despite his strong high school grades, Brandon knew the odds of his being admitted to Howard were slim. Of the thousands who applied each year, only about 3 in 10 got in. When he called the admissions office and a woman told him he'd been accepted, he was in such disbelief that he asked her to repeat herself.

Brandon entered college at the onset of a student debt boom. By the end of his first semester, student debt across the U.S. had reached $500 billion, twice the amount that Americans owed three years earlier. That sum was quickly approaching that which Americans owed on credit cards and auto loans. The media and policy makers were waking up to the problem. Author Anya Kamenetz helped put the issue on the map with her book *Generation Debt*, released during Brandon's freshman year.

Student debt was soaring in part because a greater share of Americans were going to college. The college-wage premium had reached an all-time high by the time Brandon enrolled, as employers increasingly demanded that job applicants hold a bachelor's degree for jobs that several years earlier didn't require one. Brandon was one of 15 million undergraduates across the U.S. in 2006.

The rise in college enrollment was driven by students like Brandon. They were disproportionately poor, Black, Hispanic, and the first in their families to go to college. They mostly attended schools with low or no admissions standards—community colleges, for-profit schools, and a number of historically Black colleges—schools that opened their doors to students who lacked the grades or test scores to get into more selective universities. The schools provided students a huge opportunity to move up on America's economic ladder.

Most of those students relied on debt. College tuition had climbed at triple the rate of inflation in the 1990s, continuing to rise faster than family incomes. The increase fell hardest on the poorest families, such as Brandon's, who had little to no savings. Poor students who could get into the most elite universities, such as Ivy League schools, often got free rides, because those schools had the resources—such as large endowments and alumni donations—to waive tuition for them. But most colleges lacked such resources and relied heavily on tuition dollars, including from poor students, to pay the bills.

For Brandon, Howard was a steal compared to Washington's other universities, like George Washington University and Georgetown University. But it still cost a fortune—$28,000 a year after living costs were factored in. Brandon qualified for Pell Grants and partial benefits under the G.I. Bill. But neither program provided enough money to cover tuition at many state schools, let alone a prestigious private school like Howard. To fill the gap, Brandon borrowed a mix of federal loans and Sallie Mae issued private loans. His total student debt tab: nearly $40,000 in federal loans and $60,000 in private loans. Interest pushed it thousands of dollars higher by the time he graduated.

During his sophomore year, in late September 2007, a professor gave Brandon and his classmates an assignment to attend a speech on campus. When the speaker stepped to the podium, the crowd rose to its feet. Quick to smile and at ease behind the podium, Barack Obama delivered a speech polished to a gleam, and Brandon could feel the waves of admiration washing over the crowd.

Brandon had heard of this senator from Illinois who was running for president. Like Brandon, Obama was a Black man raised by a single mother and had taken out loan after loan to attend college and law school. Obama had come to Howard on his campaign tour with a vision for revitalizing America's economy, which was in distress as the housing market crumbled. He talked about criminal justice reform, and about making society more equal. Above all, he wanted to create opportunity for society's most disadvantaged, particularly the Brandons of the world.

Just over a year after that speech, Obama stepped to a lectern outside the U.S. Capitol on a frigid day on January 20, 2009, to be sworn in as the nation's 44th president. America's economy was in tatters. The housing bubble—and the illusory era of inflated real estate that defined it—had burst, bringing financial markets to a halt and sending the economy into a tailspin. Voters had elected Obama to steer the country out of the worst crisis since the Great Depression.

The housing crisis was created by loose credit, lax regulation, and a reach for the American Dream. Mortgage lenders, believing the value of homes would only go up, had spent years lending bigger and bigger sums to borrowers whose credit histories or incomes indicated they had little hope of repaying. One in five loans in 2007 and 2008 was to borrowers with subprime credit. Federal regulators looked the other way. Government-sponsored enterprises Fannie Mae and Freddie Mac bought up many of those mortgages, fueling banks with cheap cash. Lenders sold home loans to investors as securities, using intricate financial instruments that obscured the loans' risk. Undergirding this boom was the belief that homeownership was a surefire investment for the poor and middle class.

Home prices did rise, and borrowers for a while could afford their monthly payments—until they couldn't. In 2006, a wave of homeowners fell behind on payments, and banks realized they had a pile of debt on their books that wouldn't be repaid. Home prices had risen too high, too fast. Ultimately Congress came to the rescue, spending hundreds of billions of dollars to bail out financial institutions and steady the economy.

When the bubble burst, the human consequences were devastating. Ten million people lost their homes, most to foreclosure. Nearly nine million lost their jobs over the recession. Entire cities and towns were decimated. Big banks, car companies, and small businesses failed. The stock market crashed.

The hardest-hit families tended to be Black, Hispanic, and

headed by someone without a college degree. The very people who were meant to be helped by homeownership were harmed. Instead of reducing inequality, the aggressive push by elected leaders and the private sector to get Americans into homes increased it.

Obama viewed the crisis not just as an economic disaster but as a moral one. As a state senator in Illinois in the late 1990s and early 2000s, he'd been an early critic of predatory lending, which broadly refers to banks extending risky loans to unwitting borrowers who are unlikely to repay them, given their incomes or the size of the monthly payments. Senator Elizabeth Warren (D., Mass.) recalled meeting Obama at a political fundraiser in 2003 when he was running for the U.S. Senate and she was a Harvard professor specializing in consumer finance. He greeted her with the words *predatory lending*. "On and on and on, and I never got a word in," Warren told *U.S. News & World Report*.

A month after his inauguration, in February 2009, Obama delivered his first address to a joint session of Congress, in which he laid out his plan to pull the nation out of the severe downturn and return it to prosperity. The country would educate its way out of the recession, he said. "In a global economy where the most valuable skill you can sell is your knowledge, a good education is no longer just a pathway to opportunity—it is a prerequisite," he noted.

He asked every American to spend at least one year in college—whether it be a four-year liberal arts school or a community college—to meet a bold goal: for the U.S. to have the world's most educated workforce. The country had the world's most college graduates as a share of its workforce in the early 1990s, but in the new century other countries had surpassed the U.S. Just as Lyndon Johnson had worried about Russia overtaking the U.S. in education and global leadership, Obama worried about countries like South Korea doing the same in the new millennium. "By 2020,

America will once again have the highest proportion of college graduates in the world," he vowed.

Obama framed his goal as a way to help keep alive the U.S. ideal of upward mobility, echoing the goal of Clinton's 1995 drive to increase homeownership. Under the nation's first Black president, one who'd inspired millions of followers with a message of hope and change during the 2008 campaign, the country was turning away from one cornerstone of the American Dream, homeownership, while doubling down on another, higher education, that also relied on debt.

A few weeks after Obama's speech, Obama's top economic adviser, Larry Summers, settled into his seat at Boston's Fenway Park under a gray afternoon sky. It was late April and the Red Sox were playing the New York Yankees. Summers, a former Treasury secretary under President Clinton, was spearheading the administration's efforts to dig out of the recession.

He turned to his friend sitting next to him, Harvard economist Larry Katz, and asked if he had any ideas on how to get more Americans into college. Katz thought of the 13 million unemployed workers, many from blue-collar industries like construction, manufacturing, and mining. "You need to go where the money is," Katz told Summers.

"The money" was unemployment insurance. Most of those jobless workers drew checks from state unemployment offices. Find a way to nudge them into college, Katz said. Summers was so excited by the idea he called Rahm Emanuel, Obama's chief of staff, during a rain delay. Days later, the government embarked on one of the biggest pushes ever to get Americans to go to college.

The administration urged state unemployment offices to send a letter to every person receiving jobless benefits, telling them they could get financial aid, such as Pell Grants, if they enrolled in their local college. "While the economy recovers, this is a great time to improve skills and lay the foundation for a stronger economy in the future," one of the state letters read. "Studies have shown that workers with more education and training have more secure jobs and higher wages."

Obama's advisers believed getting people into college would help not only workers but the economy, in the short and long run. The U.S. economy relies heavily on consumer spending—Americans going out to buy stuff, from cars and groceries to medical checkups and education—to fuel economic activity, and Obama's economic team envisioned college students' spending on tuition as one way to get the economy growing again.

"The top priority was fixing the economic crisis," says James Kvaal, Obama's top adviser on higher education at the White House. "If we gave low-income students scholarship dollars, they would spend, and that would ripple through the economy. We were looking for projects where the dollars would be spent quickly, not saved, and the dollars could get in the hands of people quickly."

This massive push would require huge sums of money. The stock market crash and recession had wiped out trillions of dollars in Americans' wealth, leaving most families with little savings to pay tuition. While Obama wanted to increase scholarship money for the poor, his plan inherently relied on a surge in student debt.

The sweeping economic stimulus law that Obama championed and Congress passed in 2009 increased the maximum Pell Grant award that a modest-income student could receive over a year from $4,700 to about $5,600. But that sum wasn't enough to cover a fraction of expenses even at public community colleges, the cheapest of higher education institutions. On average, attending a public two-year college—after grants were factored in—cost $12,000 a year in tuition and living expenses in 2010, or about a fifth of the typical household income.

Obama himself had relied on student loans to get through law school, as he had mentioned frequently on the campaign trail. He and Michelle Obama each owed $40,000 from their time at Harvard Law School, debt they had paid off debt only a few years earlier with the advance from a book deal.

Obama, like other presidents before him, found himself hemmed in by the federal deficit. Spending had soared under George W. Bush as the nation fought two wars. The taxpayer-funded bailouts of Wall Street and auto companies had stirred a populist uprising known as the Tea Party movement, which opposed big government spending. Obama himself had raised concerns about rising entitlement program spending.

And he had other priorities. While his Democratic Party controlled both chambers of Congress, Obama spent his early political capital on other initiatives—an economic recovery bill and a sweeping health care law—instead of pushing for a big increase in scholarship money to ease Americans' reliance on student debt.

Obama continued a bipartisan tradition of relying on student loans as a way to finance other initiatives. In 2010, he attached a provision to the Affordable Care Act, his signature health care law, to eliminate the Guaranteed Student Loan program, which since 1965 had insured student loans originated by private lenders. Ending the program would save taxpayers $60 billion over 10 years since the government would no longer have to pay banks a spread over their own borrowing costs. All federal loans from 2010 onward would be originated by the Treasury Department, using Bill Clinton's Direct Loan program.

"We can't afford to waste billions of dollars on giveaways to banks," Obama said as he signed the bill in March 2010. "We need to invest that money in our students." Not all the savings went to students, though; some financed Obama's national health care law.

Republicans accused Obama of "nationalizing" the student loan program. Some suggested the move encouraged reckless lending to students by removing "underwriting"—the process of banks screening borrowers' credit histories, incomes, and other details to determine whether they were likely to default. It was a misleading claim. It didn't matter whether the loans were originated by the Treasury Department or banks. The eligibility criteria were identical, and minimal. Obama's move merely cut out the middlemen.

But his move had a fundamental flaw: It kept in place a structure that required nothing of colleges to gain access to tens of billions of dollars in taxpayer money each year. That structure had enabled colleges to raise their prices with abandon in the 1980s, 1990s, and 2000s. By encouraging all Americans to go to college, through debt if they needed to, he had opened the spigot up further.

That spigot created both opportunity and hardship.

It enabled tens of millions of students to attend college. In Brandon's case, it opened the doors to Howard, whose graduates— many of whom had grown up poor—tended to land high-paying jobs. But for Brandon, as well as for millions of other students, it also meant an unconscionably high debt burden.

Brandon continued to suffer from anxiety at Howard. His biggest source of worry was his student loan debt. He borrowed tens of thousands of dollars each year—a mix of federal loans and private loans from Sallie Mae—watching anxiously as the interest accrued.

Brandon hadn't realized when he matriculated that he would have to borrow so much. Students accepted early each year are more likely to get financial aid from schools. Students like Brandon who come in late in the admissions process—after most of the school's scholarship money has been doled out—are often left to pay most or all of the sticker price, despite their families' lack of wealth. The only option for those students and their parents is to take on debt. They are in the worst position to repay debt but the ones most reliant on it.

While G.I. Bill funds and Pell Grants went toward Brandon's tuition, much of Brandon's debt went toward living expenses. Howard had overbooked its on-campus dorms and Brandon didn't get a room. Instead he rented an apartment for $980 a month in Prince George's County, Maryland, a half-hour drive from the school. He needed a car, and money for gas, parking, and maintenance.

Brandon could only pay for school if other family members took out debt as well. His great-grandmother co-signed his private loans from Sallie Mae. By the time he graduated in the summer of 2011, Brandon and his great-grandmother owed $148,000 in student debt, including interest. At the graduation ceremony, his great-grandmother was so proud she wept.

Brandon was part of one of the biggest graduating classes nationwide in history—and also one of the most indebted. Higher education enrollment—college and graduate school—had just hit a peak of 21 million students. Two in three graduating seniors owed debt—$27,000, on average. A small but fast-growing share, like Brandon, owed large balances—$50,000 and up.

Numerous factors collided to make this happen, some economic, some policy-related. One was a change the government made in the 1990s to begin charging interest on many student loans while borrowers were in school, driving up their balances by as much as 20 percent by graduation. Decades of lax regulation had enabled colleges to raise tuition to excessive levels. The recession also had wiped out household wealth. At a time when college was most important, it seemed, Americans were least able to pay for it. So they borrowed.

Brandon and his peers were graduating at one of the worst possible times. Even though the recession had ended two years earlier, unemployment remained exceptionally high. For most of 2011, it was above 9 percent, among the highest levels since the Great Depression. Many young college graduates lucky enough to find work were "underemployed," stuck in jobs that traditionally didn't require a college degree and paid modest wages.

Millions of young Americans had taken out debt with the belief that it was the ticket to a secure middle-class job. They were falling behind on their bills in droves. Student debt—which had for years been seen as an investment—stirred resentment among the hordes of new grads, fueling a populist movement. In September 2011, protesters crowded Zuccotti Park in New York, launching the Occupy Wall Street movement. Protesters criticized the greed of Wall Street and universities and demanded that their student debt be forgiven.

"I think this is a movement about economic justice," a woman named Stacey Patton told USA Today in October 2011. "I think it's pretty obvious what people are protesting. They are protesting greed, recklessness, illegal behavior, home foreclosures and rising student debt. We can't get jobs, but we have mounting student debt."

Student debt was rising fastest among Blacks, and particularly students at historically Black colleges. Black families had the least amount of wealth of any racial group in U.S. society. Black students tended to enroll at universities that had smaller endowments than flagship universities and selective private colleges. The schools relied on tuition for a greater share of funding than many of their peers. Roughly three in four students at private historically Black colleges had to borrow for tuition.

During college, Brandon had worked on the side at the Thurgood Marshall Fund, a nonprofit group that lobbies for historically Black colleges and universities. After he got his diploma in 2011, he told his mentor and the head of the fund, Johnny Taylor, how much he owed. Taylor sighed. He told Brandon he was going to give him a job to help him pay it off. Brandon started out earning $55,000 a year answering phones, organizing events, and assisting Taylor, working out of the group's office just a few blocks from the Howard campus.

A few months into his new job, Brandon started getting phone calls from frantic students at Howard and other Black colleges. They said their parents had unexpectedly been rejected for federal Parent Plus loans. Congress had created the program in 1980 to shift costs onto parents rather than students, who had been defaulting at high rates. The idea was that parents—with their well-established jobs—would be better positioned to repay debt than their children. By the 2000s, the loan program had become a lifeline for many Black college students.

The Education Department in 2011 had discovered that, under the old Guaranteed Student Loan program, banks mistakenly approved loans for parents who didn't meet federal eligibility criteria. Now, with banks out of the program, the department enforced the criteria, which, among other rules, blocked loans from going to parents who had declared bankruptcy within the prior five years. Hundreds of thousands of students—many at historically Black colleges—were now being denied access to the program because of the change.

The students needed the Parent Plus loans on top of their own federal student loans to cover the schools' tuition. Financial aid officers at their schools told them that unless they found another way to pay, they would have to drop out. Brandon had no idea what to tell them.

Even with the new criteria for Parent Plus loans, the government continued to give loans to parents at a high risk of default. Many had little or no savings; some were unemployed; others were close to retirement and thus would be out of work. This was part of a broader phenomenon. The risky lending wasn't just at historically black colleges, and it wasn't just to parents.

Across the country, another loan crisis was playing out. Millions of workers who had lost their jobs during the recession had trouble finding work. Newly unemployed and searching for a solution, many flooded community colleges to apply for aid. Student loans—intended to finance Americans' education, an investment leading to well-paying jobs—became something else entirely: a ready source of money to those who desperately needed it. They took it, as any rational person would do.

Inside an office building at Mohave Community College in northern Arizona, Shannon Sheaff held the receiver away from her ear as an irate woman on the other end screamed into the phone.

In early 2012, Sheaff had just started a new job as head of financial aid at the small community college in Kingman, a town about an hour and a half south of Las Vegas. Officially, the recession had been over for nearly three years. Yet unemployment remained exceptionally high, particularly in areas of Sun Belt states like Arizona, where the economy had boomed and crashed.

In Mohave County, thousands of jobs tied to the construction industry—in building, real estate, trucking—had vanished virtually overnight. When the laid-off workers applied for unemployment checks, they also received Larry Summers's letters urging them to go back to school and apply for federal student loans and grants.

Sheaff had a firsthand look at the despair in her new community. Her office filled up daily with workers desperate for student aid so they could eat and pay rent. There were homeless people, parents with their adult children, a group of senior citizens from a neighboring county an hour away.

On this particular morning, the woman on the phone had called demanding to know why she hadn't received her student loan check. Sheaff told her that she first needed to produce a document showing she had a GED or a high school diploma. Unable to do so, the frustrated woman began screaming at Sheaff.

It was hardly the only angry tirade unleashed on Sheaff. There were many altercations involving irate and desperate unemployed workers showing up at Mohave. The campus hired a security guard to protect the financial aid office. On three occasions, the campus administration shut the school down for the day due to death threats.

Mohave Community College wasn't alone. Research shows that Summers's letter had led to the enrollment of at least 500,000 students who otherwise wouldn't have enrolled. Many students weren't just taking out Pell Grants—they were also taking out loans. A significant number—it's impossible to know precisely how many—didn't plan on graduating; rather, they needed the money to live.

Many of those who did plan to graduate weren't ready for college-level work. Two-thirds of students at community colleges needed to take remedial courses, making college essentially a repeat of high school. Such students were among the most likely to drop out. They didn't earn the degrees or certificates that employers required. Yet these students now owed student debt. They got none of the benefits of college while taking on all of the costs.

Student loan money had become a form of welfare. In South Florida, a 30-year-old former retail clerk who was unemployed enrolled in his local community college to borrow thousands of dollars to live. In Montana, a father of five who had been making

$10 an hour as a security guard enrolled in his local college to learn new skills and borrowed the maximum in loans so he could feed his children.

There were also cases of outright fraud and abuse. The Education Department's inspector general reported on so-called Pell runners, people who enrolled in college to collect Pell Grants with no intention of getting a degree. They'd drop out and walk away with the money.

States cut funding by as much as 25 percent to public colleges during the recession. To soften the blow to their budgets, schools raised tuition. This accelerated a decades-long trend in which the burden of paying for higher education shifted from state governments to households. Families turned to student debt to cover those higher costs. This put college further out of reach for those who wanted an affordable and local education.

Student debt hit a milestone in early 2012—$1 trillion—stirring headlines across the U.S. A big chunk of that debt had been taken out by students at community colleges. Now many of those students were falling behind on their loans.

In late 2013, the problem that Brandon heard about on the phone from frantic students had gotten the attention of President Obama's economic advisers. Those advisers were looking for the first time at the risk that federal loan programs such as Parent Plus posed—to both taxpayers and families—and they were alarmed by what they found.

The Parent Plus loan program initially capped how much a parent could borrow for their children. In the 1990s, as tuition skyrocketed, Congress removed the ceiling, allowing parents to borrow whatever was needed to cover their children's higher education. It was another instance of how Congress responded to students' repayment troubles by simply expanding lending. For a while, most parents had little trouble repaying loans under the program. But in the 2000s, as a greater segment of society entered college, a greater share of parent borrowers were poor.

Schools lobbied to overturn the new underwriting standards that had led so many parents to be rejected in 2011 and 2012. Black colleges and universities like Howard were particularly vocal. Parent Plus and other federal loans were often the only financial lifeline for their students. By cutting off access to loans, they argued, the government was pinching off one of the only routes to higher education for low- and middle-income students.

Jordan Matsudaira, the chief economist for Obama's Council of Economic Advisers, hired a private consultant to study the characteristics of Parent Plus borrowers and the likelihood of default. The government, one of the world's biggest consumer lenders, had never performed such an analysis.

The consultant came back with a stark message: If the government continued lending to parents in such difficult financial circumstances, defaults would soar. The government risked creating the same type of crisis that had occurred in the 2000s housing bubble, when banks made predatory loans to poor families who were destined to default.

The Council of Economic Advisers called a meeting in the Roosevelt Room of the White House to review the findings. The meeting turned into a heated debate over the underlying intent of the student loan program. Top figures on the council—including its chairman, Jason Furman—argued that the government needed to rein in risky student lending to prevent families from defaulting and suffering economic ruin. Others, such as Deputy Secretary of Education Jim Shelton, contended that expanding access to education for Black families was a moral imperative, and that cutting off college loans would deprive Black families of educational opportunities widely available to whites.

When the meeting broke up, the question was unresolved. The Education Department convened a panel to study the policy, and the following year, in 2014, it rolled back the more restrictive underwriting rules. Federal policy makers followed the same path they had followed for 40 years. They continued to extend loans to families they knew would very likely default.

In the short term, the loans gave families access to higher education. In the long run, the loans would suck up a big portion of their limited incomes and ruin many families' credit. Policy makers pretended they were doing families a favor by extending the debt. In reality, they were taking the path of least resistance—while pushing the problem on to future generations, leaving families with piles of debt.

Obama kept hearing from constituents about student debt.

"I can't tell you how many letters I get from people who say, 'I did everything I was supposed to and now I'm finding myself in a situation where I have debts I can't pay off, and I want to pay them off,'" Obama told a group of college students in June 2014. He said he had received a letter from a young woman named Ashley from Santa Fe, New Mexico. "She told me that because of her student loan debt, she's worried she'll never be able to buy a car or a house," Obama said. "It's a point that all of us need to pay attention to. In America, no young person who works hard and plays by the rules should feel that way."

In 2014, Obama expanded a plan to make it easier for students to pay back their loans. He sweetened the terms of a plan known as income-based repayment. Obama tweaked an early 1990s law that allowed borrowers to cap their monthly payments at 15 percent of their discretionary income. Obama, through executive action, lowered the percentage to 10 percent. Under his plan, borrowers would make monthly payments for 20 years—or 25 years if the balance included graduate school debt. Any remaining debt would then be canceled. Interest would accrue as the borrower made payments.

Obama's plan was a form of insurance. It ensured that borrowers' payments would rise or fall with their income; if they lost their jobs, they wouldn't have to pay anything. If they landed a lucrative job, they'd pay more. But his plan left some borrowers worse off. By extending loans over 20 or 25 years, many would pay more in total. And the new plan did nothing to address the underlying causes of soaring student debt and high tuition. If anything, income-driven repayment made the causes of the student debt crisis worse. By reducing borrowers' monthly payments, it threatened to desensitize new students to higher debt amounts and make it easier for universities to further raise tuition.

By 2014, seven million people had defaulted on student loans. Millions of others had fallen months behind on payments and were headed toward default. If the definition of those defaulting is expanded to include borrowers in "forbearance"—those who have received permission from the government to suspend payments during times of hardship—4 in 10 borrowers weren't sending in checks each month.

During President Obama's two terms, student debt doubled to $1.31 trillion. Those years showcased his—and the nation's—unquestioned faith in higher education as a vehicle for societal change, upward mobility, and achieving the American Dream. But well-intentioned policies led, once again, to detrimental outcomes for families.

Obama's unprecedented push to get people into college—including the mailings to unemployed workers—boosted the nation's ranks of educated workers. But it left tens of millions of families deep in debt. Obama unintentionally made the student debt crisis worse by putting in place an income-driven repayment plan that drove up many borrowers' long-term costs while allowing colleges and universities to raise tuition.

During the two terms of the nation's first Black president, Black families who borrowed got into debt more than families of any other racial or ethnic group.

Brandon entered the income-based repayment program that Obama created, which lowered his payments to $1,100 a month but stretched them out over a longer repayment period. He found work in D.C. as a real estate agent earning $75,000 a year.

In 2019, Brandon was living out of a studio apartment in southwest D.C., delaying saving for retirement, and paying down his student debt. He felt ashamed. In his early 30s, he didn't feel in a position to start a family, to get married, to have children. Debt carried a societal stigma, like it was a personal failing.

His former boss from the Thurgood Marshall Fund, Johnny Taylor, asked him to help recruit inspirational speakers for his organization, the Society for Human Resource Management. Brandon proved adept, and signed up Martha Stewart and Lionel Richie as speakers, earning a hefty commission. He used the unexpected dividend to pay off his entire loan debt at once. But the college experience changed Brandon. He lost his wide-eyed admiration of Howard and now has a cynical view of higher education, President Obama, and his alma mater.

He recalled how when he worked at the Thurgood Marshall Fund—a source of Howard scholarships—Howard administrators didn't respond to requests to meet with Taylor, Brandon's boss at the fund. It wasn't clear why, but Brandon interpreted the refusal as a sign of elitism—that the leaders of Howard University were too good to meet with a lobbying organization that was trying help students getting deep in debt at the school.

"I do not go back to Howard. I do not go to homecoming," Brandon says. "I did not have a great experience at Howard."

It all came flooding back to him one day in 2018—before a stroke of luck allowed him to escape his huge debt—when he was walking in D.C.'s upscale Georgetown neighborhood with Taylor. They were at a shop on M Street when they spotted Wayne Frederick, who took over as Howard's president in 2013, coming toward them. They stopped to chat.

Brandon's mind raced as he faced the president of the school that he felt had failed him. There were so many things Brandon wanted to say—namely that Howard exploited students for their loan money. That Obama was not the savior of higher education that he was made out to be.

Instead, he just gave Frederick a frosty handshake, greeted him curtly, and said nothing.

SEVEN

The Great Unequalizer

(2014–2015)

Derek was sitting at the dining room table in his mother's house when an email arrived that would change his life. It was a summer evening in 2014, and he had just finished a stint teaching English in South Korea. He had returned home to Warner Robins, Georgia, to figure out how to propel himself and his family into economic security. The modest house with a brick and vinyl façade was wedged into a row of identical cookie-cutter homes. To distinguish themselves, some neighbors stuck objects atop their mailboxes. Derek's mother had set a gold angel atop hers.

At 31, Derek was tall and sinewy with sparkling brown eyes. He had applied to law school months earlier. No one, including himself, thought he'd get in. He scored low on the LSAT and had already received several rejections. He expected more of the same when the email appeared from Arizona Summit, a law school in Phoenix owned by a corporation named InfiLaw.

The email contained unexpected good news: He'd gotten in. Just like that, Derek had a path to America's upper class—a path that for generations had been blocked for many Black men like Derek. His mother, a college graduate and hospital chaplain named Shannon, shrieked.

"This is a blessing from God!" she told Derek's skeptical stepfather. Derek pulled up a map on his computer to see where Phoenix was. Growing up in the South, he had always heard that life was more exciting and interesting in western U.S. states, and he couldn't believe he was about to go to law school there. As he and his mother celebrated, his stepfather paced in the living room, worried.

Derek had always felt there were two worlds: the one of food stamps and struggle that his family inhabited, and the one of security and luxury, mostly inhabited by workers with graduate degrees. He wanted to move to the latter world. Law school offered a path to get there. His mother had always thought he'd be a lawyer, ever since he was little, because he often spoke what was on his mind and seemed uncommonly ambitious. Now, despite his low LSAT score, Arizona Summit was offering him a shot he never thought he'd have.

Standing in the way was Arizona Summit's $65,000-a-year price tag. Derek was broke and in default on $4,500 in debt, most of it in doctors' bills. One of the few rules to qualify for federal student loans was that borrowers could not be in default on any existing debt. Derek's failure to pay his doctor's bills put federal loans out of reach, and, as he feared, his application for federal loans was denied. He beseeched Arizona Summit for help. "I have begged and pleaded with family members for a co-signer," Derek wrote in an email to an Arizona Summit financial aid officer.

His dream of living in the West crashed when Arizona Summit informed him that the school couldn't help. But then a glimmer of hope emerged. Arizona Summit's sister school, an InfiLaw startup in North Carolina called Charlotte School of Law, came through. The school said it would pay off his medical debt so that he could qualify for a student loan. Once the loan was approved, the school would get its money back plus tens of thousands of dollars to cover Derek's first semester of tuition. Months later, in early 2015, the student loan check was approved, and Derek boarded a bus to Charlotte. He wasn't just leaving for law school, he believed. He was also leaving behind a life of struggle. That student loan check was his ticket out.

The legal field has long been among the least diverse professions. Black Americans compose 13 percent of the nation's population but just 5 percent of lawyers. In theory, higher education and the student loan program were supposed to narrow this gap. Colleges and universities were supposed to be the great equalizer. The student loan program would open the pathway for disadvantaged Americans to those schools. But for generations, law schools admitted only a select few students, and seldom took risks on students who grew up without the advantage of good schools, test-prep courses, and stable homes.

In the 1990s, a lawyer named Don Lively wanted to change that.

Lively was a white law professor in his 40s at a public university in the Midwest. Tall and lean with spiky gelled hair, he played pickup basketball to stay in shape.

Lively wasn't a natural fit for the rarified world of legal training. He had grown up in a trailer community outside of Santa Barbara. His father repaired telephone lines for AT&T; his mother worked for the company as a secretary. After his father won a promotion, the family moved to Oakland. To young Don, their new neighbors seemed rich. They drove around in Chevy Impalas and Ford Mustangs; Lively's parents had a Rambler. It was the early 1960s, and the nation's middle class, along with its aspirations, was expanding rapidly. "Status consciousness really was peaking," Lively says. "The whole phraseology of 'keeping up with the Joneses' became part of our social currency. I felt on the fringes rather than part of the 'in' crowd."

Lively graduated from Berkeley and got a master's in journalism at Northwestern. After a short time as a public-television producer in California, he moved to Alabama in the early 1970s to work as a reporter for a CBS affiliate, covering the administration of the segregationist Democratic governor George Wallace. Lively moved back west to go to UCLA's law school. After a stint at a law firm, he became a professor at a public university in the Midwest.

He found the law school culture stifling. Faculty members gossiped behind each other's backs. Professors chased self-promotion rather than honing their teaching skills and preparing students to be good lawyers.

The school's leaders obsessed over moving up in national rankings, which required attracting students with the highest test scores. Lively believed the practice deepened racial inequality. Those with the highest LSAT scores were predominantly white students who grew up in privilege. Law schools had "this perspective that certain people aren't cut out for this—they can't do it," Lively says. "They *can* do it if as an institution you're willing to make the commitment to enable them to catch up with those persons that have a more privileged heritage and background life experience."

"We could be the Harvard of northwest Ohio," one professor told him. That was the problem, Lively felt. Harvard epitomized elitism, the country club of higher ed. "Ego and vanity become a priority," Lively says.

He decided to make a career move after a clash with the school's dean. Lively had proposed to have students work for members of a local Black church who couldn't afford lawyers. The students would gain valuable experience and meet the state bar exam's pro bono requirements while helping the poor. Lively was energized by the idea and wanted the school to sponsor the program. The dean said no. "If you want to do it on your own time, we won't stop you," the dean said.

Lively decided to try to open his own law school. It would enroll mostly Black and Hispanic students who didn't have the grades and LSAT scores to get into most other law schools but who had the drive to succeed. It would focus on teaching practical skills that students could use in the courtroom, rather than focusing solely on how to pass the bar.

Lively traveled throughout the South, where he believed the school would have a natural constituency, pitching universities and local chambers of commerce, hoping they would invest. "I wrote letters to more university and college presidents than I can count," Lively says. "I didn't get a single response."

He kept at it for two years. In 1994, Lively was about to give up when a friend told him about a retired couple in Naples, Florida, who might be interested. Lively drove down.

Bernie and Rita Turner had acted on an impulse similar to Lively's back in the 1970s, when they were labor activists in New York City and believed corporations had gained too much power at the expense of their workers. Bernie, a union worker who served as a college instructor on the side, had been denied a promotion at his school because he lacked a Ph.D. He didn't have the time to get a graduate degree. Hoping to help workers like himself, he and Rita used their savings of $15,000 to open a graduate school in an abandoned motel overlooking a pond in Naples. They called it Walden University, named after Henry David Thoreau's pond, and catered to midcareer professionals, holding classes in the summer. The school grew rapidly. In the 1980s, the Turners sold it to Wall Street investors, who expanded it nationally.

Lively pitched his plan.

"What do you do with this mass of people that don't have the breaks that the more affluent have?" Bernie Turner recalls. "One of my thoughts was at least give them the opportunity to get in and try."

The Turners knew that if the venture worked, they'd make a lot of money. They told Lively they had sold Walden at too low a price and that his venture would offer them a measure of redemption. They invested $600,000 in Lively's project.

Two years later, in 1996, Lively opened Florida Coastal School of Law in a former massage parlor in a strip mall in Tallahassee.

If one wanted to make money in higher education, law school was a prime target.

Postgraduate programs—master's degrees, Ph.D.s, MBAs, law school, medical school—charged far higher tuition than associate's and bachelor's programs. That in part reflects the value of graduate degrees in the labor market. Workers with graduate degrees earn far more than workers with only college degrees. In 2017, the typical worker with a master's degree earned 20 percent more than the typical worker who only had a bachelor's. A worker with a professional degree from a medical or law school earned 57 percent more. Thus, universities charge a premium for those degrees—on the premise that the cost to students is a down payment on a lucrative career. The government allows students to borrow tens of thousands of dollars more each year for postgraduate programs than for college.

Entrepreneurs figured this out in the 1990s. While thousands of for-profit colleges had sprouted up in the 1980s, almost all offered six-month or two-year programs in trades like auto repair, hairstyling, or trucking. A small share offered four-year degrees in the liberal arts. A few had opened alternative medicine schools, such as those training chiropractors.

But for those entrepreneurs, the glittering prize of starting up for-profit law schools was out of reach. Until 1996, for-profit schools weren't allowed to receive money from the federal student loan program. Their students had to find other ways to pay for tuition. The reason had to do with accreditation. Universities are only allowed to collect students' federal loan dollars—as a form of payment for their tuition—if they are accredited. The accrediting body for law schools is the American Bar Association. The ABA prohibited for-profit schools from receiving accreditation, believing such schools would place the interests of investors over those of students. The schools would provide education on the cheap, sacrificing quality to increase profit margins, the ABA thought.

In 1996, the Clinton Justice Department believed that the nation's law schools behaved like a cartel, and it blamed the ABA. Law school professors, moonlighting on the ABA's accreditation committee, demanded that law schools raise faculty salaries as a condition for staying accredited. Committee members, as professors, stood to benefit from the salary increases. Deans complied, raising salaries—and then raising tuition to pass the costs onto students.

The Justice Department believed the process caused a never-ending spiral of rising tuition. It thought the ABA's ban on for-profit schools made matters worse by inhibiting competition among law schools. If for-profit schools received accreditation, students would have more options, forcing nonprofit and public law schools to lower their tuition to attract students. The department sued the ABA, and in 1996, the organization agreed to a consent decree. The ABA agreed to stop fixing faculty salaries—and to lift the ban on for-profit law schools. In one swoop, the Clinton Justice Department carved out an opening for a new for-profit graduate education sector.

Florida Coastal opened in the same year. It initially lent directly to students, using its own money. In 1997, the school won ABA accreditation to become the nation's first accredited for-profit law school. That allowed students to take out federal loans to cover the school's tuition. By 2004, the school had grown to 900 students. Disproportionately Black and Hispanic, with below-average LSAT scores, its graduates outperformed most of their peers. That February, 80 percent of Florida Coastal graduates who sat for the state bar exam passed—the second-highest success rate among Florida's eight law schools, behind only the University of Florida.

The school outgrew its building. It hired valet parking because the lot only had 350 spaces. The parking lot suffered from flooding, requiring staff to take off their shoes and roll up their pant legs as they entered the building. Lively wanted to move into a bigger, more modern space. He wanted to increase salaries to compete with other law schools for the best professors. "We couldn't get to the level we needed to with a mom-and-pop investor group," he says.

Lively hired a company to request bids from potential investors. Unlike a decade earlier when he had to go begging for money, 18 groups made offers. Times had changed.

With higher education enrollment rising and the government backing student loans, education earned ever more attention from Wall Street. Lively met with a company called Sterling Partners. The Chicago private equity group was building a $5 billion portfolio of investments heavily centered on education. Sterling owned stakes in Sylvan Learning Centers, a test-prep company, and Laureate, the corporate owner of Walden, the national provider of graduate schools founded by Rita and Bernie Turner.

One of Sterling's co-owners, Rick Inatome, had made a name for himself in the tech industry in the 1980s. Inatome and Sterling's other co-owners saw a big investment opportunity. Each year, about 100,000 people applied to law school, but only about half won admission. That left tens of thousands of potential customers. With federal student loans, those customers could borrow freely to cover the famously high tuitions of law schools.

When Lively met with Sterling investors, he said he needed money to expand Florida Coastal. *Think bigger*, they said. *Let's open law schools around the country—Las Vegas, Phoenix, Charlotte.* Lively liked what they had to say. Sterling bought out the Turners and gave $1 million to Lively, who maintained a stake of less than 1 percent the new company and became vice president.

Sterling, which named the new company InfiLaw, opened Phoenix School of Law—later renamed Arizona Summit—and Charlotte School of Law, in North Carolina. It rounded up additional investors, including the endowments of Ivy League schools such as Harvard. Prestigious schools like Harvard served a different clientele than InfiLaw. They imposed tough admissions standards that kept out the students with low LSAT scores that InfiLaw targeted. Investing in InfiLaw was a way for Harvard to do what Sallie Mae, banks, and for-profit schools had done: make money while arguing they were contributing to a social good.

In 2005, Sterling's chances of making money from the venture grew. Congress created a program known as Grad Plus, which lifted the ceiling on how much an individual student could borrow to attend a graduate or professional school. Congress had once again responded to constituents' concerns about rising costs of education by simply allowing them to borrow more. Congress created the law to allow graduate students to borrow at lower interest rates than they would if they had to take out private loans. But by allowing students to borrow more, Congress provided a potential windfall for companies like Sterling, which could set tuition even higher now. The program amounted to a blank check—a school could set its price however high and a student could borrow that amount, no questions asked.

* * *

In the spring of 2007, Derek did something very few people from his background were able to accomplish. He graduated college.

Derek was born in 1983 in Shreveport, Louisiana. His parents split when he was young, and for much of his childhood he and his three siblings were raised by his mother. From age five, he stuttered. Classmates teased him. He felt like an outcast in school and struggled academically.

But his mother pushed him to aim high and go to college. He got into her alma mater, Texas College, a historically Black college 90 minutes east of Dallas. Derek beat the odds there. The vast majority of its students drop out, but Derek graduated with a degree in English literature—and a lot of debt. The $6,000 he received in Pell Grants was not enough to cover tuition for one semester at Texas College, let alone living expenses. He had to borrow each year. By the time he graduated, he owed $70,000 in student loans—more than three times the national average for graduating seniors.

Derek was part of a disturbing trend. The typical Black family had roughly $25,000 in wealth in 2004, while the typical white family had $180,000, indicative of a racial wealth gap that has persisted for decades. The lack of wealth among Black people meant they had to rely more on debt than white households to attend college. Blacks who graduated college in 2008 owed an average of $52,726 in student debt four years later—compared to $28,006 for white students.

Though Derek was inspired by the nation's first Black president and had read his book *Dreams from My Father*, he graduated as the economy was crumbling after the housing crash. Unemployment skyrocketed. Derek fell into two categories hit particularly hard—young Americans, and Black Americans. The unemployment rate among workers 24 and under soared to 19 percent in the wake of the recession, as did the unemployment rate for Black men. That figure was nearly double the peak rate of 10 percent among all workers.

After graduation, Derek taught prekindergarten in Texas for a while. The meager paycheck wasn't enough to pay the bills and he defaulted on his student loans. In search of an emotional escape, he moved to South Korea to teach English for two years. Though Derek had done everything he was encouraged to do, by President Obama and his mother—go to college, work hard, contribute to the economy—he had been trapped by the same cycle of high loans and low salaries that many young people experienced at the end of the 2000s.

The weak economy that sent Derek overseas turned out to be a boon for for-profit colleges. While enrollment grew across all types of colleges during the recession—as Americans sought to escape the weak labor market by learning new skills—it grew fastest at for-profit schools. The colleges offered more online courses than traditional nonprofit and public colleges. This gave them more reach, allowing them to recruit students in far-flung locales—rural areas, small towns—that were so-called education deserts, with no physical campuses. These types of places also were some of the hardest hit by the housing bust and recession, which left millions of workers unemployed and in search of new training.

Meanwhile, for-profit colleges of the 2000s—unlike the mom-and-pop-owned schools of the 1980s—faced intense pressure from Wall Street investors, who had poured in money and demanded a profitable return. In response, the colleges recruited aggressively—far more aggressively than their nonprofit and public peers.

The administration of President George W. Bush loosened regulations to allow schools to pay recruiters based on how many students they enrolled. Companies responded by hiring more recruiters. At public and nonprofit schools, 1 percent of employees are salespeople; at for-profit schools, that figure is 7 percent. Many schools skimped on education-related spending—including the number and quality of instructors—to keep costs low and boost profit margins. History repeated itself: As in the 1980s, investors discovered how lucrative the student loan program could be, and recruited students aggressively to make money while insisting they were providing opportunity. Once those students were enrolled, the schools often failed to provide resources to ensure they succeeded. The schools didn't have to. Congress, after heavy lobbying from the for-profit college industry, had watered down regulations over the years, reducing the risk of consequences for schools that saddled their students with high debt for degrees of dubious quality.

The Obama administration tried to crack down on for-profit schools through a regulation called "gainful employment" that shut off access to student loans if too many students defaulted or ended up in high levels of debt relative to their salaries. The industry's main trade group sued the administration, claiming the rule was illegal, and the regulation remained tied up in court for years. That allowed the industry to prosper despite the administration's misgivings.

The for-profit higher ed industry grew swiftly in the absence of regulation. In 2010, enrollment peaked at 2.4 million students, or just above 1 in 10 students in all of U.S. higher education. Few were as big and profitable as InfiLaw. By 2012, the company was the biggest law school provider in the country. Combined, its three schools taught more than 4,000 students that year. Most of its money came from federal student loans. No sector of higher ed received more money from the Grad Plus program than law schools, and no law school received more money from it than InfiLaw. By 2017, InfiLaw's students had borrowed $1 billion in federal loans—$700 million from Grad Plus—most of which went to the school to cover tuition.

After the recession ended in 2009, colleges and universities were hit hard. College enrollment generally goes in the opposite direction of the economy. When the economy shrinks, enrollment in higher education rises as Americans have fewer job opportunities and figure it's a good time to go to school. When the economy grows, enrollment goes down as potential students opt for jobs.

In 2010, as U.S. employers stepped up hiring, workers who otherwise would have enrolled in college or grad school went to work instead. Higher education enrollment, which hit an all-time peak that year, fell for the first time in decades in 2011. Law schools were hit particularly hard. The number of first-year law students in the fall of 2010 fell to the lowest levels since the early 1990s. Desperate to maintain enrollment and profits, law schools around the country lowered admissions standards. In 2010, law schools collectively admitted slightly more than a third of all applicants. In 2013, they admitted half.

InfiLaw followed suit. It already had among the lowest admissions standards of all law schools, and it now lowered its standards even further. In 2010, the typical incoming first-year student had scored 149 on the LSAT, placing in the bottom 40 percent of test takers. In 2016, the typical first-year student had a score of 144, placing in the bottom quarter. InfiLaw believed that because it had succeeded in training the first batch of students to pass the bar, it would succeed in teaching the second.

Outside voices disagreed. In 2014 Dave Frakt, a lieutenant colonel in the air force and a lawyer, interviewed to become Florida Coastal's dean. Before the job interview, he asked InfiLaw to send him the academic backgrounds of the incoming batch of students.

He was shocked: Over half the students ranked in the bottom quarter of LSAT test takers. Many also had earned mediocre or low grades in college. "It was just horrifying," Frakt says. His conclusion was chilling. "They were simply admitting hundreds of students with little or no aptitude—no demonstrated aptitude—for the study of law," he says. The school aggressively recruited them, even though many were bound to drop out or fail the bar exam, Frakt says. They'd never repay their loans. This was predatory lending, he felt.

As a finalist for the deanship, he was invited to the school to present his vision for Florida Coastal. One of his PowerPoint slides pointed out the school's problems and flagging morale, low admissions standards, and falling enrollment. Frakt got a chilly reception. Midway through the presentation, the school's president interrupted Frakt and ordered him to leave, saying that if he didn't, security would escort him off the campus. The school, to say the least, didn't offer him the job.

Lively says InfiLaw believed it could help the new batch of students graduate in the same way it had helped disadvantaged students in prior years. Nearly three in four InfiLaw graduates between 2007 and 2014 who scored 145 on the LSAT passed the bar, InfiLaw says.

"We showed the world that our students could outperform," says Lively, who served for a period as Charlotte School of Law's president. "I'm in the business of wanting to change things." Societal change usually takes decades. Lively believed they were doing it within years.

Charlotte School of Law's instructors earned praise from American Bar Association regulators, who wrote after visiting the school in 2014 that instructors were engaging and used a good mix of teaching techniques.

However, shortly after that, the school faced new pressures and the environment for students changed, state documents show.

Enrollment at Charlotte School of Law plummeted. Between 2014 and 2016 it fell by more than half, from slightly over 1,400 students to about 640. As InfiLaw lowered its admissions standards to mitigate the enrollment decline, it faced financial pressure. By 2014, InfiLaw owed more than $300 million in debt, much of it at high interest rates of 9.5 percent or higher, *The State* newspaper in Columbia, South Carolina, reported at the time. A chunk of that debt was set to come due over the next few years.

Charlotte School of Law dramatically cut costs around this time, according to a report commissioned by North Carolina authorities as part of a review of the school's state operating license. Between 2012 and 2016, the amount the school spent per student for educational programs dropped more than 20 percent. Meanwhile, the amount the school earned per student—much of it through student loans—nearly doubled. In short, the school slashed its spending while allowing in students at a high risk of dropping out, and charging those students high tuition. By 2014, Charlotte School of Law's tuition exceeded $40,000—and that didn't include the tens of thousands of dollars students needed—and often borrowed—for living expenses.

"The data suggest that CSL's [Charlotte School of Law's] cost management initiatives may be designed to maintain profitability at the expense of CSL's core educational programming," state documents show.

Research shows that when private equity investors get involved in higher education, often, the outcomes among students are troubling. Economists at New York University and the University of California Merced analyzed 88 private equity deals involving more than 640 campuses in higher education in the 1990s and 2000s. They found that after such deals, graduation rates deteriorated and students relied more on federal loans to cover tuition. But company profits doubled. The schools allowed in more students and raised tuition.

At InfiLaw, the case was much the same. Tuition rose sharply. Many students left the school owing over $200,000. As Frakt warned, the share of students who passed the bar exam fell sharply. In 2010, 8 in 10 Charlotte School of Law graduates passed the state bar exam on their first try, according to American Bar Association data published by the website Law School Transparency. By 2015, just under half did.

There is a blurry line between predatory recruiting of vulnerable students and providing opportunity to them. Nonprofit schools like historically Black colleges and community colleges have long recruited disadvantaged students—those who lack the grades to get into selective colleges, students who are behind academically, who are jobless or homeless, who come from poor families.

But federal laws designed to crack down on schools that fail to serve their students have often been weakly enforced. And the evidence suggests InfiLaw didn't do enough to ensure the success of Derek and many other students it enrolled.

Derek's score of 137 on the LSAT placed him in the bottom tenth of all test takers. If it had been several years earlier, no law school would have accepted him. But Charlotte School of Law promised him that his scores wouldn't be a problem. "Don't Let Your LSAT Keep You from Law School," read the subject line of an email Derek received.

"The LSAT score is not a measure of whether someone will pass the bar," says Penny Willrich, Arizona Summit's dean of academic affairs. "What the LSAT generally determines is how well someone's going to do their first semester of law school. What really determines whether someone is going to pass the bar is their ending law school grade-point average. We have had graduates that have very low LSAT scores and then they go on and pass the bar the first time around because they were stellar students."

Left unsaid here is that students with low LSAT scores are also at the highest risk of dropping out. Lively says it was the school's responsibility to provide help to those students—tutoring, mentoring, intensive one-on-one instruction—to ensure they succeeded.

"The whole system broke down," Lively says in retrospect. "We weren't ready to deliver on a scaled basis. To be successful at this level, you've got to have a really strong academic support program. And we haven't built up our academic support program to a level that would enable us to deliver those things that we were convinced we could deliver."

Concerned about the school's recruiting and admissions practices, the Obama administration in 2016 prohibited the school from awarding any more federal loans to students. In 2017, North Carolina's attorney general opened an investigation of the school, focusing on its recruiting practices. In the summer of 2017, Charlotte School of Law, suddenly without access to the loan program, shut down. Florida Coastal and Arizona Summit were still open as of early 2021.

InfiLaw's schools did train thousands of minority students who went on to become lawyers. But it also left thousands of students without a degree and deep in debt. Thousands dropped out or failed the bar. Among the class of 2016 alone, fewer than one in five students passed the bar and got a job that required a law degree, even though those students spent $100,000 at the school, North Carolina's attorney general said in a statement. Altogether, InfiLaw's three schools awarded more than $1 billion in federal loans to students. Most of that money went to the schools as payments for tuition.

Lively says that as soon as the school saw the sharp drop in students failing the bar, it raised admissions standards again. But by then the damage was done.

Ultimately, for-profit law schools were a risky endeavor for both the students and the schools. Both lost out—schools like Florida Coastal wound up in a downward spiral of declining standards and battered reputations, while students often ended up without a degree and with piles of debt. That's not to say that both are victims. For the schools, the risk is more theoretical—they keep making risky decisions as long as those decisions make money, until they don't. For students like Derek, the outcome of that risk means damage to their financial stability, their prospects for the future, and even their self-esteem.

Derek's low LSAT score should have been a blinking warning signal. Several months into his first semester, Derek couldn't keep up with the work and was failing his classes. Desperate, he plagiarized a paper. The school found out and put him on academic probation. He continued to struggle and dropped out. He moved back to his mother's house in Warner Robins, where he headed to his room and stayed in bed for a month, depressed.

Derek's five months at Charlotte School of Law were costly. He borrowed more than $30,000 to attend the school. His loans carried a high interest rate of 7.21 percent. Research shows how big a problem this was in schools run by private equity investors. Between 1987 and 2015, such schools taught only 5 percent of students but accounted for 18 percent of all student loan defaults across the U.S.

Lively insists InfiLaw provided Blacks and Hispanics with opportunities, and that while the company grew too fast, it wasn't due to greed. "The thing that concerns me is attributions of motive," Lively says. "I don't have any quibble with anyone who would criticize us for our outcomes."

While Lively may have had good intentions, he profited from students like Derek, whose student loans afforded Lively a comfortable life. He split time between houses in Phoenix and Naples.

Three years after dropping out of law school, Derek lived in New York City in a friend's studio apartment, no bigger than 300 square feet, atop a dollar store in Harlem, a place he called his "escape." The bills kept coming from two contractors that the government paid to collect his loans: Navient, a former subsidiary of Sallie Mae; and the Higher Education Loan Authority of the State of Missouri, a nonprofit better known as MOHELA. Those two groups are among about 10 organizations the Education Department pays to collect debt and provide customer service for borrowers. He put his loans in "deferment," which meant technically he wasn't in default but he wasn't making payments. The balance grew as the interest piled up. Including his undergraduate debt, it was up to well over $100,000. His credit score fell to 520, a severely low mark that will likely haunt him for years, preventing him from borrowing for a car, getting a credit card, or qualifying for a home loan.

Instead of equalizing opportunity, Derek's student debt reinforced the class divide. It lowered his net worth, rather than increasing it. It will likely hang over him for decades. Beyond the economic harm, it damaged his psyche, his confidence, his self-worth. It's the most underappreciated aspect of the student debt crisis—the shame that comes with owing so much, simply for trying to do the right thing.

By 2019, thousands of other students dropped out of InfiLaw's schools. Many owed over $100,000 in student debt.

"As I look back on it, it was just too good to be true," Derek says. "I thought I could be Superman. I could save the family from being in poverty."

EIGHT

State U Inc.

(2014–2018)

Weeks into his freshman year of college, Thomas was bored. In the fall of 2014, the 19-year-old freshman found campus life dull at the Marion Military Institute, a public two-year college in Alabama. The campus, in the sleepy, hard-luck town of Marion, lacked the glitzy amenities of modern-day universities. To escape the institute's starchy military uniforms and rigid schedule, Thomas would jump in his truck on weekends and head to Tuscaloosa, home of the University of Alabama.

The University of Alabama had a meticulously groomed campus and stately redbrick buildings with white colonnades that conveyed scholastic gravitas. It had a championship-caliber Crimson Tide football team and legendary game-day tailgating with students swilling beer on fraternity-house rooftops. It featured amenities like a state-of-the-art recreation center with a climbing wall and a "lazy river" pool complex with a 30-foot water slide. Fraternities hosted world-class rock concerts. A campus dining hall served steak cooked to order.

Everything on campus—from the student tour guides dressed in red polo shirts riding around with parents in the back of golf carts, to the tulips carefully arranged at the school's main entrance—was designed to appeal to young students like Thomas and their parents.

The legacy of Carl Elliott, the congressman who championed the first student loan program in Congress in the 1950s, was stamped on the university. Elliott's papers, including his correspondence with congressmen during the drafting of the National Defense Student Loan program after Sputnik, were archived in a campus basement. Across campus in senior housing, Mary Jolley, Elliott's chief aide who helped him write the bill at the Tutwiler Hotel in downtown Birmingham, lived in a cluttered apartment. A portrait of Elliott hung near her kitchen.

Like Elliott eight decades before him, Thomas and his eight siblings faced seemingly insurmountable economic barriers. Tall and muscular, with pale skin, rosy cheeks, and thick, jet-black hair, Thomas was one of nine children raised in a turbulent home in Bradenton, Florida, a suburb on the Gulf of Mexico. His native Manatee County had the tragic title of opiate capital of the U.S., having the nation's most opioid-related deaths per capita. When Thomas was in high school, one of his brothers died of a heroin overdose.

Money was tight. Neither of his parents had gone to college. His father once owned a construction business but lost everything during the housing bust and now toiled as a construction worker. His mother worked 12-hour shifts as an emergency-room nurse. His family moved 11 times during his childhood. He and his siblings shared rooms crammed with bunk beds.

Thomas stayed out of trouble, earned good grades in high school, wrestled and swam competitively, and bagged groceries at the local Publix from age 14. "In our household, it was made clear that we'd provide for ourselves once we turned eighteen," Thomas once wrote in an online essay. "One after one, I watched my brothers and sisters choose to not attend college—not because they didn't want to, but because they couldn't afford it. The basic goods my peers took for granted, such as food, gas, and car insurance, were only possible because I worked full-time in high school."

Pell Grants and a scholarship covered his tuition and living expenses at Marion. But Thomas yearned for the American college experience of living on a big campus, going to Division I football games, socializing with other students. After he spent a few months at Marion, Alabama's allure closed the sale. In spring 2014, he enrolled at the state flagship university.

He would need to borrow to do so. By 2014, nearly 20 million students were enrolled in higher education, most of them at public colleges. Unlike just two decades earlier, borrowing was the norm. More than two out of three undergraduates needed student loans to help cover their tuition.

The debt Thomas accumulated was far beyond what Elliott could possibly have imagined when, as a U.S. lawmaker, he pushed the government to get into student lending in the 1950s. Elliott was worried about economic barriers blocking children from getting a higher education. Now his alma mater was causing, rather than removing, another set of economic barriers. Thomas's need to take on debt did not happen by accident. It resulted from a strategy the university's leaders embarked on a decade earlier—one that relied on families to get into deep student debt. It was working just as planned. The University of Alabama was acting like a for-profit institution.

In the long interval between Elliott's and Thomas's years at Alabama, higher education had morphed in ways Elliott never would have imagined. During the 1970s and '80s, mom-and-pop for-profit colleges sprouted across the country. In the 1980s and '90s, tuition skyrocketed at private nonprofit universities. In the 2000s, Wall Street–owned universities and colleges became hot commodities for investors. Then, after 2010, the nation saw the emergence of a new brand of commodified education, the Disney-fied state U. No university epitomized that last era more than Alabama.

By the time Thomas enrolled, Alabama had become the fastest-growing public university in America. It also represented the avarice and indulgence that define today's universities. It was in the thick of a construction and hiring boom—intended to improve the quality of education and the student experience. The school achieved that goal, but it was financed on the backs of students and their parents, who turned to federal student loans, with no assessment of the borrowers' ability to repay their mountainous debt.

The University of Alabama opened in 1831, with a class of just 52 students. It was one of the first American universities to offer engineering courses. In 1860, it became a military school that trained Confederate troops. Days before the Civil War ended, in April 1865, Union troops burned down the campus. The university didn't shed its sympathies to the antebellum South and segregation; in 1910, the school named one of its buildings for a Grand Dragon of the Ku Klux Klan.

As the civil rights movement gained momentum in the 1960s, two Black students, Vivian Malone and James Hood, sought to enroll at Alabama in June of 1963. Governor George Wallace staged a protest, standing defiantly in front of an auditorium door in the center of campus, blocking the students from enrolling as news crews aimed their cameras at him. President Kennedy federalized the Alabama National Guard and sent an army general to confront Wallace, who stepped aside that afternoon.

For decades, the university lagged in the competition for federal research and development dollars that flooded universities after World War II to develop technology to win the Cold War. While the University of Alabama was the state flagship, it stood in the shadow of the University of Alabama in Huntsville, which in the 1960s opened a research center to aid NASA.

Until 2000, Alabama was known more for its game-day parties than academics. Faculty felt underpaid. School leaders deferred repairs or upgrades to campus facilities while downsizing or eliminating departments. Asking the state legislature for more money was a long shot; Alabama was one of the poorest states in the U.S.

Enter Robert Witt, a visionary who was about to radically shift the university's trajectory. Witt grew up in a blue-collar family in Connecticut. Both of his parents had dropped out of high school. His father made a decent living at a local factory. Witt earned a bachelor's degree from Bates College in Maine and an MBA from Dartmouth University.

In 1968, he joined the faculty of the business school at the University of Texas at Austin. He worked his way up to dean. The university's president told him to do whatever it took to land the business school on the cover of *BusinessWeek*, which had just started publishing an annual ranking of the nation's top business schools. A *BusinessWeek* cover would lead big firms like Goldman Sachs to send recruiters to the campus. Witt succeeded. The business school rose in prestige. Student applications soared. In 1995, Witt became president of the University of Texas at Arlington, where he worked similar wonders, leading to a spike in enrollment and revenue.

Eight years later, Witt was in his early 60s and thinking about retirement when a recruiting firm called to discuss the vacant presidency of the University of Alabama, his wife's alma mater. When members of the university's board of trustees traveled to Texas to sell Witt on the job, they stated a bold goal: Make the University of Alabama a national brand.

Could Witt do for Alabama what he did for the University of

Texas? Could he turn an afterthought in the world of higher ed into a national brand? It was similar to what Sterling Partners sought out to do with InfiLaw. The university's board wanted Alabama to grow, and fast. Witt agreed to take on the challenge, accepting the job in early 2003. Hired at a $400,000 annual salary, he embarked on a strategy that would transform the state college's mission— and in the process, adopt a new model for getting students on the hook for debt.

A generation ago, public colleges like Alabama received the vast majority of their funding from state legislatures and were thus relieved of the need to charge students high tuition. In California, public colleges remained tuition-free to in-state students until the late 1960s. As early as 1980, the money that public colleges received from student-paid tuition made up only a fifth of their revenues, on average.

Over the years, the responsibility of paying for public college shifted from state governments to students. The shift accelerated in the new century. By 2019, tuition dollars made up nearly half of all money state colleges collected each year.

Colleges like Alabama say they have been forced to raise tuition because state governments cut direct funding of schools. During the 2007–2009 recession state governments radically cut funding for higher education to deal with a severe drop in tax receipts. (State governments, unlike the federal government, are generally prohibited by law from running a deficit.) But many state colleges have raised tuition even when times were good and state funding was stable or increasing. In Alabama, per-student funding in higher ed was stable in the late 1990s and early 2000s, after adjusting for inflation.

Another theory better explains why public-college tuition has risen so fast. The idea, outlined in the early 1980s by a former college president named Howard Bowen, is simple: Colleges will find a way to spend money, no matter how much of it they have. There is no specific amount of state funding that colleges can cite as the appropriate level. Their appetite is never sated.

The biggest cost for public colleges is their employees' salaries. Pressure from university faculty and administrators for raises often leads college presidents to raise tuition. Faculty have for decades—as early as the 1950s—complained about not getting paid enough. Student loans enabled college presidents to extract more money from students to pay professors more.

That pressure existed at Alabama. A week into his tenure, Witt called Judy Bonner into his office. Bonner had worked at the university for decades, starting as a professor and working her way up to dean of the College of Environmental Sciences. Witt asked Bonner to be provost. She accepted, and then delivered a dire message to her new boss. "The fat had been trimmed out of the budget and we were down to which limb was going to be removed," Bonner says. Committees were deciding which new programs to cut. "We're going to have to cut something really big," she told Witt.

"I did not come here to cut the budget," Witt replied. He wanted the school to grow. The school needed a new source of cash. Bonner's task was to find it.

For Bonner, figuring out how to rescue Alabama from its funding crisis was personal. She grew up in Camden, Alabama, a tiny town in one of the poorest counties in the nation. After graduating Wilcox County High School in 1965, "I never really considered going anywhere else to college except the University of Alabama," she says. Her parents paid her tuition. She graduated in 1969, earned her master's at the school, and earned a doctorate at Ohio State. She returned to Alabama for good in 1981.

Throughout her career, she and other faculty complained of being underpaid. Compared to other professions they weren't doing bad. In 2003, University of Alabama professors earned an average of $81,000 over nine months, well above the nation's typical household income of $43,000 over 12 months. What mattered to the university's professors was that Alabama paid less than its competitors. Other universities in the southeastern United States had raised faculty salaries faster than Alabama. The school had trouble keeping professors from fleeing to those schools for bigger paychecks.

Witt told Bonner he was determined to raise faculty pay, so that Alabama's professors earned more than their peers at the dozens of universities in the region that spanned from Texas to Delaware. "My heart raced as I listened to him say that," Bonner says. Prior presidents had aspired to raise salaries, "yet we had never gotten there in any discipline or any rank," she says.

Witt needed money to fulfill his vision. The state legislature had for years rejected the university's requests for big funding increases. Witt concluded he had to raise tuition and expand the student body. The more students the school enrolled, the more money it would make.

Witt and Bonner came up with a strategy. There weren't enough college-eligible in-state students, so they'd expand the pool of applicants by recruiting from outside the state. Alabama at the time had about 19,500 students, three-quarters of them from the state.

Not only would they expand the number of applicants, they'd recruit students who would pay far more than if they had come from Alabama. The University of Alabama, like most state flagships, charges much higher tuition—up to three times as much—for out-of-state students. Many of those students would pay that tuition through student loans. Because the federal government capped how much undergraduate students could borrow, many parents had to take out loans, too. Without the Parent Plus loan program, many of those out-of-state students had no way to cover the school's tuition.

The strategy changed the university's identity. The leaders abandoned the school's role as a state flagship whose main mission was to teach in-state students, giving an economic lifeline to the poor from rural areas. Instead, it became a regional, and eventually national, franchise.

Witt looked at what national elite universities were charging and determined Alabama was underpriced. His first year, he raised tuition by $1,000.

"We didn't approach what we'd charge from a particularly sophisticated level," Witt says. "We increased it $1,000. It was a fairly significant percentage increase. Applications and acceptances continued to go up. We basically systemically started taking it up $1,000 a year. Our thinking was, if we begin to notice a softening in applications, acceptances, and/or matriculation, we'll know that we need to start backing off a little." That never happened.

Like Stephen Joel Trachtenberg at George Washington University more than a decade earlier, Witt learned that he could raise tuition in perpetuity. He speaks of doing so with pride, reciting how much he raised tuition on out-of-state students. When he started in 2003, the school charged them about $9,500 a year. That figure had more than doubled by the time he left.

The amount of debt that students and their parents shouldered rose commensurately. The school did not analyze whether students would have any trouble repaying their debt. Like so many advocates of higher education before them, Witt and Bonner assumed that attending Alabama was a good investment for students, who would benefit from higher incomes after graduation.

Raising tuition was one prong in the strategy. Witt and Bonner also had to geographically broaden the student body to get prospective students from around the country to pay attention to Alabama and apply.

"He was a president who very much understood brand and return on investment," says Roger Thompson, who at the time was Alabama's head of enrollment management. "If you give us a million dollars more to recruit, we're going to turn that into $6 million more in tuition."

Witt foresaw a domino effect. Recruiting out-of-state students begot more out-of-state students. Once someone from, say, Oregon committed to Alabama, they'd tell their friends or younger siblings, who would then be more likely to apply.

Alabama hired three dozen recruiters stationed all over the country.

"We worked very hard to not only recruit students aggressively, but to recognize that to the right or left of that student is a parent or parents, and you need to recruit them also," Witt says. "You need to, in effect, recruit the high school counselors who advised many of these students. And you need to put together a field of recruiting operations that needs to be managed exactly the way you manage a field sales organization."

Each recruiter knew precisely how many high school graduates were in their territory and how well they scored on standardized tests. "We told the recruiters, your job is not done until that student is registered and sitting in class," Witt says. "They were managed the way you managed a sales force. If someone wasn't producing quality results, they were very quickly replaced."

The first job was getting students to visit campus. The second was selling them once they got there.

Witt transformed the university into a wonderland of higher ed, and not in a figurative sense: He used Disney World as a model. Research indicated that many families decide whether to apply to a school within 20 minutes of arriving on its campus. First impressions were everything. Witt concluded the grounds had to be pristine. To lead the grounds crew, he hired a retired air force colonel, who went to Disney World to study how the theme park managed its grounds.

When he went recruiting in wealthy enclaves in the North-east, Witt discovered that students often had their own bedrooms growing up, instead of sharing them with siblings. He believed he needed to cater to those students by building dorm room suites. The university built 10 residence halls during Witt's tenure, along with a state-of-the-art recreation center, new academic buildings and a baseball field, and expanded the football stadium. A new building opened every 90 days.

"We have packaged and promoted the University of Alabama as very much a quintessential traditional university experience," Witt says.

The university didn't just want to increase the student body. It also wanted to attract students with strong academic credentials—high SAT and ACT scores—who tended to come from wealthier families. Those students would raise the university's national profile and ranking.

But those students were also hard customers to land, because they tended to have more higher education options and greater financial flexibility. They could shop for their ideal college. The University of Alabama needed to have exactly the right pitch to lure them in and close the deal. So the university did what more and more schools had quietly started to do since the early 2000s. They turned to consultants who specialized in tailoring tuitions for individual students. Specifically, a consultancy owned by Sallie Mae that plugged student data into algorithms that coughed out custom-made tuition plans. Witt wanted the campus to look like Disney World, but he wanted to treat tuition like airline fares.

Alabama turned to an Iowa-based company called Ruffalo Noel Levitz, which was among half a dozen firms in a cottage industry known as "enrollment management." These firms, largely unknown to the public, set the true price of college tuition, using a calculus hidden to applicants.

The industry sprouted in the 1970s. At the time, colleges faced a crisis on two fronts: a demographic slowdown and the end of the Vietnam War. As baby boomers aged into their 20s and 30s, the generation replacing them wasn't nearly as big, ending a period of growth that had served colleges well. Between 1960 and 1970, the number of Americans graduating high school soared by more than 50 percent, from almost two million in 1960 to nearly three million in 1970. By 1976, the figure increased another 9 percent. In the late 1970s, that pipeline of high school graduates fell for the first time in decades, and continued falling through most of the 1980s. Between 1976 and 1990, the proportion of high school graduates shrank by 18 percent.

On top of that, many young men had avoided the draft by enrolling in college or graduate school. The end of the Vietnam War in 1975 meant that younger Americans no longer had to worry about the draft. That cut off another stream of customers. Fewer customers meant fewer tuition dollars.

Colleges, worried about losing money, got creative about how they charged tuition to extract more money from those who did enroll. Consulting firms cropped up to help them do that.

At the start, schools mailed cards to prospective families, asking that they fill them with personal details. Schools also harvested the data that students provided on their student loan application forms. Early on, private universities primarily used enrollment management consultants. In the 1990s, this practice went into overdrive because of a move by Congress that effectively made more middle-class families look poor on paper. Congress prohibited schools from considering the equity in a family's primary residence to determine tuition discounts. "That was the shock to the system," says Kevin Crockett, Ruffalo Noel Levitz's CEO.

What began was an era of "gapping." The gap refers to the difference between a school's tuition—its advertised sticker price—and the amount, as determined by a federal formula, a family is expected to pay toward tuition, based on its wealth. The latter figure is known officially as "expected family contribution." The government wants families to pay something out of pocket toward tuition.

Before 1992, a family's home equity counted toward wealth. But that year, Congress barred schools from using home equity in calculating the family contribution, and the "gap" per family suddenly became bigger—often thousands of dollars bigger. If a school's sticker price is $50,000 a year, and the family's expected contribution is $20,000, the gap is $30,000. When families are faced with a gap, as most are, they can turn to federal student loans. But the school can also cover that gap by using its own money to provide a scholarship, offering a discount off the sticker price.

Firms like Ruffalo Noel Levitz help schools determine how much to discount for each student to make as much money as possible overall. The firms use hundreds of variables—including race, home address, SAT scores, parental education level and wealth, and even how many times the student visited campus during recruiting—to gauge each student's "price sensitivity." That phrase refers to how much his or her family might be willing and able to pay. The firms study the behavior of the past three years of freshman classes and then suggest, down to the dollar, what the school should charge students of different characteristics.

The most price-sensitive students tend to be those with the most options: students who scored well on standardized tests, got high GPAs, and thus are likely to be fielding offers from multiple colleges. Schools like Alabama want to give these students a discount big enough—but not a penny more—to convince them to choose their institution over other schools.

The least price-sensitive students tend to be those without options, students who aren't high academic achievers. Often they'll get less scholarship money, known as "merit aid," because the school knows they will likely enroll without it. For example, a student who only applied to one school and late in the application cycle fits that category. Some students, like Thomas, applied only to Alabama and wanted to attend at any price.

Colleges, including Alabama, have a love-hate relationship with enrollment management. They recognize that the industry has made public colleges into a cutthroat business that treats education as a commodity. But they also recognize that they need the firms if they want to make money. Schools like Alabama didn't have Wall Street investors breathing down their necks, like InfiLaw, but they had other pressures, including the board of trustees and faculty.

During one conference of college officials in 2005, Thompson, Alabama's head of enrollment management, compared his job to car sales. "I hate it. It's almost like buying a car. But the rankings are driving so much of that. You have to have X number of National Merit Scholars and all that. The ranking thing is out of the barn."

At the same conference, Alabama's enrollment management team demonstrated how, while recruiting out-of-state students, "they overlaid income data from the U.S. Census on maps of high schools in Texas to target wealthy students." Thompson said those students would raise the school's profile. "There are some kids that we'll buy," he said, unironically using the same salesperson's term he derided. "The National Merit kids, they're going to get a full ride. But if you're sitting at a private high school in Florida, where they pay twenty grand to go, we don't even bring financial aid material. What's the point? You don't even need to talk about cost."

The airline-type pricing, the out-of-state recruitment, the meticulously planned campus scenery—it all paid off. The University of Alabama's enrollment started to climb, and so did its prestige. By 2005, it had climbed 12 spots up the *U.S. News* rankings. But Alabama and other public colleges soon faced the same existential threat that schools did in the late 1970s: a smaller number of students. This time, it was largely economic.

Alabama's legislature—and those of most other states—cut higher education funding after the 2008 recession. Alabama had to rely on tuition revenue even more to pay the bills. State funding levels hadn't returned to prerecession levels even though the U.S. had been in an economic expansion since mid-2009.

By 2014, Witt had moved on to become chancellor of the state university system, and Judy Bonner succeeded him as president. She continued the strategy of recruiting out-of-state students and jacking up tuition. The university would need even more students to offset the state funding cuts. Thomas would be one of them.

Thomas had cheaper options than Alabama. He could have gone to a state school in Florida for a lot less. But he was responding to incentives built into the student loan system—and so was Alabama.

The situation exposed an inherent contradiction in the student loan system. Historically, state schools are supposed to serve the students of their home states. Yet the whole idea of the student loan structure resembled a voucher system in that it enabled students to go to the school of their choice—whether that be an in-state school, an out-of-state school, a private university, or a for-profit college. Thomas's top choice was Alabama, and that voucher-type system enabled him to attend regardless of whether he'd be able to repay his debt.

That system also incentivized Alabama to aggressively recruit students, raise tuition, and drive up the university's own costs with a construction binge. By 2014, out-of-state tuition at Alabama had risen more than 150 percent since Witt had taken over roughly a decade earlier.

Like many young high school graduates in the U.S., Thomas had little idea of what he wanted to do in life. In earlier generations, it was mainly elite and upper-middle-class students who expected to go to college. By the time Thomas graduated from high school, college had also become the default for students of more modest means like Thomas. And like so many others, Thomas was convinced college would lead to economic security and a higher standard of living than that of his parents.

Thomas was a lot like Lisa, developing into a rock of stability despite all the chaos around him. He avoided drugs and stayed out of trouble. His parents divorced when he was young and he was raised mostly by his mom and his stepfather. The couple would fight and she'd sometimes move out with the kids, only to move them back in. No one in his family had ever earned a four-year college degree. He came from a family of blue-collar workers, and Thomas had seen what such work did to their bodies and spirits. He had only to look to his father, who once made a good living as owner of a business that cleared land for developers. But one day in the early 2000s, a tree fell on him as he was operating a bulldozer, injuring his back. He never fully recovered. To make ends meet, he returned to construction in his 50s, this time working as a foreman.

Higher education would be Thomas's way out of that hard life.

His father had no money to give to his son. Meanwhile, Thomas's stepfather had the means to help but felt Thomas needed to work his way through school on his own. He preached personal responsibility and self-sufficiency. If the public school system— and the student loan program—was designed to serve anyone, it was Thomas.

Thomas wasn't a "price sensitive" student. He was a transfer student. He had decent grades but not great ones. And he really wanted to go to Alabama. The school had leverage over him. As a result, he got little scholarship money. The financial aid "package" that the school provided to cover his gap included a big Parent Plus loan. Thomas would have to borrow the maximum in loans himself, and then ask his mother to borrow to make up the difference.

When the first student loan bill came, the school said his mother would need to take out tens of thousands of dollars of loans herself. Thomas didn't think much of it. This was a government program, after all. And this was the University of Alabama, a state flagship school, not some fly-by-night for-profit college in a strip mall. How risky could this investment be?

Thomas, like most high school graduates, didn't have much experience with money. He had a credit card with a $2,000 limit and a checking account with a small balance. But he felt incurring college debt would pay off. In 2003, the year Witt took over as president, Alabama charged about $11,300 for out-of-state tuition per year. By 2015, Thomas's first year, it had more than doubled, to $26,000. Room and board was another $9,000. Each year he was there, tuition rose 4 percent, more than double the rate of overall inflation. Room and board also rose.

Debt was passing upward from the young to the old, and not just in Thomas's family but in thousands of University of Alabama families and millions across the U.S. For a long period of the 20th century, families like Thomas's would have passed wealth downward to younger offspring. But now, for a shot at the American Dream, the opposite is occurring—debt is being passed upward to older generations. Congress, and the Obama administration, were partly to blame. In 2010, when the administration killed the Guaranteed Student Loan program, it projected that the government would "save" $60 billion over 10 years. Those projected profits helped fund the Affordable Care Act and other programs. Some of that money would come from people like Thomas's mother. The government charged higher interest rates on Parent Plus loans so it could make a profit. And the price families would pay was high—in Thomas's case, so high that it would stand in the way of the very moment of triumph he craved.

One Monday in December 2017, Thomas missed a call from his father. It was finals week, and Thomas, by now a 23-year-old senior, was studying in his dorm room just before sunset. His cell phone rang at 5:11 p.m. He ignored it, letting the call go to voicemail.

When Thomas listened to the message, it was his father, Robert, rambling. Robert was broke financially and broken in spirit, but one hope sustained him: watching his son grab his college diploma and cross the stage that spring. "I might have enough money saved to go to your graduation in May," Robert said. "I might just surprise everybody. I'm proud as shit of you, buddy."

The call reminded Thomas just how much was riding on his success and on finishing what he'd started four years earlier. Thomas was already living out a version of the American Dream—he'd fulfilled the rite of going to college. He would be the first in his family to get a bachelor's degree.

That February, weeks before graduation, Thomas got another call from his father. He sounded distraught. He was being mistreated at work, he told Thomas, and was depressed. After the call, Thomas felt uneasy. Days later, he texted his brother. "U heard anything from dad? His phone still going 2 voicemail."

Three days later, police in Fort Myers found his father's body in his pickup truck at a gasoline station, a dose of heroin injected in his arm. Thomas texted his brother again: "Call me asap dad is dead bro. Bro call me back please." In between classes, he was on the phone, arranging to have his father's remains cremated, paid for with his federal loan money.

A month later, the university's financial aid office notified Thomas that he owed $2,800 in back fees. When the Education Department disbursed Thomas's student loan funds to the school, the university took its cut to cover tuition and fees and gave him the rest to cover living expenses. But because of an apparent clerical error in the school's financial aid office, one of Thomas's fees had gone unpaid. Thomas had already spent his student loan money for the semester—he paid his rent six months in advance—and had no money. "You assume that if you get the refund check, that your student bill is paid," he says.

The financial aid office insisted the bill be paid. The price for not covering the fee: Thomas would receive his diploma, but he wouldn't be allowed to participate in graduation festivities or cross the stage.

The University of Alabama—the school with the highest-paid public employee in the country, football coach Nick Saban, who earned $10 million in 2020, and with an endowment of nearly $1 billion—wouldn't permit Thomas to cross the stage over a $2,800 debt. It didn't matter that he already had gotten himself and his family into a mountain of debt.

On the day of graduation, Thomas put on his gown and mortarboard. Instead of lining up with his classmates, he walked around the immaculate campus and posed as his stepfather snapped photos of him in front of various campus landmarks, while the ceremony went on inside an auditorium without him.

Alabama alum Carl Elliott had pushed through the nation's first student loan program designed to put a degree within reach of people like Thomas. He had pushed for student loans as a way to democratize higher education, to lift the poor out of poverty and elevate the nation's level of education.

In one sense, Elliott's vision had worked for Thomas—he had his degree. But it came at a steep price. At graduation, Thomas and his family owed $153,000. For transferring to that lush campus with its lavish amenities, he personally owed about $30,000, near the national average for graduating seniors, while his mother and brother owed the rest. (Parent Plus isn't just restricted to parents; other relatives, including siblings, can borrow from the program.) Each had gotten into other forms of debt and filed for bankruptcy. Millions of other Americans similarly found student debt to be more an anchor than a buoy.

After graduation, Thomas sold life insurance, earning $50,000 a year. His employer offered no retirement plan. To get assistance with his student debt, he joined the National Guard, which within several years forgave a chunk of his student debt. But that did nothing for the debt of his mother and brother, who collectively owed $160,000 in student loans by late 2020, as interest mounted.

The three set up a joint bank account, each agreeing to pay $400 a month toward the remaining debt. The debt had created a fissure among them, and Thomas says he was no longer talking to either of them. In late 2020, Thomas was thinking about going to law school in the hopes of getting a well-paid job as a lawyer to pay off the remaining balance. To do that, he would need to take out still more loans.

In 2020, the Trump administration, for the first time, published how much parents like Thomas's were going into debt at each university. At Alabama, the typical parent who borrowed owed $55,000 upon graduation. That was on top of the typical debt of between $18,000 and $27,000, depending on the major, that undergraduates accrued.

Witt and Bonner's plan to boost faculty pay through higher tuition had worked. Alabama used the debt that families like Thomas's took on to drastically raise the pay of its professors, who in 2020 earned an average of $152,000—nearly double what they earned when Witt became president in 2003.

Two years after he graduated, in 2020, Thomas had a broader perspective about his college experience. He was no longer enamored of the university that had beckoned him to hop in his truck on the weekends.

"The fact that they were willing and able to give me hundreds of thousands of dollars in debt—it's mind-boggling," he says. He recalled going online to apply on his mother's behalf to take out student debt. "She just gave me permission—she never went online and did it. She just gave me her Social Security number. She was like, 'Here, go ahead and do it.' I just went online at nineteen years old"—to apply for student loans—"just with the click of a button."

NINE

The Trap

(2016–2018)

On a cold, dreary day in February 2016, Lisa turned her car into the lot of an office park in West Chester, Pennsylvania. She circled among real estate offices and doctor's offices and a furniture-refinishing business until she found the address she was looking for plastered on the side of a drab, 1970s-era brick building. She got out of her battered Subaru and walked to the entrance, cars roaring on West Chester Pike behind her. She took the stairs to the second floor, trying to collect her thoughts as she approached the door to a law office with a plaque that read "Lohr & Associates."

On the other side of the door was the cluttered office of Bob Lohr, a burly lawyer in his 50s with his hair parted to one side, and a lopsided smile. Despite the title suggesting a stable of lawyers, it was a solo legal practice. Precarious stacks of file boxes surrounded Lohr's desk, a barricade of legal documents related to his specialty, Chapter 7 and Chapter 13 bankruptcies. Lohr waved her over, and Lisa took a seat. Holding back tears, she spilled out her story. Lisa was uncomfortable talking about her financial woes. She had made a career out of counseling clients in crisis, providing therapy for people grieving over the loss of a job or a wife or a sibling. Now she was the one who needed help. She had tried to avoid this moment for years. With nowhere left to turn, she was about to do something she once thought unthinkable. She was going to file for bankruptcy.

The day that Lisa walked into Lohr's office, the U.S. was seven years into the nation's longest economic expansion on record—one that began as a recovery from the Great Recession, which was caused by the bursting of a debt-fueled housing bubble. Ten million Americans lost their homes during the housing crisis, most of them through foreclosure, a devastating process that gave beleaguered households a fresh start to rebuild their lives. Congress passed reforms to regulate banks and reduce the risky lending that allowed so many Americans to take on debt they'd never repay.

By 2016, the economy was well into a steady recovery. And yet, Lisa was part of another debt crisis. Millions of Americans with student loans had fallen behind on their payments and saw no way of repaying. Others paid dutifully, yet saw their balances rise because they couldn't cover interest, let alone principal. Each day, 3,000 people defaulted on a student loan; by the end of 2016 some eight million Americans were in default. Several million others were on the brink of default.

That the system had been broken for generations was a reality many borrowers knew but policy makers had refused to acknowledge. The evidence of that broken system piled up, and it had become impossible for the nation's leaders to deny the crisis that the government, schools, Sallie Mae, and the banks had wrought. Unlike homeowners felled by the housing crash, this new population of vulnerable Americans had no escape hatch. They were mired in a crisis.

Those in default spilled across every demographic category.

Some were single millennials; others were parents and grandparents, some of whom owed their own college debts or defaulted on Parent Plus loans. Defaults occurred in every region of the country. They were Black, they were white. They were Latino and Asian. They were men and women.

Beyond the defaulters, many borrowers, like Lisa, were technically in good standing but engulfed in crises that touched every corner of their lives. Their debt prevented them from moving to cities they dreamed of, it prevented them from buying homes, it deferred their hopes of starting families.

For millions, higher education was no longer a ladder up—it had become a slide *down*. Young college graduates had lost their wealth advantage over those who never got an education beyond high school, research by the Federal Reserve Bank of St. Louis showed. College grads made more than nongrads. But many who graduated in the 2000s, like Lisa, barely had any more *wealth* than nongrads because of their towering education debt. Many devoted so much to debt that they couldn't afford other investments. Grads bought fewer homes compared to prior generations. Like Lisa, many saved little or nothing for retirement because their loans gobbled up their income.

Student loans even prevented borrowers from getting the jobs the degrees promised to facilitate. Bad credit resulting from student loans prevented thousands of borrowers from obtaining occupational licenses in some states, a *New York Times* investigation showed.

Many borrowers were worse off for having gone to college—particularly those who went to for-profit colleges, whose alumni represented a disproportionate share of all defaulters. Researchers at George Washington University and the Treasury Department tracked 1.4 million students who either graduated from or dropped out of a for-profit college between summer 2006 and summer 2008.

On average, those students—many of whom were older adults—earned $600 to $700 a year less in the six years after leaving school compared with what they earned at jobs in the six years before enrolling in college. Most owed student loans—an average $13,000 for those who sought a bachelor's degree. The problems weren't limited to for-profit college alums. A study by the think tank Third Way showed that almost 4 in 10 students who had enrolled at the average nonprofit college in 2005 earned no more than workers with only a high school degree six years later—$25,000.

Cracks appeared in the whole system. In February 2015, as the Obama administration put together its annual budget, one of the first clear indications of impending trouble became obvious. The amount of money borrowers collectively sent to the government to repay their loans had plummeted. Students weren't paying down their balances. The administration downgraded its long-term revenue projections for the federal student loan program by $22 billion. The program was drowning in an ocean of red ink.

Lisa's debt was just one drop in that ocean. As for many other Americans who found themselves in dire financial straits, there was no straight line to her insolvency and bankruptcy, no single action or decision that led to her dreadful outcome. Rather, it was a series of decisions, coupled with unpredictable mishaps, that amplified the consequences of the student debt.

When Lisa earned her Ph.D. in 2001, she owed $119,000. More than a fifth was interest that built up while she was in school. She owed more than twice as much as the average annual salary of $55,000 for college graduates that year.

She was part of a national trend: borrowers with big balances, exceeding $50,000. There were five million such borrowers in 2014. While a minority, their ranks were growing rapidly. In 1990, they represented just 2 percent of all borrowers, after adjusting for inflation. By 2014 they represented 17 percent.

Debate on the student debt crisis among policy makers and in the media focuses on undergraduate debt. But graduate school debt has been one of the biggest drivers of student debt. Graduate debt is about 40 percent of all student debt. The Grad Plus loan program has become a cash cow for universities, while driving up some borrowers' balances to mortgage-like levels.

Lisa is a prime example of how graduate debt compounds undergraduate debt. Back when Lisa was an undergraduate, she had been surprised to learn that she would need an advanced degree to practice in her field. Rather than seeing that hurdle as an insurmountable obstacle, she was determined to get the required degree and reach her goal. After Lisa earned her graduate degree, her monthly payment easily exceeded $1,000. She couldn't afford that.

Congress, at the direction of President Clinton, had created a repayment plan in the early 1990s that was supposed to help borrowers like Lisa. That plan, known as income-based repayment, set a borrower's monthly payment at 15 percent of her "discretionary" income, defined as a borrower's adjusted gross income minus 150 percent of the poverty level. After 25 years of payments, the government would cancel any remaining balance.

But Lisa, along with millions of other borrowers, didn't qualify for income-based repayment in the early 2000s. Congress limited the repayment program to borrowers under Clinton's Direct Loan program and excluded those under the Guaranteed Student Loan program.

Lisa had only one option to lower her bills. She could refinance her debt with a new 30-year-term loan, known as a "consolidation loan." On its face, consolidation seemed like a good option. It allowed borrowers to collapse their debts into a single new loan, hopefully with better terms. Lisa's consolidated loan carried an interest rate of 6.4 percent, based on a formula under federal law that averaged out the interest rate of her prior loans. If she spread her loans out over a longer period, her monthly payments fell to $759. But the loan was far costlier in the long run, and far more profitable for Sallie Mae. She would pay $150,000 in interest. In total, including all interest and principal, the loan she signed called for her to pay $270,314.88 for her education.

Unforeseen factors placed new burdens on Lisa. In the spring of 2002, she and her husband separated, with Lisa retaining custody of their two children. He failed to pay court-ordered child support. She hadn't yet opened her practice and didn't earn enough to support her family and pay her bills. "Everything was crumbling financially," she recalls.

She called Sallie Mae to ask about options to reduce her monthly payment. The customer service rep reassured her there was an easy fix. "Just go into forbearance for a year," the rep told her. Forbearance allowed borrowers to suspend payments temporarily without any damage to their credit.

"Oh, I can do that?" Lisa asked, incredulous. She had never heard of this option, and felt relieved.

"Not a problem whatsoever," the woman replied.

Lisa signed up. The woman on the other end of the line didn't tell her an important detail: While forbearance gave short-term relief, it would drive up the total amount Lisa owed because interest would continue to accrue. A year later, when Lisa resumed payments, her balance had grown by thousands of dollars. "I look at it and I start getting physically ill," she says.

The financial pressure became so great that she began resorting to money-saving measures that have become common practice for millions of cash-strapped Americans. During snow days or school holidays, she would bring her kids to work because she couldn't afford a babysitter, for example.

"You're always trying to pull from somewhere to pay it down. I would obsess over this stuff. I would be up all night to stay on top of things. My credit meant something to me."

Despite the obstacles, Lisa was determined to repay her debt. Lisa's estranged husband had taken debt, mostly in real estate, and discharged it in bankruptcy in 2009. After they divorced in 2011, Lisa remained on the hook for a $233,000 mortgage that her ex-husband had used to purchase a commercial property in the early 2000s.

In August 2012, as she drove home after driving her daughter to stay with a friend at the Jersey Shore, she pulled to the side of the road during a violent thunderstorm. The storm moved on and the sun came out, and she continued home. Her phone rang. It was her son. "Mom, something bad happened," he told her.

When she got to the house, local television news trucks were parked outside, satellite dishes pointed skyward. A massive poplar tree had toppled, falling onto her daughter's bedroom and splitting the house. Her son had been in the next room. Though no one was hurt, the house was destroyed. Lisa, in a daze, took her son to a friend's house to spend the night. The next morning, she got up and went to see clients at her private practice so she could earn money to stay on top of her student debt payments. Clients who had seen her house on the news were incredulous that she was at work. "I have to. There's no cushion," she told herself.

Insurance covered most of the home repairs, but not all. She took out a credit card to cover the rest, charging thousands of dollars. In 2013, Lisa downsized, moving herself and the two kids into a 1,000-square-foot condo so she could keep up with the student loan payments. Her new mortgage payment of $900 was almost the same as her student loan bill. She felt guilty raising two children in an apartment. But she told them they had to live frugally so she could repay her student debt.

The office that her husband had purchased fell into disrepair. The ceiling caved in, revealing structural damage. The previous owner had sold the property under false pretenses, but too much time had passed for her to go after him. The bank took possession of the property. She still owed $100,000 on it. "At that point, I was so beaten down," she says.

All the while Lisa kept making student loan payments. Her loan balance was barely going down and she was paying mostly interest, thanks to the longer 30-year term on her consolidation loan. She wanted to reach a deal with the government to settle for less than what she currently owed. But her calls with Sallie Mae went nowhere.

The customer service reps were often outright rude. "What do you expect? You're barely even paying the interest," she remembers one saying. Another told her, "Who told you to have kids?"

With mortgages, borrowers eventually had a way out—foreclosure. Americans with student loans have no such option. Borrowers like Lisa are trapped. That's what led her to Bob Lohr's office in February 2016.

Lohr had a warm demeanor and walked with a slight limp. He had heard many stories like Lisa's, from clients desperate to get out from under their student debt. He knew she couldn't repay her student loans and the rest of her debts on her $70,000 salary. But he knew he'd have the talk with her, the same talk he'd had with prior clients. Lohr explained that unlike other forms of debt, student loans were nearly impossible to discharge in bankruptcy. "I almost always tell my clients, 'The odds are really against you. This is a very high standard in the bankruptcy code,'" he told her. But he said it was always worth a try—perhaps a sympathetic judge would rule in her favor.

Bankruptcy was intended to give the hopeless a fresh start, avoiding decades or even a lifetime of being stuck in place, physically, financially, and mentally. Except, that is, for student borrowers. Until 1976, borrowers with student loans had the same bankruptcy rights as those who owed mortgages, auto loans, and credit card debt. If they could prove to a judge that they were insolvent, they could get their loans wiped away or reduced.

But as more and more borrowers defaulted on student loans in the 1970s, Congress looked askance at them, believing that young grads were using bankruptcy to escape their obligations without trying to repay. Congress believed bankruptcy created an incentive for borrowers to discharge debts that they'd easily be able to repay as they progressed in their careers.

In 1976, Congress tightened the law to treat student debt differently from other debt. Student loan borrowers would be able to wipe away their debts in bankruptcy only after making five years of payments—or if they proved they faced an "undue hardship." Congress left it to judges to define what *undue hardship* meant. In 1985, a New York judge did that. A borrower named Marie Brunner had tried to cancel student debt she racked up while earning a master's degree in social work. The judge said she had to prove three things to show undue hardship: she couldn't maintain a minimal standard of living based on her income and expenses; her situation wasn't likely to improve anytime soon; and she had made a good-faith effort to repay. She lost the case. The three-pronged test became known as the "Brunner Test," which other judges adopted.

In 1998, Congress made undue hardship the main bankruptcy threshold, adopting the Brunner Test while striking the provision that allowed federal student loans to be discharged after five years of payments. In 2005, Congress set the same standard for private student loans, those originated by banks with no federal guarantee. After 1998, discharging student loans became nearly impossible, and many bankruptcy lawyers told their clients as much. Few borrowers tried to declare bankruptcy, knowing the standard was so high.

Removing the bankruptcy option allowed the government to assume that it will ultimately get back all of the money it lent to borrowers like Lisa so long as they live a normal life expectancy. Thus, removing the risk of bankruptcy translates into higher projected profits for the government when it puts together its long-term budget estimates. There was money to be made in preventing bankruptcy.

Lisa walked out of Lohr's office crying. Despite his earnest demeanor and kindness, the lawyer was not reassuring when he described the stark reality of bankruptcy for student debt. After leaving him, she worried about losing everything. "I was most afraid of losing my home at that point," she says. In August, the day she dreaded finally arrived when Lohr filed Lisa's paperwork in bankruptcy court, arguing that she should be allowed to shed her debts because of undue hardship. She had no idea how much worse her hardship was about to become. Two weeks after she filed for bankruptcy, Lisa visited her doctor. She was in an examination room, making small talk with a nurse. As she chatted about her dating life and how she was about to become an empty nester, her doctor walked into the room. She looked at an image and gently touched Lisa on the shoulder. She had a serious look on her face. "I think this might be cancer." Lisa was diagnosed with breast cancer.

Up until that moment, Lisa had been battling to keep her head above water financially. Now, with a frightening diagnosis, the stakes were even higher. She was fighting for her life. Her situation felt so bleak that when the family's adopted collie died, she didn't get a new dog because her future felt so uncertain.

Her physical fate rested with God. Her financial fate now rested with an obscure agency in New Jersey.

When Lisa filed for bankruptcy, she set in motion a series of transactions that shifted her debt from Sallie Mae to a separate, nonprofit guarantee agency called the New Jersey Higher Education Student Assistance Authority. Working on behalf of the federal Department of Education, the New Jersey authority essentially bought the loan, reimbursing Sallie Mae for the total principal and accrued interest. The New Jersey agency now owned Lisa's loan.

When Lisa filed for bankruptcy, she was waving a red flag to the Department of Education signaling that she was unable to repay her debts, triggering the machinations of student debt collection. If her bankruptcy case failed, the agency could use various tools that Congress had created to collect the debt, including calling her repeatedly and garnishing her wages, tax refunds, and even—if she was old enough—her Social Security retirement checks. In other words, there'd be no escaping her obligation to repay. In another level of irony, Lisa's interest would continue to accrue during the bankruptcy proceedings, meaning that the agency could make still more money from Lisa's loan even as her case lingered in bankruptcy court.

Lisa hoped that with her cancer diagnosis, she would meet the undue hardship threshold. Already in a crisis, she now had the terrifying specter of cancer treatment. She had lost two of three siblings to cancer. Her health insurance came with a $7,000 annual deductible. As awful as the cancer diagnosis was, perhaps it would be enough to get her out of her student loan obligations.

It wasn't. Lisa's case went through 10 months of fact-finding known as "discovery," with Lohr and the New Jersey agency exchanging the evidence they planned to show a judge. The New

Jersey Higher Education Student Assistance Authority argued that Lisa did not meet the threshold for undue hardship, and should not be allowed to walk away from her mountain of debt.

At one point, Lohr told Lisa that the only way she could get out of her debt was to convince the judge that she was spiritually hopeless. Lisa was shocked. As a psychologist, she had counseled many clients over the years who were truly beyond all hope, sunk into a helpless pit of despair. Her whole job was to give them hope. Now the government was forcing her into the position that she had counseled clients to stay out of—that of effectively becoming suicidal.

"They basically said, 'No way,' for two years," Lisa recalls. "I'm going through all these cancer treatments. I had no hope in sight."

Meanwhile, she was blocked from making payments on her loans, and she worried that if she failed in bankruptcy, she'd be faced with a far bigger balance than before, just as had happened when she'd gone into forbearance. She started researching online, trying to understand the history of student debt, why the system, at every step of the way, seemed so tilted against borrowers like her.

When Lisa declared bankruptcy, she had joined eight million Americans who defaulted on federal student loans. She was at the crest of a national wave of student debtors. During the 2007–2009 recession and the subsequent recovery, Americans had put faith in higher education as a way to restore the American Dream and the nation's economy. Since 2007, student debt had nearly tripled to $1.4 trillion. There were nearly as many student borrowers in default as there were homeowners who lost their homes after the housing crisis. Americans became delinquent on student debt at twice the rate that homeowners became delinquent on mortgages at the height of the housing crisis.

Every tale of student debt woe is unique, but there were also system-wide flaws and failures that caused enormous numbers of students to fall into default at once. One of those systemic collapses came in mid-September 2016, a month after Lisa filed for bankruptcy. The huge for-profit chain ITT Technical Institute collapsed amid investigations into allegations that it had defrauded students with deceptive advertising. It had taught about 40,000 students across the U.S. A year earlier, Corinthian Colleges, another big chain that owned schools like Everest, Heald, and Wyo-Tech, had gone bankrupt amid similar accusations and lawsuits. Both ITT and Corinthian denied wrongdoing. The broader for-profit college sector had collapsed. The big companies could escape their obligations in bankruptcy, but most of the borrowers couldn't. It was the cruelest of ironies.

With bankruptcy viewed as a nearly impossible option for borrowers, student loan activists found a potential back door to student loan cancellation—an obscure, decades-old law that entitled borrowers to have their loans forgiven if they proved their schools had defrauded them. The law had been used successfully on only a handful of occasions. By 2016, with so many for-profit school students feeling deceived, thousands had petitioned the Education Department to forgive their loans. The agency was overwhelmed by the sudden surge in applications, and the law was so vague—it didn't specify the level of proof borrowers had to provide of school fraud, most notably—that the Obama administration embarked on a rulemaking process and hired a special master to help adjudicate claims.

Meanwhile, the IRS and federally hired debt collectors aggressively pursued defaulted borrowers. More and more, the government garnished Americans' Social Security checks to collect unpaid student debt. The government collected more than $1 billion from Social Security recipients since 2001, the Government Accountability Office reported in late 2016. Millions of people faced a life sentence of indebtedness and even poverty, trapped in a prison without walls. Had she been a decade older, Lisa might have been one of those aged debtors, still paying money to the federal government for loans that had long ago proven impossible to pay. One day, unexpectedly, she was handed the key to get out.

In the summer of 2018, Lisa was depressed and distraught as she drove down I-95 to drop her daughter off at freshman orientation at the University of South Florida. She was sending her daughter off to college while being ruined by her own higher education experience.

It should have been a joyous road trip with Drake blasting over the stereo. Instead, Lisa's normally buoyant daughter was solemn and quiet, leaving Lisa alone with her thoughts as the highway rolled past, mile after mile. It had been almost two years since she had filed for bankruptcy, and all that she had gained from it was endless wrangling with the seemingly unmovable New Jersey loan agency, and more accrued interest. The case was still in the extended discovery phase, and a judge had not ruled on her request.

Deflated, she told Lohr in August to tell the agency she was ready to give up.

"I had a spiritual acceptance of, 'It's done. Any hope of financial peace is over for me. What else can you get from me?'"

Judges had begun to notice this trend of desperate student loan borrowers. Noting the impossible position of these students and how they lacked any legal recourse, judges started taking a looser interpretation of the bankruptcy code to allow student loan borrowers out of their debt obligations. "More than 50 current and former bankruptcy judges, frustrated at seeing borrowers leave federal courtrooms with six-figure debts, say they or their colleagues are more open to chipping away at the decades-old guidelines that determine how such debt is treated," the *Wall Street Journal* reported in June 2018.

"If the law's not going to be improved by Congress, we have to help these young people who are drowning in student loan debt," said U.S. Bankruptcy Court judge John Waites in South Carolina. After they arrived in Tampa and Lisa dropped her daughter at college, she proposed to Lohr that she hand over her retirement account to the government. It was a desperate gambit to end the Sisyphean task of ridding herself of debt. Lohr said he would take the offer to the lawyers for the New Jersey Higher Education Student Assistance Authority, and see what they said. He wasn't optimistic, but it couldn't hurt to try.

Two weeks after she dropped off her daughter, Lisa was sitting with a client in her office on Main Street in Chester, Pennsylvania, when her cell phone rang. She ignored the buzz. After the client's session ended, she looked down at her phone. She had missed a call from Bob Lohr. He had sent her an email almost simultaneously.

Uh-oh, she thought. A call from Lohr usually wasn't a good sign.

Expecting more bad news, she recited a mantra that she often used to calm herself. "I could see peace instead of this," she said out loud, to steady herself and quiet her thoughts. Then she read the email. She couldn't quite believe what it said, so she dialed her lawyer back.

When Lohr answered, he told her he had just gotten off the phone with the lawyer for the New Jersey guarantee agency. Lohr had filed a motion in Lisa's case asking for summary judgment, which essentially meant Lisa was asking the judge to decide in her favor and discharge her debts without going through the whole bankruptcy proceeding. The lawyer for the guarantee agency had been brief. "My orders are to not contest the motion for summary," the lawyer had told Lohr, who now relayed the message to Lisa.

Lisa paused. "What does that mean?" she asked.

"It means we're going to win by default," Lohr said.

"What does that mean?" Lisa asked again, louder.

"You're going to get your student loans discharged," Lohr said. If the guarantee agency didn't oppose Lisa's motion, then the judge would simply decide in her favor, and Lisa's debt would disappear. "That's what it means."

When Lohr delivered the news, it was like a dam broke within her. Years of welled-up anxiety spilled out in a flood of emotion. For two decades, she had struggled to get out of debt, and it had been like trying to claw her way out of quicksand. Suddenly, the fight was over. She began to weep uncontrollably, still clasping the phone. "Oh my God," she gasped in between the sobs that wracked her body. "Oh my God." Lohr laughed in joy as she struggled to get out her words. "It's really nice to hear tears of happiness," he said.

That night, she sent a text with the good news to her daughter, who had just had her first day of classes as a freshman. "MOM!!! THAT'S SO EXCITING!!! I'm so happy for you!!!" her daughter texted back. "I'm so happy!!!" Lisa wrote back. "We just need a dog now." Soon after, she adopted a sweet three-legged mutt named Balboa, a rescue dog with soulful eyes.

Later, Lisa and Lohr tried to guess why the New Jersey agency had suddenly dropped the case. Lohr remembered a conversation with the agency's lawyer in which he had brought up Lisa's cancer. The lawyer's tone had changed, and he mentioned that a close cousin had recently died of cancer.

Lohr and Lisa believed he dropped the case out of sympathy for Lisa because of her cancer. The law had no sympathy. But a stranger—hired by the government to go after her—apparently did.

＊　＊　＊

Lisa had found an unexpected route out from under her mountain of debt. But it wasn't because of a tripwire in the law designed to extend mercy to those who were suffering. It wasn't because of a policy change intended to rectify the opaque and tragically unforgiving nature of student debt. It wasn't even because a bankruptcy judge—the arbiter of such cases—had ruled that she was a worthy candidate for forgiveness. It was perhaps because of a random act of clemency on the part of a lawyer who held Lisa's fate in his hands and had decided to give her a break.

In a way, Lisa's case resembled that of Brandon, who was relieved of his Howard University debt because of a sudden job bonus, or that of Barack Obama, whose book deal wiped his financial slate clean. Lisa was one of the lucky few. Millions of other Americans would have no such good fortune. For the vast majority of borrowers, programs created to help those in financial trouble in fact prolonged their indebtedness and piled on new interest, or proved too difficult to navigate. Unemployed workers, desperate for a route back into the workplace, followed Larry Summers's advice and tried to go back to school, only to fail out with new debt. Black, Hispanic, and poor students asked their families to help them reach for a degree, only to be declined for new Parent Plus loans and forced to drop out. Lisa found a way out, but millions of others would not.

As Lisa sat in her quiet office with its facing love seats and pictures of trees on the wall, the familiar surroundings felt different, unreal, as though she had been suddenly transported to a place that she didn't recognize. The office was peaceful and still, and for a moment, she sat stunned on the love seat, reflecting on the significance of what had happened. A massive burden had been lifted, but she didn't feel elated or triumphant.

She felt a vague sense of embarrassment, the feeling of shame that had haunted her since she first realized she was underwater with debt. Here she was in her mid-50s, talking with friends about retirement, and she had none of the savings that someone of her age and education might assume. In a month or two, Bob Lohr would take her out for a celebratory dinner. For now, there was no bottle of bubbly to uncork, or plane to board for a long-awaited vacation on the beach, or glass of wine to savor.

Instead, she collected herself, blew her nose, and calmed her racing thoughts to get ready for the next client who would come in the door shortly to sit across from her. That client would have struggles and doubts and traumas of their own to work through, and she needed to be ready to listen attentively and help them navigate their own labyrinth. She had work to do. She had money to make. There was a difference, though. For the first time in decades, the money she made would finally be her own to keep.

Conclusion

In the summer of 2018, Betsy DeVos, President Donald Trump's education secretary, called Jamie Dimon, the CEO of JPMorgan Chase. She needed his help.

The student loan program was in shambles. For years, federal budget officials had said that the government would make money from student loans. They assumed students would borrow, graduate, land well-paying jobs, and repay their loans with interest.

But the Education Department spotted a disturbing trend. A huge number of borrowers' balances were rising, not falling. They owed more than they had originally borrowed. They were unable to pay enough each month to cover interest. Their debt was turning into quicksand. Millions of borrowers were in distress, and the country's biggest consumer-loan program—bigger than what Americans owed on credit cards or auto loans—was hemorrhaging money.

For decades, Congress and various presidential administrations had ignored warning signs that their no-questions-asked lending practices would submerge borrowers in a crisis and saddle taxpayers with hundreds of billions of dollars in losses. Now they couldn't ignore the warning signs.

Dimon sent Jeff Courtney, one of his former deputies, to Washington to investigate the program. Courtney, a married father of two from Delaware who had previously overseen JPMorgan's private student loan practice, discovered that the government had been charging interest in ways that doomed borrowers to default. It had charged interest while borrowers were still in school, making the balances so high that many couldn't afford the monthly payments once out of school. When borrowers defaulted, the government continued to charge interest, increasing the balance.

By charging more in interest, and allowing them to take out bigger loans, Congress thought it was doing borrowers a favor—giving them access to higher education—while also making taxpayer money. A win-win. Instead, the government had sunk millions of borrowers into a crisis.

And it left taxpayers to cover a staggering amount of bad debt. Borrowers would pay only two-thirds of the debt on the books—leaving taxpayers on the hook for more than $500 billion, according to consultants the agency hired to help Courtney assess the portfolio. By comparison, private lenders lost about $535 billion in subprime mortgages when the housing market crashed. DeVos concluded the figures proved the program needed a major revamp, though the Trump administration didn't act on that impulse, leaving any such effort to the incoming Joe Biden administration.

The idea that the government could lend freely—looking the other way as borrowers took on tens and even hundreds of thousands of dollars in debt, despite numerous warning signs—with only positive outcomes was a myth.

Unlike with the 2008 financial crash, most of the debt was on the government's books, not the private sector's books. In the housing decline, banks couldn't cover the losses, causing a financial crash that brought down the economy. This time, the federal government could borrow trillions of dollars at ultra-low interest rates and easily absorb the losses. There was no "systemic" risk here. There wouldn't be a financial crash. But the evidence was clear: The second consumer debt bubble of the 21st century had burst.

In one sense, the federal student loan program achieved its mission. It opened up higher education to the masses. Anyone who has wanted to go to college has been able to, rich or poor. Today, half of the U.S. adult population has an associate's or bachelor's degree, because student loans gave people the money to pay for it. Without loans, many would have never gone to college.

The American economy has, in one respect, benefited. The education of America's workforce propelled the U.S. to become the world's most prosperous nation in the latter half of the 20th century. Higher living standards, a reduction in poverty, the rise of the world's biggest and most innovative companies in the U.S.—all of those positive developments resulted, in a big way, from the country's investment in higher education.

But those benefits have come at a steep cost. It has contributed to income inequality. Student debt has held back some Americans from saving for retirement, buying homes, and starting businesses. It has caused stress and hardship for borrowers like Lisa. It has widened inequality, leaving many borrowers worse off, particularly those who took on debt but never earned a degree.

The struggles of borrowers—along with the sharp rise in tuition enabled by the loan program—have eroded Americans' faith in higher education. In 2017, a *Wall Street Journal* poll asked whether going to college was worth the cost. Just under half of the respondents said yes. Only four years earlier, a solid majority thought college was worth it.

This, in some ways, is a good thing. Many families have concluded that college isn't worth any price, and have demanded discounts from their schools or sought cheaper options. In recent years, schools that once raised tuition without restraint have frozen or cut tuition, desperate to lure students.

The coronavirus pandemic that hit the country in March 2020 accelerated this trend. As colleges across the U.S. were forced to shut their campuses and hold classes online, many could no longer justify charging $40,000 and up for tuition and discounted tuition further.

Meanwhile, members of both political parties acknowledge something is wrong. In the 2020 Democratic presidential primary, Senator Bernie Sanders of Vermont called for canceling student debt entirely, while proposing that state colleges be tuition-free. Senator Elizabeth Warren of Massachusetts called for writing off up to $50,000 for every borrower—canceling $640 billion in total debt.

In the spring of 2020, the day after Sanders dropped out of the primary, Joe Biden, as the presumptive Democratic Party presidential nominee, came out in support of forgiving at least some student debt. He later backed a plan to cancel $10,000 for every borrower. He also called for making public college tuition-free for all students from families earning $125,000 or less a year.

It isn't just Democrats who acknowledged that the system was broken. Wayne Johnson, the former chief operating officer of the federal student loan program under DeVos, ran as a Republican for a U.S. Senate seat in Georgia on a platform of forgiving student debt. Senator Ron Johnson, a Wisconsin Republican and Trump ally, told me he believed the student loan system was fundamentally broken. "It's causing real economic harm," Senator Johnson says. "It is causing young people to delay a full life. This is a huge disservice we've done to our young people, telling them they had to get a college education, and the way to do it is you all have to have a student loan. That's just not turning out to be the truth."

Suddenly, the politics of personal responsibility that had dominated congressional debates over how to pay for higher education for generations had now shifted toward an acknowledgment that Congress had erred in allowing students to borrow so freely.

Identifying a problem is a crucial first step. Fixing it is much harder. And the fix that Democrats have zeroed in on could make the problem worse.

Canceling student debt would help borrowers. But it wouldn't solve rising tuition, low-quality programs, and indebtedness for future students. The government is on track to lend another $1 trillion to students and their parents over the next decade. Without reforms, the country will end up where it started—deep in student debt with another wave of defaults.

The student loan crisis is about perverse incentives. Schools had the incentive to raise tuition to unsustainably high levels—and profited wildly from access to free student loan money. Banks had the incentive to push money out the door—and made untold billions from their involvement. Sallie Mae had the incentive to give banks money—and became a multibillion-dollar hegemon on Wall Street. Congress had the incentive to finance the whole operation—since it helped their constituents gain access to college without acknowledging the expenses of doing so. All of those institutions significantly reduced the risk that they'd lose money. A real fix would change those incentives, particularly for schools. It's no coincidence that when universities such as Stanford University and the University of Minnesota made loans to students directly—in the first half of the 20th century, before the government got into the loan business—default rates were low. When schools—or banks—put their own money at risk, they are more careful with it, and less likely to extend loans at amounts that will be impossible for borrowers to pay off. If student loans continue to be one of the primary ways that the U.S. finances higher education, schools should put more of their own money at risk and suffer some losses if borrowers default. Congress, meanwhile, should come up with a more accurate accounting system to assess the likelihood of borrowers to repay. With a proper assessment of risk, Congress can better target aid programs to the neediest borrowers.

I came to that conclusion after eight years of reporting for the *Wall Street Journal* on student debt—and after conversations with hundreds of people tied to the system, including those harmed by it and those who profited from it.

In January 2018, I met Derek, the former Charlotte School of Law student, in New York City at a café. He wore a diamond stud in each ear, a black hoodie, and skintight black jeans. When he arrived at my table I stood up and extended my hand. Even though it was our first time meeting face-to-face, he ignored my hand and gave me a warm hug.

I asked him about his childhood and his time at Charlotte School of Law. He said his biggest regret was that he wasn't able to fulfill his dream of landing a white-collar job that would come with a secure income. In the middle of our conversation, his cell phone rang. It was a robo-call. I heard a woman's automated voice on the other line: "I'm calling to see if you're interested in a home loan." He hung up and rolled his eyes.

He was living with a friend above a dollar store in Harlem. The studio was spartan. The closet contained his wardrobe. He said the clothes made him feel wealthy.

The prior week, he said, his roommate, who also owed student debt, had received a call from his servicer, bugging him to make a payment on his $10,000 balance. "Do you think ten K is a lot of debt?" his roommate had asked Derek. Derek laughed at him.

While we were on the subway heading to Union Square for lunch, Derek mentioned that his sister was deep in debt from attending a for-profit art school in Atlanta. She was working as a flight attendant. He told me he was thinking of moving to Europe, to escape the stress of living under student debt.

As I talked with him I couldn't help but think of just how dysfunctional the student loan system has become. Derek had grown up poor and incurred medical debt; he had a subprime credit score when he applied to Arizona Summit, which knew he was at a high risk of defaulting on a student loan. He had a low LSAT score. Yet the government readily extended him tens of thousands of dollars in debt—on top of the tens of thousands of dollars it had extended him to go to college—to attend a law school that was already under investigation for alleged misbehavior. (The school denied wrongdoing; it closed before the results of that investigation.) He was stuck with that debt, which he would never be able to repay. On top of that, his loans for law school carried an extra-high interest rate, set by Congress so it could use the money it made from him and other graduate students to balance its own books. Yes, there were good intentions: Schools like InfiLaw and members of Congress who approved loans stressed the need for educational opportunities for "high-risk" students like Derek. Yet by doing so, with so much evidence that students like Derek wouldn't be able to repay and that the consequences would be devastating and long-lasting, the government was in its own way engaging in a form of predatory lending.

I've learned just as much by talking to the people who made money from the student loan system. The two biggest architects of the student loan industry were Al Lord and Ed Fox. They are two of the most vociferous critics of the higher education industrial complex I've met.

Lord profited from the student loan system as much as anyone. I reached out to him multiple times for an interview. For a year, he ignored me. Finally, he agreed to meet.

He's retired and splits his time between an estate in Maryland and a house in Naples, Florida. In the spring of 2020, just after the pandemic began, we met in a restaurant in downtown D.C., for what would be the first of four meetings. The first thing he told me was how much he resented the cost of higher education. He's a grandfather putting three grandchildren through college.

"Forty years, I've been listening to people say, 'Well, sooner or later it will get so high no one's going to be able to go to school,'" Lord says. "Well, they still are."

For a moment, he sounded not like the former CEO of the company that made untold billions from student loans but like a working-class parent struggling to ensure his children had a shot at the American Dream. Lord considers colleges greedy, charging exorbitant amounts while building up huge endowments to pay professors to work fewer and fewer hours and construct amenities to attract students. Until a few years ago, he served on the board of trustees at Penn State, and he said he was outraged at how much the school charged in tuition as well as in room and board, despite having a multibillion-dollar endowment.

In the 1980s and '90s, schools started experimenting with raising tuition by high amounts each year to test the waters—to see if students would pay it, which they did. Because they were rewarded for it, they kept raising fees each year. Students kept paying. And Congress, attempting to help students with costs, allowed them to borrow more. But because Congress attached no strings to the money—it didn't require schools to prove the quality of their education or to suffer consequences if their loan amounts were too high—Congress made the problem worse.

I asked Lord if he felt responsibility for this dysfunctional system. He got defensive, talking fast and accusing me of asking leading questions. He initially characterized himself as an "observer" in the student loan system.

But he wasn't just an observer—he was one of the main actors on the stage. While he told me that he blamed Congress for the mess, I reminded him that he couldn't separate himself from Congress—Sallie Mae and Congress were inextricably linked. Sallie Mae—and Lord himself—spent heavily on lawmakers' campaigns and lobbying them to shape legislation to the industry's benefit, often to the detriment of borrowers. If Congress passed laws that harmed many students—which Lord and I both agree Congress did—it was in part directly because of the heavy influence of Sallie Mae.

After one of our meetings, Lord sent me an email, in which he seemed to acknowledge responsibility—a little. "For me to criticize the rapidly growing dependence of [*sic*] education establishment and government largesse seemed presumptuous and certainly inimical to all our interests," he wrote, recalling his time as Sallie Mae's swashbuckling CEO. "It was difficult to bite my tongue and I did not always."

Lord would have never gotten where he was without the seeds planted by Ed Fox, Sallie Mae's first chief executive, who is now retired and living with his wife, Carmen, in a penthouse condo at the Ritz-Carlton in Georgetown, the upscale neighborhood in D.C. Their condo overlooks the Potomac River. Their living room features modern artwork including a giant sculpture of a human body by the artist Joel Shapiro, whose artwork sells for hundreds of thousands of dollars. The sculpture in Fox's living room could fetch twice what Lisa paid for her education. As I interview Fox, his red-haired Maine coon, Sasha, saunters around the living room.

Fox criticizes Congress. But as much as he wanted to blame Congress for the student loan mess—and Congress deserves as much blame as anyone—Fox accepts some blame. He acknowledged he and Mary Whalen lobbied for and shaped the major higher education laws passed in the 1970s and '80s. Late in 2020, I called him to ask if he had any regrets. "I don't regret that we did what we were asked to do and did it successfully from the corporate point of view," Fox told me.

I said I felt like he was holding back, and asked more pointedly: Had he ever reflected on his role in the dysfunctional system he believed had screwed over a lot of students?

For the only time in my 12 hours in interviews, he raised his voice and swore. "If you're looking at the broader overview, it was a big fuckup," he said. "Eventually you wind up with $75,000 tuitions at institutions that have $40 billion in reserves.

"Don't you agree?"

There's no one actor to blame for the crisis. Each institution is responsible, which makes the monster systemic. So what do we do to fix it?

Any reform needs to achieve two separate goals. The first is to continue to ensure all Americans have access to a quality higher education, regardless of their financial background. The second is to remove the current incentives for schools to raise tuition to unconscionable levels without any regard to how those prices will impact families.

Policy makers should take two steps: First, deal with those who already have student debt; second, take steps to prevent another run-up in student debt and another wave of defaults.

Forgive interest on student loans. Congress should write off the interest that has accumulated on student loans. Many borrowers tell me they don't want their entire loans forgiven—they just want a fair shot at paying off their debts. Their balance has grown so high because of interest that they see no hope of repaying the full balance, so they see no point in paying at all.

Make four-year schools put up their own money. For too long

Washington policy makers have been swayed by university lobby-ists who are asking for more money without being willing to make sacrifices. Lyndon Johnson's original vision was to have schools and the government contribute to an insurance fund that would guarantee student loans made by banks. If the borrower failed to repay, both schools and the government would suffer the losses. Instead, the federal government covered almost all of the losses on defaulted student loans and schools suffered few consequences. Requiring that schools be on the hook for at least a portion of defaulted loans would make them think twice about raising tuition too high or awarding unbearable loan amounts to students.

Make community college truly free. Millions of Americans attend K-through-12 school without receiving an adequate educa-tion. High schools need to be improved, and community college should provide a second chance for those who grew up with an educational disadvantage. Today, one year of community college—including tuition and living expenses—costs $15,000 after grants are factored in. Four in ten community-college students go into debt, and they are nearly twice as likely to default as their peers at four-year public and private schools. These students are among the likeliest to default. Most drop out—for a variety of personal, academic, and economic reasons—and are left with debt but no de-gree. As a result, the student loan program has reinforced societal inequalities, rather than reduced them.

For both political and practical reasons, I don't support four years of free college. But I do support at least one or two years of free college. Give students a chance to try college and see if it works for them, without automatically anchoring them with debt. Once they've persisted after one or two years, then provide them the opportunity to borrow. If students last at least one year in college, they're far less likely to default.

Revise the idea of the American Dream to respect and reward

alternatives to the four-year degree, particularly apprentice-ships. The research is clear: Apprenticeship programs are effective at getting students well-paid jobs. In Kentucky, Toyota and other employers in 2010 started a program called the Federation for Advanced Manufacturing Education to train workers how to operate machinery. The average graduate earned $98,000 five years after the apprenticeship.

The government should stop subsidizing grad school. The Grad Plus program is perhaps the most dysfunctional of all types of student loan programs. It has enabled grad students to borrow as much as their schools charge, and schools have taken advantage, jacking up graduate school tuition to obscene levels. The program has become a cash cow for universities, and has led to a growing number of borrowers with six-figure debts. Grad school could benefit from private sector discipline. The returns on graduate degrees—how much borrowers earn after college—are far clearer than on undergraduate degrees. Without the federal government's near-monopoly on student lending, private lenders would be able to assess the quality of different graduate school programs and lend amounts commensurate with students' ability to repay. That would prevent tens and potentially hundreds of thousands of dollars from being heaped on students who'll never be able to repay it. And it would force universities to keep their graduate school tuition in check.

States, cities, and communities should step up. In Kalamazoo, Michigan, a group of wealthy philanthropists—worried about their town's decline in the early 2000s as globalization walloped American manufacturing—started a program that guaranteed city residents free college. They believed the plan would encourage people to move back into the city, and upgrade the workforce.

It paid off—to an extent. The city's population started growing again, reversing a long decline, and more of the city's youth enrolled in college—and graduated. It was an example of how a local community invested in its youth instead of relying solely on the federal government to pay for higher education.

While reporting on the program, I met a 19-year-old woman named Caitlyn, who wore a nose ring and had long blond hair tucked under a baseball cap. She was earning $9.75 an hour working behind the counter of a coffee shop in Kalamazoo's town square.

The scholarship program had allowed her to attend the local community college for free, with all of her living expenses covered. She found herself aimless and suffering anxiety, in part because of a breakup with a boyfriend. She dropped out after a semester.

Like so many Americans, she tried college but it didn't work out. But unlike millions who enrolled in other cities in recent years, she didn't have debt hanging over her. She said she would consider going back to school. "I'd need to figure out why I would, other than just 'You need a degree to function,'" she said.

I spotlighted Lisa's story because I identified with it.

My mother, Kathleen Diane Mitchell, was born about a decade earlier than her, in Harrisburg, Pennsylvania, in a working-class family with no college graduates. She ran away from home at 17, moved to the suburbs of Washington, D.C., and got a job as a secretary. A dozen years later, at age 29, she gave birth to me and my twin brother, David. Eighteen months later, she and my father divorced. My mother raised the two of us.

She never made more than $30,000. She moved us from apartment to apartment, chasing cheaper rent. A Sunday-evening ritual involved her driving us to the local bank, withdrawing a $20 bill—our lunch money—and showing us the receipt, which usually showed a balance of a few dollars and change. It was her way of saying the $20 had to last until her next paycheck.

She lacked the financial stability that once came with having a college degree and white-collar job. She could never save for a down payment on a house or for her retirement. She hadn't gone on vacation in decades. In late 2016, she texted me while I was at work, saying that she was in the hospital with what appeared to be the flu, but not to worry, she'd be okay. She had lupus, an autoimmune disorder. Seven months later, she died.

Despite decades of working in tedious jobs, sacrificing so much to raise my brother and me, she died poor, with several hundred dollars to her name.

Poverty is generational—the data is clear on that. I was, in all likelihood, headed for the same life as my mom. But while we lived paycheck to paycheck, I had a tremendous advantage that few other Americans had. I always knew college would be free.

My grandfather on my father's side, Elliot Mitchell, grew up in Connecticut, the son of Jewish immigrants from Lithuania. The Mitchell family ran a neighborhood grocery store. My grandfather worked there as a teenager, stocking shelves. One day a female customer close to the family saw something in him and insisted he go to college. She gave him a bit of money, and he enrolled at Harvard University, the same class as John F. Kennedy. To save money, he transferred after two years to the College of William & Mary in Virginia and later became a Defense Department scientist. In late 1958, months after Lyndon Johnson pushed through the Space Act that created NASA, my grandfather served as a founding member of a board at NASA that doled out research money to support rocket technology in response to Sputnik.

My grandfather squirreled away a college fund for his grandchildren. I attended the University of Maryland and graduated debt-free thanks to that fund.

My mother's death, in the months before I embarked on this book, caused me to reflect on how she struggled to raise two kids on a secretary's salary in America. I always wanted more for my mother. It's easy for me to imagine her getting into the same awful predicament as Lisa, drowning in debt with no way out.

Lisa tried to avoid the same fate of women like my mother. I understood why Lisa found it so important to send her children to college, but also why she was so stressed about debt.

When I met Lisa in her office, she took me to a back room, where years of Sallie Mae bills had piled on a desk. They sat underneath a vertical picture plastered to the wall, of her and her two children making funny faces in a photo booth.

She said she had repeatedly told her own children not to get into debt. Her daughter Stephanie told me that the message got through. Stephanie was so determined to get a scholarship she took the ACT seven times to improve her score. It paid off when she received a $38,000 scholarship to the University of South Florida. She borrowed $4,000 her first year to cover the remaining tuition and living costs. She said she was determined not to get deep into her debt like her mother. "She worked really hard," Stephanie told me. "I could tell that was really hard for her."

As I walked out of Lisa's office, she said she wasn't in favor of free college. She didn't want a handout. She expressed the desire to pay her own way. Lyndon Johnson had that concept in mind when he launched the student loan program. He looked up at the stars in October 1957 and worried that America had lost its greatness—a greatness tied to America's commitment to education. He took pride in the fact that he upheld those dual values, personal responsibility and education. Lisa had wanted the same thing—a fair shot at college, at a reasonable price.

Acknowledgments

I am so grateful to the characters in this book who all shared their stories with me over many hours in person and by phone. They all provided whatever I asked to verify their stories: emails, loan documents, text messages, voicemails. All interviews were conducted on the record. I have used pseudonyms for the four borrowers—Lisa, Brandon, Derek, Thomas—profiled in this book. It was a privilege to tell their stories.

I would like to thank Stuart Roberts, my editor at Simon & Schuster, for being such a thoughtful, creative, and compassionate editor. His assistant, Emily Simonson, worked tirelessly on this project and never failed to ask thoughtful questions that greatly improved the manuscript. Thank you.

I would like to thank Jon Cox, my first editor at Simon & Schuster, who saw right away that this was an important topic affecting tens of millions of lives, that there was a story to tell, and that I was the one to tell it. I am grateful for the team at Simon & Schuster that played various roles to see this project through: Brigid Black, Sherry Wasserman, Carly Loman, Stephen Bedford, Larry Hughes.

I am grateful for my agent, Howard Yoon, whose brilliant vision for the book provided the foundation for this project.

I would like to thank two people who helped me conceive, outline, structure, and write the manuscript—Theo Emery and Evelyn Duffy. They provided crucial support, creatively and emotionally, and without them I wouldn't haven't finished this book.

I am every day inspired by my editors and colleagues at the *Wall Street Journal*. I am grateful for Greg Ip, an amazing mentor who was the first person to encourage me to pursue this project. Likewise, many other colleagues at the *Journal* encouraged me to write about this topic and enthusiastically discussed and promoted story ideas. Chief among them: Nell Henderson, Jon Hilsenrath, Neil King, Sudeep Reddy, Becky Bowers, Mark Anderson, Chris Wellisz, Eric Morath, Erich Scwhartzel, Melanie Trottman, Gary Fields, Andrea Fuller, the whole economics team at the *Journal*. The *Journal*'s D.C. bureau chiefs, first Jerry Seib and then Paul Beckett, provided me a long leash to pursue this topic while upholding the *Journal*'s rigorous, unparalleled standards of fairness, thoroughness, and thoughtfulness. I am particularly grateful for Brody Mullins, who read multiple versions of my manuscript and tirelessly offered ideas big and small. Thank you all.

Thank you so much to these people who encouraged me every step along the way to start and finish this project, and who contributed in some fashion: Tom Burke, Christopher Johnstone, Adam Chudy, Teal Baker, Alex Messmer, Bill Ghent, Thomas Cluderay, Chad Byron, James Hafferman, John Grant, Mike Van Opstel, Jamie Vasquez, Ronnie Rojas, Melody Feldman, Rebekka Ellman, James Allen, James Holdorf, Vicki Stewart, Steve Tuttle, Jonathan Mable, Thomas Richards, Brian Zang, Chris Urena, Bill Moran, Kevin Murphy, John Murawski, Adam Looney, Tamar Jacoby, Kevin McGilly, Jeremy Hube, Matthew Wiggins.

Above all I would like to thank my family: My father, Stephen Mitchell, and my stepmother Susan Mitchell; my sister, Stephanie

Mitchell, and my brother, Zachary Mitchell; my first stepmother, Vicki Mitchell; my aunt Jane Mitchell, my aunt Nina Mitchell, my uncle Jason Mitchell; my cousins Arin Mitchell and Brian Mitchell. And last, I would like to thank my twin brother, David, my best friend, who has always supported me.

Notes

All details in the intro are primarily from interviews with Lisa and her lawyer, Robert Lohr. I interviewed Lisa at length in her office and in multiple phone conversations. I independently verified her account through her bankruptcy documents, text messages, and Navient, her student loan servicer, which, after receiving Lisa's permission, gave me her entire student loan history, including the original amounts she borrowed, the interest she was charged, and all of her payments.

In this section, as throughout the book, I use quotation marks when a character remembered clearly what was said. Otherwise, I italicize a character's statement in a given scene to paraphrase, conveying the broad message of what he or she said.

Figures on student debt are typically drawn from two sources. The first is the Federal Reserve Bank of New York's quarterly *Household Debt and Credit Report*, which can be found here: https://www.newyorkfed.org/microeconomics/hhdc.html. This report is based on a sampling of consumer credit reports from a private-sector credit firm and includes both federal and private student debt. The second source is the U.S. Department of Education's Federal Student Aid data center, which releases a quarterly

report on the federal student loan portfolio, found here: https://
studentaid.gov/data-center/student/portfolio. This source also
provides figures on total outstanding federal debt, number of borrowers, number in default and forbearance, etc.

Figures on college and graduate school enrollment are drawn
from the Education Department's National Center for Education
Statistics, which can be viewed here: https://nces.ed.gov/programs
/coe/ataglance.asp.

Other sources are cited below.

Introduction

5 *owing an average of $29,000*: "Student Debt and the Class of 2019," The
   Institute for College Access & Success, https://ticas.org/interactive-map/.
5 *At least a hundred owe over $1 million*: Josh Mitchell, "Mike Meru Has
   $1 Million in Student Loans. How Did That Happen?," *Wall Street
   Journal*, May 25, 2018, https://www.wsj.com/articles/mike-meru-has-1
   -million-in-student-loans-how-did-that-happen-1527252975.
5 *The number of people who lost their homes after the housing crash*: "The End
   Is in Sight for the U.S. Foreclosure Crisis," Federal Reserve Bank of St.
   Louis, December 2, 2016, https://www.stlouisfed.org/publications/housing
   -market-perspectives/2016/the-end-is-in-sight-for-the-us-foreclosure-crisis.
6 *3,000 people a day*: Josh Mitchell, "Student-Loan Defaults Rose by
   1.1 Million in 2016," *Wall Street Journal*, March 14, 2017, https://www
   .wsj.com/articles/student-loan-defaults-rose-by-1-1-million-in-2016
   -1489498222.
6 *Black households with student loan debt typically owe*: U.S. Federal
   Reserve, *2019 Survey of Consumer Finances*, last modified November 17,
   2020, https://www.federalreserve.gov/econres/scf/dataviz/scf/chart
   /#series:Education_Installment_Loans;demographic:racecl4;population:
   1,2,3,4;units:median.
6 *Black borrowers are three times as likely . . . to default*: Judith Scott-Clayton,
   "What accounts for gaps in student loan default, and what happens after,"
   Brookings Institution, June 21, 2018, https://www.brookings.edu/research
   /what-accounts-for-gaps-in-student-loan-default-and-what-happens-after.
6 *Nearly 4 in 10 Black borrowers . . . defaulted*: Ibid.

6 *The homeownership rate among young Americans*: Zachary Bleemer et. al.
   *Echoes of Rising Tuition in Students' Borrowing, Educational Attainment,
   and Homeownership in North America*, Federal Reserve Board of New
   York Report 820, July 2017, https://www.newyorkfed.org/medialibrary
   /media/research/staff_reports/sr820.pdf?la=en.

6 *Couples are delaying marriage*: Fenaba Addo, Jason Houle, and Sharon
   Sassler, "The Changing Nature of the Association Between Student
   Loan Debt and Marital Behavior in Young Adulthood," *Journal of
   Family and Economic Issues* 40, no. 1 (March 2019): 86–101, https://doi
   .org/10.1007/s10834-018-9591-6.

6 *They are holding off on starting businesses*: Brent W. Ambrose, Larry
   Cordell, and Shuwei Ma, "The Impact of Student Loan Debt on Small
   Business Formation" (working paper, Federal Reserve Bank of Philadelphia, July 2015), https://www.philadelphiafed.org/the-economy/the
   -impact-of-student-loan-debt-on-small-business-formation.

6 *They are delaying saving for retirement*: Matthew S. Rutledge, Geoffrey
   T. Sanzenbacher, and Francis M. Vitagliano, "Do Young Adults with
   Student Debt Save Less for Retirement?" (working paper, Center for
   Retirement Research at Boston College, Chestnut Hill, MA, June 2018),
   http://crr.bc.edu/wp-content/uploads/2018/06/IB_18-13.pdf.

6 *They are choosing jobs soley for higher salaries*: Jesse Rothstein and Cecilia
   Elena Rouse, "Constrained After College: Student Loans and Early
   Career Occupational Choices" (working paper, National Bureau of
   Economic Research, May 2007), https://www.nber.org/papers/w13117.

6 *Among Americans born in the 1980s*: William Emmons, Ana Hernández
   Kent, and Lowell Ricketts, "Is College Still Worth It? It's Complicated,"
   On the Economy (blog), Federal Reserve Bank of St. Louis, February
   9, 2017, https://www.stlouisfed.org/on-the-economy/2019/february/is
   -college-still-worth-it-complicated.

6 *hundreds of thousands of senior citizens*: "Social Security Offsets," U.S.
   Government Accountability Office, December 20, 2016, https://www
   .gao.gov/products/GAO-17-45.

7 *borrowers are on track to pay back*: Josh Mitchell, "Student loan
   losses seen costing U.S. more than $400 billion," *Wall Street Journal*,
   November 21, 2020, https://www.wsj.com/articles/student-loan-losses
   -seen-costing-u-s-more-than-400-billion-11605963600.

8 *Universities employ more lobbyists*: "Industry Profile: Education," 2019,
   Center for Responsive Politics, https://www.opensecrets.org/federal
   -lobbying/industries/summary?cycle=2019&id=w04.

8 *Eighty-one university leaders*: Dan Bauman, Tyler Davis, and Brian O'Leary, "Executive Compensation at Public and Private Colleges," *Chronicle of Higher Education*, last modified July 17, 2020, https://www .chronicle.com/article/executive-compensation-at-public-and-private -colleges/#id=table_public_2019.

9 *She didn't hesitate*: Alice Rivlin, interview by the author, February 2019.

Chapter One: The Visionary

11 *After nightfall*: Johnson, *The Vantage Point*, 272.

11 *For Lady Bird*: Lady Bird Johnson, audio diary and annotated transcript, November 23, 1968, Lady Bird Johnson's White House Diary Collection, LBJ Presidential Library, https://www.discoverlbj.org/item/ctjd -19681123.

12 *"I also remember the profound shock"*: Johnson, *The Vantage Point*, 272.

13 *Private colleges charged the equivalent*: Goldin and Katz, *The Race Between Education and Technology*, 276.

14 *"Everything from automobile"*: Walter J. Greenleaf, *Self-Help for College Students* (Washington, D.C.: U.S. Department of the Interior, 1929), 11, https://archive.org/details/ERIC_ED540098/mode/2up.

14 *"honesty, character"*: Ibid., 11.

14 *One of those early bank borrowers*: Robert Caro, *Means of Ascent* (New York: Alfred A. Knopf, 1990), 142–43.

14 *His local bank*: "School Days," Texas State University Archives, accessed February 8, 2021, https://exhibits.library.txstate.edu/univarchives /exhibits/show/lyndon-b-johnson/school-days.

15 *only 9 in 100*: Snyder, *120 Years of American Education*, 76.

15 *when unemployed World War I*: "Bonus Expeditionary Forces March on Washington," National Park Service, last modified September 3, 2019, https://www.nps.gov/articles/bonus-expeditionary-forces -march-on-washington.htm.

15 *the law provided*: The text of the original G.I. Bill can be found here: https://www.loc.gov/law/help/statutes-at-large/78th-congress/session-2 /c78s2ch268.pdf.

16 *set up "trailer towns"*: Multiple articles have been written on the trailer towns that colleges set up to accommodate veterans. One such article is Ellen Glover, "GI Trailer Towns Podcast," *Voices from the IU Bicentennial* (blog), Indiana University, January 17, 2017, https://blogs

.iu.edu/bicentennialblogs/2017/01/18/bicentennial-podcast-gi-trai
ler-towns/.

16 *"Fly-by-night" schools*: A detailed look at the for-profit college abuses
resulting from the original G.I. Bill—along with a link to the Teague
report—can be found on the Century Foundation's website at https://
tcf.org/content/report/truman-eisenhower-first-gi-bill-scandal/.

16 *The G.I. Bill had another flaw*: Jill Lepore, *These Truths: A History of the
United States* (New York: W.W. Norton & Co., 2018), 527–30.

16 *The so-called Zook Commission called*: A copy of the Zook Commission report can be found here: https://archive.org/details/in.ernet
.dli.2015.89917/page/n355.

17 *"There's probably never"*: Urban, *More Than Science and Sputnik*, 47.

17 *Eisenhower and his wife, Mamie, settled in*: Dickson, *Sputnik*, 21.

18 *"one small ball"*: David S. F. Portree, "One Small Ball in the Air: October
4, 1957–November 3, 1957," in *NASA's Origins and the Dawn of the
Space Age*, Monographs in Aerospace History, no. 10 (Washington, D.C.:
NASA History Division, 1998), https://history.nasa.gov/monograph10
/onesmlbl.html.

18 *Reports focused on*: Clowse, *Brainpower for the Cold War*, 15.

18 *"They could pass us swiftly"*: Dwight D. Eisenhower, *The White House
Years* (Garden City, N.Y.: Doubleday, 1963–65), 211.

18 *the Russians launched Sputnik 2*: "Sputnik II," NASA, https://nssdc.gsfc
.nasa.gov/nmc/spacecraft/display.action?id=1957-002A.

18 *Flopnik*: "60 Years Ago Vanguard Fails to Reach Orbit," NASA,
December 6, 2017, https://www.nasa.gov/feature/60-years-ago
-vanguard-fails-to-reach-orbit.

18 *"We were finally"*: Johnson, *The Vantage Point*, 275.

19 *Milton Friedman wrote*: His 1995 essay "The Role of Government in
Education" can be found here: https://la.utexas.edu/users/hcleaver
/330T/350kPEEFriedmanRoleOfGovttable.pdf.

19 *Devereux Josephs*: "Colleges Are Too Cheap," *Fortune*, September
1957, https://fortune.com/2011/04/17/colleges-are-too-cheap-fortune
-classics-1957/.

19 *Eisenhower proposed*: Dwight D. Eisenhower, "Special Message to the
Congress on Education," January 27, 1958, The American Presidency
Project, https://www.presidency.ucsb.edu/node/233942.

19 *The son of tenant farmers*: Elliott, *The Cost of Courage*, http://www.ency
clopediaofalabama.org/article/h-2377.

20 *"The House denounced"*: Stewart E. McClure, interview by Donald

Ritchie, January 28, 1983, interview 4, transcript, Oral History Interviews, Senate Historical Office, Washington, D.C., https://www.senate.gov/artandhistory/history/resources/pdf/McClure4.pdf.

21 *Harvard economist Seymour Harris*: "More Student Loans Are Urged," *New York Times*, March 22, 1959, B9.

21 *"Half of all American families"*: John F. Kennedy, president's news conference, February 7, 1962, transcript, The American Presidency Project, https://www.presidency.ucsb.edu/node/236998.

22 *A front-page story*: Marjorie Hunter, "Colleges to Cut Student Loans," *New York Times*, September 14, 1963, 1.

22 *On the evening of*: Johnson, *The Vantage Point*, 69.

22 *"Higher education is no longer"*: Lyndon B. Johnson, special message to the Congress: "Toward Full Educational Opportunity," January 12, 1965, transcript, The American Presidency Project, https://www.presidency.ucsb.edu/node/238600.

23 *"Many educators who advocate"*: written analysis of Allan Cartter, submitted for the congressional record, at a hearing before the U.S. House Special Subcommittee on Education, Washington, D.C., February 1, 1965.

26 *Walker's mother*: "An S.O.B. with Elbows," *Time*, August 7, 1978.

26 *By 1965*: testimony of Allen D. Marshall at a hearing before the U.S. House Special Subcommittee on Education, Washington, D.C., March 8, 1965.

26 *"Parent and student"*: testimony of Armour Blackburn in a hearing before the U.S. House Special Committee on Education, Washington, D.C., March 9, 1965.

27 *"His intention was"*: Walker's personal notes, provided to me by a former colleague of Walker's, Pınar Çebi Wilber, who collaborated on a book idea.

27 *"I don't think"*: Ralph Yarborough, speaking during a hearing before the U.S. Senate Subcommittee on Education of the Committee on Labor and Public Welfare, Washington, D.C., March 16, 1965. Library of Congress, Washington, DC.

27 *"You are never going to be able to get enough money"*: Wayne Morse, speaking during a hearing before the U.S. Senate Subcommittee on Education of the Committee on Labor and Public Welfare, Washington, D.C., June 1, 1965. Library of Congress, Washington, DC.

28 *Johnson returned to his alma mater*: "Higher Education Act Media Kit," LBJ Presidential Library, http://www.lbjlibrary.org/mediakits/highereducation/.

29 *"the thick doors"*: "700 College Aides Meet on U.S. Funds," *New York Times*, December 10, 1965.

29 *"your goddamn banks"*: Charls E. Walker, interview by Ted Gittinger, September 16, 1999, interview 1 (I), LBJ Library Oral Histories, LBJ Presidential Library, https://discoverlbj.org/item/oh-walkerc-19990916 -1-14-15.

31 *In 1968, the Carnegie Foundation*: Fred M. Hechinger, "Carnegie Panel Asks U.S. to Send Poor to College," *New York Times*, December 13, 1968, page 1. See also Earl F. Cheit, *The New Depression in Higher Education*, A General Report for the Carnegie Commission on Higher Education and the Ford Foundation (New York: McGraw-Hill, 1970).

31 *"marriageable age"*: Alice Rivlin, "An Interview with Alice Rivlin," by Hali J. Edison, date unknown, American Economic Association, https:// www.aeaweb.org/about-aea/committees/cswep/about/awards/bell/rivlin.

32 *College groups argued for direct aid to schools*: Gladieux and Wolanin, *Congress and the Colleges*, 43.

32 *Rivlin's panel supported*: *Toward a Long-Range Plan for Federal Financial Support for Higher Education* (Washington, D.C., U.S. Department of Health, Education and Welfare, 1969).

34 *Johnson called outgoing Treasury secretary Joe Barr*: Walker, interview by Gittinger.

Chapter Two: When Ed Met Sallie

I interviewed Edward Fox for more than 10 hours during four visits at his home in Washington, D.C., and additionally on the phone and by email, in 2019 and 2020. Most details and direct quotes are directly from him. I tried to independently verify them through news accounts; public documents, including Sallie Mae's financial statements; interviews with other Sallie Mae executives, including Albert Lord; interviews with congressional aides, including Bill Ford's longtime chief of staff, Dave Geiss; and congressional testimony obtained at the Library of Congress.

35 *Samuel Welch*: Interview with a relative and another with knowledge of the murder. See also: Associated Press, "Home Loan Director Is Shot, Killed," *Cumberland* (Md.) *News*, November 4, 1969.

39 *Nixon's advisers proposed*: Finn, *Education and the Presidency*, 57–59.

40 *scathing memo*: Ibid., 59.

40   *"Some members of the working group"*: Ibid., 59.

44   *"Almost from the beginning"*: Lois D. Rice, ed., *Student Loans, Problems and Policy Alternatives* (New York: College Entrance Examination Board, 1977), 15.

45   *Hundreds of corporate-owned correspondence schools*: David Whitman, "Vietnam Vets and a New Student Loan Program Bring New College Scams," The Century Foundation, February 13, 2017, https://tcf.org /content/report/vietnam-vets-new-student-loan-program-bring-new -college-scams/.

45   *Advance taught students*: Details about Advance Schools Inc. can be found in this December 31, 1974, memo, at the Ford Presidential Library: https://www.fordlibrarymuseum.gov/Library/document /0005/1561325.pdf.

46   *"I could go down"*: Larry Van Dyne, "The FISL Factories," *Chronicle of Higher Education*, August 4, 1975: 4, https://drive.google.com/file /d/0B7aqIo3eYEUtSzVERHVsS3BhMm8/view.

47   *"They understood the value of education"*: Tamara Henry, "Legislator's Lessons in Education Advocacy," *USA Today*, September 28, 1994.

48   *When Ford was a young adult*: Dave Geiss, interview by the author, December 20, 2019.

49   *"We knew that trouble was developing"*: Statement of Bill Ford at a hearing before the U.S. House Subcommittee on Postsecondary Education, Washington, D.C., June 19, 1991.

51   *"In the process everybody who touches it"*: Statement of Bill Ford, U.S. Subcommittee on Postsecondary Education, Washington, D.C., May 30, 1979.

53   *"You were a fool"*: Terry Hartle, interview by the author, February 28, 2019.

55   *"I just sensed a surge"*: Willie Schatz, "Sallie Mae's First, Only President Resigns," *Washington Post*, May 15, 1990, D1.

57   *"With just plain people"*: Nelson, *The History of Sallie Mae*, 88.

57   *"We were shocked to find"*: *Lessons Learned from the Privatization of Sallie Mae* (Washington, D.C.: U.S. Treasury Department, 2006), https://www.treasury.gov/about/organizational-structure/offices /Documents/SallieMaePrivatizationReport.pdf.

58   *"Since day one we have run this corporation as a business"*: Nancy Ross, "Sallie Mae Works a Risk-Free Arena," *Washington Post*, February 21, 1983, WB1.

59   *"Everybody dealt with her with kid gloves"*: Terry Hartle, interview by the author, February 28, 2019.

59 *"They were so far ahead of everybody"*: Thomas Stanton, interview by the author, December 21, 2018.

59 *One lender offered Sony Walkmans*: David Brock, "Banks Push Loans to College Students," *Wall Street Journal*, August 20, 1985.

61 *"a small key to Fort Knox"*: Nelson, *The History of Sallie Mae*, 53.

62 *"Its luxurious Georgetown offices"*: Waldman, *The Bill*, 52.

63 *"We protected them"*: Ibid., 146.

Chapter Three: Our Greedy Colleges

65 *Students crowded the hallway*: Eleanor Hill, interview by the author, October 21, 2019.

67 U.S. News & World Report: Jeffrey Selingo, *Who Gets In and Why* (New York: Scribner, 2020), 79, iBooks.

67 *president of Kalamazoo College*: David Breneman, interview by the author, January 9, 2019.

69 *"It's going to kill us"*: George H. W. Bush, remarks of the vice president at the Annual Republican Senate-House Dinner, April 7, 1981, transcript, The American Presidency Project, https://www.presidency.ucsb.edu/node/246635.

71 *"Our Greedy Colleges"*: Bill Bennett, "Our Greedy Colleges," *New York Times*, February 18, 1987.

72 *"more palatable food"*: Maureen Harrington and Diane Carman, "Amenities Abound on Campuses," *Denver Post*, September 4, 1989.

72 *"I would have taken"*: Stephen Joel Trachtenberg, interview by the author, March 1, 2019.

73 *"The Ivy schools are part"*: Gary Putka, "Do Colleges Collude on Financial Aid?," *Wall Street Journal*, May 2, 1989.

74 *A company owned by two brothers*: "Abuses in Federal Student Aid Programs," U.S. Senate Permanent Subcommittee on Investigations of the Committee on Governmental Affairs, May 17, 1991. The report can be found on the Century Foundation's website: https://tcf.org/content/report/president-george-h-w-bush-cracked-abuses-profit-colleges/.

74 *"There is no way to escape"*: Ibid.

76 *Schools have been*: *Abuses in Federal Student Aid Programs: Hearings Before the Permanent Subcommittee on Investigations of the Commit-*

tee on Governmental Affairs (Washington, D.C.: U.S. Senate, 1990), https://files.eric.ed.gov/fulltext/ED334955.pdf.

76 *"We have yet to hear of even"*: Nunn statement before U.S. Senate Permanent Subcommittee on Investigations, September 25, 1990. Library of Congress, Washington, DC.

76 *Between 1980 and 1990*: U.S. Department of Labor, Consumer Price Index, https://www.bls.gov/news.release/cpi.toc.htm.

76 *the Justice Department sued*: U.S. Department of Justice, "Consent Decree Settles Charge of Conspiracy to Restrain Price Competition on Financial Aid Against Universitites," news release, May 22, 1991, https://www.justice.gov/archive/atr/public/press_releases/1991/325032.pdf.

Chapter Four: American Dreamer

81 *"is now a necessity"*: Caroline Hendrie, "Colleges Face Serious Challenges," *The Record (N.J.)*, May 21, 1990.

81 *a landmark study*: Barbara Schneider, *Sloan Study of Youth and Social Development, 1992–1997*, Inter-university Consortium for Political and Social Research, last modified October 22, 2013, https://doi.org/10.3886/ICPSR04551.v2.

84 *One year at a private*: "Average Undergraduate Tuition and Fees and Room and Board Rates Charged for Full-Time Students in Degree-Granting Postsecondary Institutions, by Level and Control of Institution: Selected Years, 1963–64 Through 2018–19," *Digest of Education Statistics*, 2019, https://nces.ed.gov/programs/digest/d19/tables/dt19_330.10.asp?current=yes.

84 *Americans with student debt owed*: Waldman, *The Bill*, 29.

84 *Senator Edward Kennedy released*: John J. Fialka, "As Pressure Mounts on Sallie Mae in Washington, the Rich Loan Agency's Future Is Far from Clear," *Wall Street Journal*, March 9, 1993.

85 *"I'm going to make"*: Rob Andrews, interview by the author, June 25, 2020.

86 *threatened to veto the bill*: Hilary Stout, "Veto Is Threatened for Legislation on Student Loans," *Wall Street Journal*, October 23, 1991.

88 *"I refuse to be part"*: Bill Clinton, presidential campaign announcement, Little Rock, Ark., October 3, 1991, video, 36:06, C-SPAN, https://www.c-span.org/video/?21803-1/governor-bill-clinton-d-ar-presidential-campaign-announcement.

88   *"It was so expensive"*: Bill Clinton, *My Life* (New York: Vintage, 2004), 67.

89   *The Yale program*: William M. Bulkeley, "Old Blues: Some Alumni of Yale Realize That They Owe College a Lasting Debt," *Wall Street Journal*, February 23, 1999.

89   *"If you're asking"*: William Galston, interview by the author, April 21, 2020.

90   *"The student loan business is changed forever"*: Maggie Mahar, "How Sallie Will Survive," *Barron's*, June 14, 1993.

92   *"You figure out"*: Larry Hough, interview by the author, March 21, 2019.

93   *Clinton announced the National Homeownership Strategy*: John F. Harris, "Clinton Pushes Homeownership Strategy," *Washington Post*, June 6, 1995, https://www.washingtonpost.com/archive/politics/1995/06/06 /clinton-pushes-homeownership-strategy/f256ec84-dbf2-4a2d-b487 -2882fa157da3/.

Chapter Five: The Lord of Wall Street

This chapter draws from multiple interviews with Al Lord over five occasions, most in person, in 2020 and 2021. Lord spoke with me on the record. When possible, I verified what he told me with his former colleagues and friends, whose quotes, unless noted otherwise, were drawn from interviews by me.

105   *The decline in factory employment*: U.S. Bureau of Labor Statistics, "All Employees, Manufacturing," FRED, Federal Reserve Bank of St. Louis, last modified January 8, 2021, https://fred.stlouisfed.org/series/MANEMP.

105   *6 in 10 recent high-school graduates*: "Recent High School Completers and Their Enrollment in College by Sex and Level of Institution, 1960 Through 2018," *Digest of Education Statistics*, 2019, https://nces.ed.gov /programs/digest/d19/tables/dt19_302.10.asp.

105   *"Nobody is putting any significant money"*: Olaf de Senerpont Domis, "Sallie Mae CEO Promises Bankers Vigorous Student Loan Competition," *American Banker*, December 10, 1997.

107   *Fitzpatrick read the financial documents*: Tim Fitzpatrick, interview by the author, February 6, 2020.

107   *had nearly 70,000 students across the U.S.*: "Apollo Group Univ. of Phoenix Enrollment Up," press release from Apollo Group, via Dow Jones News Service, December 14, 1999.

107 *Its tuition in 2000 was about*: public/private college tuition average nces, February 6, 2020.

108 *"opportunity pools"*: Stephen Burd, "Borrowing Trouble; With Its Lax Oversight of Student Loans, Washington Was Asking for Problems," *Los Angeles Times*, April 10, 2007.

108 *If it could convince a school*: Tim Fitzpatrick, interview by the author, February 6, 2020.

109 *Inside Bush's vehicle*: Ari Fleischer, interview by the author, January 21, 2020.

109 *Representative Tom Davis*: Tom Davis, interview by the author, January 23, 2020.

110 *Among them was Jeff Andrade*: Jeff Andrade, interview by the author, February 2, 2018.

111 *More than 1,800 Computer Learning Centers employees*: Amy Joyce, "Help on the Way for Former CLC Students," *Washington Post*, January 25, 2001.

111 *David Bergeron*: David Bergeron, interview by the author, January 4, 2019.

112 *We have been approached*: Rene Champagne speaking on an ITT Educational Services Inc. earnings call, October 16, 2003.

119 *When Senator Edward Kennedy*: Tim Fitzpatrick, interview with the author, February 6, 2020.

120 *When Chris Flowers*: Chris Flowers, interview with the author, January 13, 2020.

122 *Jack Remondi was working*: Jack Remondi, interview with the author, March 21, 2019.

122 *A huge chunk of Sallie Mae's portfolio*: Ibid.

Chapter Six: Hope and Hubris

126 *Founded by missionaries*: A history of Howard University can be found here: https://www2.howard.edu/about/history.

127 *They mostly attended schools*: Adam Looney and Constantine Yannelis, "A Crisis in Student Loans," Brookings Institution, Fall 2015, https://www.brookings.edu/bpea-articles/a-crisis-in-student-loans -how-changes-in-the-characteristics-of-borrowers-and-in-the-institu tions-they-attended-contributed-to-rising-loan-defaults/.

128 *Obama stepped to a lectern*: Barack Obama, inaugural address,

January 20, 2009, Washington, D.C., transcript, *What's Happening* (blog), White House, https://obamawhitehouse.archives.gov/blog/2009 /01/21/president-barack-obamas-inaugural-address.

129 *The housing crisis was created*: The congressionally mandated investigation into the financial crisis, the Financial Crisis Inquiry Commission's report, can be found here: https://www.govinfo.gov/content/pkg/GPO-FCIC /pdf/GPO-FCIC.pdf.

129 *One in five loans*: Josh Mitchell, "The U.S. Makes It Easy for Parents to Get College Loans—Repaying Them Is Another Story," *Wall Street Journal*, April 24, 2017, https://www.wsj.com/articles/the-u-s-makes-it -easy-for-parents-to-get-college-loansrepaying-them-is-another-story -1493047388.

129 *Ten million people lost their homes*: The Federal Reserve Bank of St. Louis says as many as 10 million mortgage borrowers may have lost their homes as a result of the financial crisis. William Emmons, "The End Is in Sight for the U.S. Foreclosure Crisis," *Housing Market Perspectives* (Federal Reserve Bank of St. Louis), December 2, 2016, https://www.stlouisfed.org/publications/housing-market-perspectives /2016/the-end-is-in-sight-for-the-us-foreclosure-crisis.

129 *Nearly nine million lost their jobs*: U.S. Bureau of Labor Statistics, "All Employees, Total Nonfarm," FRED, Federal Reserve Bank of St. Louis, last modified January 8, 2021, https://fred.stlouisfed.org/series/PAYEMS.

130 *"I never got a word in"*: Paul Bedard, "Elizabeth Warren to Obama: 'You Had Me at Predatory Lending,'" *U.S. News & World Report*, May 23, 2011.

130 *The country had*: "Adult Education Level," Organization for Economic Cooperation and Development, https://data.oecd.org/eduatt/adult-edu cation-level.htm#indicator-chart.

131 *A few weeks after Obama's speech*: Larry Katz, interview by the author, November 2, 2018. Larry Summers didn't respond to multiple requests for an interview.

131 *The administration urged*: Graham Boone, "A Letter That Transforms: A Look at the Pell Letter Initiative," *Monthly Labor Review*, December 2018, https://www.bls.gov/opub/mlr/2018/beyond-bls/a-letter-that -transforms-a-look-at-the-pell-letter-initiative.htm.

132 *"The top priority was fixing"*: James Kvaal, interview by the author, February 6, 2018.

133 *He and Michelle each owed $40,000*: Michael Stratford, "Obamas' Own Student Debt Topped $40,000 Each," *Inside Higher Ed*, August 27, 2013,

https://www.insidehighered.com/quicktakes/2013/08/27/obamas-own
-student-debt-topped-40000-each.

136 *"I think this is a movement"*: DeWayne Wickham, "Occupy Wall Street Is
a 2nd American Revolution," *USA Today*, October 11, 2011.

136 *Student debt was rising fastest among Blacks*: Federal Reserve, *2019 Survey
of Consumer Finances*, last modified September 28, 2020, https://www
.federalreserve.gov/econres/scf/dataviz/scf/chart/#series:Education_In
stallment_Loans;demographic:racecl4;population:1,2,3,4;units:median.

137 *The Education Department in 2011*: Rachel Fishman, "The Wealth Gap
PLUS Debt," *New America*, May 15, 2018, https://www.newamerica
.org/education-policy/reports/wealth-gap-plus-debt/.

138 *Inside an office building*: Shannon Sheaff, interview by the author,
April 26, 2016.

138 *In Mohave County*: U.S. Bureau of Labor Statistics, "Unemployment
Rate in Mohave County, AZ," FRED, Federal Reserve Bank of St.
Louis, last modified January 5, 2021, https://fred.stlouisfed.org/series
/AZMOHA0URN.

139 *In South Florida*: Josh Mitchell, "Student Loans Entice Borrowers More
for Cash Than a Degree," *Wall Street Journal*, March 2, 2014.

139 *In Montana, a father*: Ibid.

140 *Pell runners*: U.S. Department of Education, Office of Inspector
General, *Final Audit Report: Title IV of the Higher Education Act*,
February 2014, Programshttps://www2.ed.gov/about/offices/list/oig
/auditreports/fy2014/a07l0001.pdf.

140 *States cut funding*: Michael Mitchell, Michael Leachman, Kathleen Mas-
terson, and Samantha Waxman, "Unkept Promises: State Cuts to Higher
Education Threaten Access and Equity," Center on Budget and Policy
Priorities, October 4, 2018, https://www.cbpp.org/research/state-budget
-and-tax/unkept-promises-state-cuts-to-higher-education-threaten-access
-and.

140 *Student debt hit a milestone*: Josh Mitchell and Maya Jackson-Randall,
"Student Debt Tops $1 Trillion," *Wall Street Journal*, March 22, 2012.

141 *a greater share of parent borrowers*: Josh Mitchell, "The U.S. Makes It
Easy for Parents to Get College Loans—Repaying Them Is Another
Story," *Wall Street Journal*, April 24, 2017.

141 *the chief economist for Obama's Council*: Various participants, interview
by the author.

142 *Obama expanded a plan*: U.S. Department of Education, "Education Department Launches 'Pay as You Earn' Student Loan Repayment Plan,"

news release, December 21, 2012, https://www.ed.gov/news/press
-releases/education-department-launches-pay-you-earn-student-loan
-repayment-plan. See also Barack Obama, "Presidential Memorandum—
Student Loan Repayments," June 9, 2014, White House Office of
the Press Secretary, https://obamawhitehouse.archives.gov/the-press
-office/2014/06/09/presidential-memorandum-federal-student-loan
-repayments.

Chapter Seven: The Great Unequalizer

148 *"I have begged and pleaded"*: Derek, email to Arizona Summit,
August 14, 2014.

149 *Black Americans compose*: American Bar Association, *ABA Profile of the
Legal Profession 2020*, 109, https://www.americanbar.org/content/dam/aba
/administrative/news/2020/07/potlp2020.pdf.

149 *Don Lively wanted to change that*: Don Lively, multiple interviews by the
author, 2017–21.

151 *Bernie and Rita Turner had acted*: Bernie and Rita Turner, multiple
interviews by the author, 2017. See also Wade Keller, *Aspire Toward the
Highest* (Marco Island, Florida: Keller Publishing, 2009).

152 *Postgraduate programs—master's degrees*: Sandy Baum and Patricia Steele,
The Price of Graduate and Professional School, Urban Institute, June
2017, http://www.urban.org/sites/default/files/publication/91016
/price_of_grad_professional_school_0.pdf.

152 *the typical worker with a master's degree*: Elka Torpey, "Measuring the Value
of Education," *Career Outlook* (U.S. Bureau of Labor Statistics), April
2018, https://www.bls.gov/careeroutlook/2018/data-on-display/education
-pays.htm.

152 *Until 1996, for-profit schools weren't allowed*: Details of the 1996
consent decree are discussed here in this Justice Department release:
https://www.justice.gov/archive/atr/public/press_releases/2006/21
6804.htm.

153 *The Justice Department believed*: Josh Mitchell, "The Rise and Fall of
a Law School Empire Fueled by Federal Loans," *Wall Street Journal*,
November 24, 2017, https://www.wsj.com/articles/the-rise-and-fall-of
-a-law-school-empire-fueled-by-federal-loans-1511544524.

154 *about 100,000 people applied to law school*: Mitchell, "The Rise and Fall
of a Law School Empire."

155 *It rounded up additional investors*: Ibid.

156 *Blacks who graduated college in 2008*: Josh Mitchell, "Black College Grads Owe Nearly Twice as Much as Whites Four Years Out," *Wall Street Journal*, October 20, 2016, https://blogs.wsj.com/economics /2016/10/20/black-college-grads-owe-nearly-twice-as-much-student -debt-as-whites-four-years-out/.

156 *the unemployment rate among workers 24 and under*: Bureau of Labor Statistics, via the Fedreal Reserve Bank of St. Louis's FRED database, https://fred.stlouisfed.org/series/LNS14024887.

157 *the unemployment rate for Black men*: U.S. Bureau of Labor Statistics, "Unemployment Rate—20 Yrs. & Over, Black or African American Men," FRED, Federal Reserve Bank of St. Louis, last modified January 28, 2021, https://fred.stlouisfed.org/series/LNU04000031.

159 *InfiLaw's students had borrowed $1 billion*: Author's calculations using annual reports to the Education Department, award years 1999–2000 through 2016–2017.

159 *In 2014 Dave Frakt*: Dave Frakt, multiple interviews by the author, 2010. See also Paul Campos, "The Law-School Scam," *The Atlantic*, September 2014, https://www.theatlantic.com/magazine/archive/2014/09 /the-law-school-scam/375069/.

162 *"Don't Let Your LSAT Keep You from Law School"*: Charlotte School of Law, email to Derek, March 7, 2014.

Chapter Eight: State U Inc.

168 *Across campus in senior housing, Mary Jolley*: Mary Jolley, interview by the author, March 26, 2018.

170 *fastest-growing public university*: Nick Anderson, "U. of Alabama Is Fastest-Growing Flagship; Others Are Standing Still," *Washington Post*, September 25, 2015, https://www.washingtonpost.com/news/grade -point/wp/2015/09/25/u-of-alabama-is-fastest-growing-flagship-many -others-are-standing-still/.

170 *The University of Alabama opened in 1831*: The university's history can be found here: https://www.ua.edu/about/history.

170 *the school named one of its buildings for a Grand Dragon*: Melissa Brown, "University of Alabama trustees vote to rename hall honoring 'ardent white supremacist,'" *Montgomery Advertiser*, September 17, 2020, https://www.montgomeryadvertiser.com/story/news/2020/09/17

/university-alabama-morgan-hall-renamed-english-hall-confederacy
-ties/3478819001/.
170 *"two Black students . . . sought to enroll"*: A description of
Vivian Malone's and James Hood's experience can be found here:
http://throughthedoors.ua.edu/vivian-malone.html.
171 *Robert Witt, a visionary*: Robert Witt, interview by the author,
February 25, 2020.
172 *Another theory better explains*: Dylan Matthews, "The Tuition Is Too
Damn High, Part VI—Why There's No Reason for Big Universities to
Rein in Spending," *Washington Post*, September 2, 2013, https://www
.washingtonpost.com/news/wonk/wp/2013/09/02/the-tuition-is-too
-damn-high-part-vi-why-theres-no-reason-for-big-universities-to-rein
-in-spending/.
173 *Witt called Judy Bonner into his office*: Judy Bonner, interview by the
author, December 19, 2018.
174 *University of Alabama professors earned an average of $81,000*: University of
Alabama salaries can be found here: https://oira.ua.edu/factbook/reports
/faculty-and-staff/average-salaries-for-full-time-instructional-faculty/.
174 *typical household income of $43,000*: U.S. Census Bureau, "Median
Household Income in the United States," FRED, Federal Reserve Bank
of St. Louis, last modified September 16, 2020, https://fred.stlouisfed
.org/series/MEHOINUSA646N.
175 *"He was a president who very much"*: Roger Thompson, interview by the
author, May 5, 2020.
178 *The industry sprouted in the 1970s*: Paul Tough, "What College Admissions Officers Really Want," *New York Times Magazine*, Sept. 10, 2019,
https://www.nytimes.com/interactive/2019/09/10/magazine/college
-admissions-paul-tough.html.
178 *"That was the shock to the system"*: Kevin Crockett, interview by the
author, August 9, 2019.
180 *"It's almost like buying a car"*: Matthew Quirk, "The Best Class Money
Can Buy," *The Atlantic*, November 2005, https://www.theatlantic.com
/magazine/archive/2005/11/the-best-class-money-can-buy/304307/.

Chapter Nine: The Trap

191 *research by the Federal Reserve Bank of St. Louis showed*: Josh Mitchell,
"College Still Pays Off, but Not for Everyone," *Wall Street Journal*,

August 9, 2019, https://www.wsj.com/articles/college-still-pays-off-but
-not-for-everyone-11565343000.

191 *Bad credit resulting from student loans*: Jessica Silver-Greenberg, Stacy
Cowley, and Natalie Kitroeff, "When Unpaid Student Loan Bills Mean
You Can No Longer Work," *New York Times*, November 18, 2017,
https://www.nytimes.com/2017/11/18/business/student-loans-licenses
.html.

191 *Researchers at George Washington University and the Treasury Department*:
Stephanie Riegg Cellini and Nicholas Turner, "Gainfully Employed?
Assessing the Employment and Earnings of For-Profit College Students
Using Administrative Data" (working paper, National Bureau of Economic
Research, May 2016, revised January 2018), https://www.nber.org/papers
/w22287.

192 *In February 2015, as the Obama administration put together its annual
budget*: Nick Timiraos and Josh Mitchell, "U.S. Boosts Estimated Cost
of Student Debt Forgiveness," *Wall Street Journal*, February 5, 2015,
https://www.wsj.com/articles/u-s-boosts-estimated-cost-of-student
-debt-forgiveness-1423174266.

192 *She was part of a national trend: borrowers with big balances*: Josh
Mitchell, "The Rise of the Jumbo Student Loan," *Wall Street Journal*,
February 16, 2018, https://www.wsj.com/articles/jumbo-loans-are-new
-threat-in-u-s-student-debt-market-1518790152.

193 *Congress . . . had created a repayment plan in the early 1990s*: Robert
Shireman, "Learn Now, Pay Later: A History of Income-Contingent
Student Loans in the United States," *Annals of the American Academy
of Political and Social Science*, April 27, 2017, https://journals.sagepub
.com/doi/abs/10.1177/0002716217701673.

197 *Congress tightened the law to treat student debt differently*: Katy Stech
Ferek, "Judges Wouldn't Consider Forgiving Crippling Student Loans—
Until Now," *Wall Street Journal*, June 14, 2018, https://www.wsj.com
/articles/judges-wouldnt-consider-forgiving-crippling-student-loans
-until-now-1528974001.

201 *The agency was overwhelmed by the sudden surge*: Josh Mitchell, "Thousands Apply to U.S. to Forgive Their Student Loans, Saying Schools
Defrauded Them," *Wall Street Journal*, January 20, 2016, https://www
.wsj.com/articles/thousands-apply-to-u-s-to-forgive-their-student-loans
-saying-schools-defrauded-them-1453285800.

202 *"More than 50 current and former bankruptcy judges"*: Ferek, "Judges
Wouldn't Consider Forgiving Crippling Student Loans."

Bibliography

Carey, Kevin. *The End of College: Creating the Future of Learning and the University of Everywhere.* New York: Riverhead Books, 2015.

Clowse, Barbara Barksdale. *Brainpower for the Cold War: The Sputnik Crisis and National Defense Education Act of 1958.* Westport, Conn.: Greenwood, 1981.

Dickson, Paul. *Sputnik: The Shock of the Century.* New York: Walker, 2001.

Elliott, Carl. *The Cost of Courage.* New York: Doubleday, 1992.

Finn, Chester E., Jr. *Education and the Presidency.* Lexington, Mass.: Lexington Books, 1977.

Gladieux, Lawrence E., and Thomas R. Wolanin. *Congress and the Colleges.* Lexington, Mass.: Lexington Books, 1976.

Goldin, Claudia, and Lawrence F. Katz. *The Race Between Education and Technology.* Cambridge, Mass.: Belknap Press, 2008.

Johnson, Lyndon Baines. *The Vantage Point: Perspectives of the Presidency, 1963–1969.* New York: Holt, Rinehart and Winston, 1971.

Mettler, Suzanne. *Degrees of Inequality: How the Politics of Higher Education Sabotaged the American Dream.* New York: Basic Books, 2014.

Ravitch, Diane. *The Troubled Crusade.* New York: Basic Publishers, 1983.

Urban, Wayne J. *More Than Science and Sputnik: The National Defense Education Act of 1958.* Tuscaloosa: The University of Alabama Press, 2010.

Waldman, Steve. *The Bill: How Legislation Really Becomes Law: A Case Study of the National Service Bill.* New York: Penguin Books, 1995.

Wilkinson, Rupert. *Aiding Students, Buying Students: Financial Aid in America.* Nashville, Tenn.: Vanderbilt University Press, 2005.

Zaloom, Caitlin. *Indebted: How Families Make College Work at Any Cost.* Princeton, N.J.: Princeton University Press, 2019.

Index

Index

About the Author

JOSH MITCHELL is a reporter in the Washington bureau of the *Wall Street Journal*, writing about the economy and higher education. In 2016, the Education Writers Association named him the nation's top education beat reporter among large publications, calling his reporting "unique, comprehensive, illuminating, and a must-read for policy makers, prospective and current college students, and their parents." He lives and works in Washington, D.C.

CPSIA information can be obtained
at www.ICGtesting.com
Printed in the USA
LVHW030808240622
721457LV00008B/8